STATISTICAL CONCEPTS FOR CRIMINAL JUSTICE AND CRIMINOLOGY

STATISTICAL CONCEPTS FOR CRIMINAL JUSTICE AND CRIMINOLOGY

Frank P. Williams III

Professor of Criminal Justice
University of Houston – Downtown

Professor Emeritus
California State University, San Bernardino

PEARSON
Prentice
Hall

Upper Saddle River, New Jersey
Columbus, Ohio

Library of Congress Cataloging-in-Publication Data

Williams, Franklin P.
    Statistical concepts for criminal justice and criminology/Frank P. Williams III.
        p. cm.
    Includes bibliographical references and index.
    ISBN-13: 978-0-13-513046-9 (alk. paper)
    ISBN-10: 0-13-513046-8 (alk. paper)
    1. Criminal statistics. 2. Criminal justice, Administration of. 3. Criminology. I. Title.
HV7415.W54 2009
364.01'5195 — dc22

                                                                        2008002531

Editor-in-Chief: Vernon R. Anthony
Acquisitions Editor: Tim Peyton
Editorial Assistant: Alicia Kelly
Media Project Manager: Karen Bretz
Director of Marketing: David Gesell
Marketing Manager: Jimmy Stephens
Marketing Assistant: Les Roberts
Production Manager: Kathy Sleys

Creative Director: Jayne Conte
Cover Design: Bruce Kenselaar
Cover Illustration/Photo:
  Getty Images, Inc.
Full-Service Project Management/
  Composition: Shiji Sashi/
  Integra Software Services, Inc.
Printer/Binder: R.R. Donnelley & Sons, Inc.

Pearson Education Ltd., London
Pearson Education Singapore, Pte. Ltd
Pearson Education Canada, Inc.
Pearson Education–Japan
Pearson Education Australia PTY, Limited
Pearson Education North Asia, Ltd., Hong Kong
Pearson Educación de Mexico, S.A. de C.V.
Pearson Education Malaysia, Pte. Ltd.
Pearson Education Upper Saddle River, New Jersey

10 9 8 7 6 5 4 3 2 1
ISBN-13: 978-0-13-513046-9
ISBN-10:   0-13-513046-8

Brief Contents

Contents

Preface

This book is about the basic concepts of statistics. Therefore, the coverage is elementary and focuses on the building blocks of statistical ideas. This is a purposeful choice. Many students today, for various reasons, have a fear of mathematics and numbers. In learning about statistics, you can't escape the numbers because statistics is a *quantitative* approach to the examination of reality. So, we're stuck with numbers. However, it is possible to avoid most of the calculation (unless, of course, your professor wants you to do that) and, here's the bottom line about this book, you only need to look at a few calculations as illustrations of the concepts involved. The statistical formulas are here for you to see, and to illustrate what a statistic does, but you can avoid them if you want (again, assuming your professor will allow that).

What does the book have then? Statistics is really about the role of variance and error. That is, how things vary (perhaps from each other) and whether that variance is real or not. So, the book begins with that. In fact, it takes a while (Chapter 11) before you will even get to techniques some people feel are "real" statistics. If you focus on the concepts involved, they will serve as a foundation for understanding what goes on when statistics are used.

Many students are convinced they will not be conducting research of their own in the future, and so they do not really need to learn how to use statistics and perform analyses. But, if you are a criminal justice or criminology major, you *will* have to use the products of research and statistical analysis. Do you know that the National Institute of Justice will not fund any program without an evaluation built into it? That means you need to know how to read statistical materials and research reports—not to understand everything, but to have a *reasonable* understanding of what was done and how the results were achieved, and even make an assessment of the quality of the information. The higher you rise in administration, assuming that might be among your goals, the more you will be faced with reading research reports. Indeed, at the higher administrative levels, you might even be creating research projects to improve efficiency, find a better way to do a job, or determine if a policy should be implemented. Actually, as a criminal justice or criminology student, you will be reading the results of statistically-based research in virtually every course textbook.

So, why this textbook? First, it is the product of over 30 years of teaching statistics and research and even more years of doing research and publishing the results. I have found that the concepts are more critical than the manipulation of numbers—and better yet for you—result in more people passing a statistics course. Second, in doing research and teaching others to do it, I found there are certain steps involved that facilitate the process and help others to understand it. In using statistics, for example, simple comes before complex and close attention has to be paid to the nature of the data collected. That's because it is easy to make mistakes by choosing the wrong type of statistical analysis. You need to understand what kind of data you have before you can make decisions about which sophisticated analyses to perform. And even more than that, a researcher needs to know when it is proper to use a statistical technique and how to interpret the results. In my own student days, I have personally had statistics courses in which we calculated the heck out of everything, but never were told when the statistics we were calculating should be used or even how to interpret the results. Consequently, this book attempts to create a more meaningful experience.

In reading this book, you will slowly go through a logical sequence of concepts beginning with the two basics: variance and error. Then you will learn about the different types of numbers and begin to explore the ways we use numbers to describe things. There is even a chapter on graphical descriptions. From these descriptive approaches, you will move to the concept of relationships and begin with the most basic forms of looking for them. Only after this will you begin to deal with hypotheses and "statistical significance" and whether differences and presumed effects are real or not. These are the "real statistics" you might have heard about. Even here, though, there are only three statistics covered. The three I have chosen are the ones used the most and, in another sense, are the most basic. Finally, after these statistics, the idea of association and correlation is introduced and two statistics are explained. This will bring you through the most elementary forms of describing data to the foundations of some of our most sophisticated types of analysis.

As much as is possible, all this is done in simple language. There are examples of when to use various statistics, what you need in order to use them, and examples of how to interpret them. Moreover, virtually all of the examples are based on real data and, in many cases, real research too. My experience has been that this approach results in most students' beginning to understand how statistics work and how generally to interpret them. However, if your professor uses this text and adds a lot of calculation or problem solving, rest assured that approach to teaching works best for him or her. Teaching statistics is a highly individualized endeavor—there is no one way to do it correctly. So, there are ways in which the chapters in this book can be assigned in a different order without having to understand too much of the preceding materials. Your professor will know how to do that.

Now, about the Appendices. In most cases, they can be left alone. They are there for those who are curious about other statistical techniques, particularly more complex ones. Or, perhaps, your professor is used to teaching some of these approaches as part of a basic course (I do). If you are an advanced student or, even perhaps a graduate student browsing through an introductory text, you will definitely want to check them out.

Finally, the SPSS statistical program has been used to create most but not all of the examples. You don't need to have access to that program or any other to understand the material in the text. If you have a statistical program assigned for the class, it makes no real difference if it is SPSS, or not as far as the text is concerned. Most programs today create quite similar statistical output. Actually, if you would like to have such a program, a very good and better yet, free, program is available on the web as part of the Open Source Project—OpenStat. Try it, you might like it.

A few academic colleagues, and I have no idea how many students, have contributed to the materials in this text, the sequencing, and the way ideas are expressed. There are too many to name or remember and, besides, I want to avoid litigation. The way I see it, if you don't like this book, blame them. On the other hand, if you like it, . . . I will, however, say that Tim Peyton, the Senior Editor at Prentice-Hall, thought the ideas I expressed would make a great statistics book. Because he didn't know much about statistics, I went with his encouragement. And, as always, I thank my patient and supporting spouse, Marilyn McShane.

I wish to thank the following reviewers:

Kristen Kuehnle, Salem State College
Larry Miller, East Tennessee State University
Ojmarrh Mitchell, University of Cincinnati
Callie Rennison, University of Missouri- St. Louis
Brion Sever, Monmouth University

CHAPTER I

Introduction to Statistics

Key Concepts

- quantitative

- descriptive statistics

- inferential statistics

- predictive statistics

- variance

- error

- constant

- power

- robustness

Most students in criminal justice and criminology put off taking a statistics course as long as possible, mostly because they assume it is very difficult and is another mathematics course. This is unfortunate, mostly because the reasons are wrong and the course can help students read and make sense of the research literature necessary for their other courses. In fact, a statistics course should be among the first courses taken in your major.

There is really no reason to fear a statistics course. Though it is a branch of mathematics, it is a *practical* branch and exists for our benefit. Think of one of those charts with little stick figures you have probably seen. The more stick figures in the chart, the more of that particular thing there is. How many times have you counted something that has more than one category? Have you used hash marks to tally up the number of things in each category? And you probably then counted the hash marks to arrive at a total like the example below?

Green balls	⦀ //	Number = 7
Red balls	////	Number = 4
Yellow balls	⦀ ///	Number = 8

What about looking at a line chart in the business section of your local newspaper showing how the stock market has changed over time, or perhaps a bar chart showing how some categories are "more or less" than others? If you have done or seen any of these things, you have used statistics. Even in the unlikely event you haven't seen any of these things, you have still used statistics. Any discussion of an "average" or the percent of something is sufficient to have used statistics. In fact, the truth is that you have been using statistics all the time and never knew it.

WHAT ARE STATISTICS?

Technically, statistics are quantitative (essentially numerical) ways of summarizing information. Some people suggest that statistics are used with *sample* information and not with population information (like the U.S. Census). However, this overlooks the fact that we use percentages and averages with populations, too. There are certain types of statistics, though, that are used only with samples. These are used to express the likelihood that an estimate derived from a sample is approximately the same as the "real" figure in the population. For example, if a political poll reports that 55% of sample respondents say they will vote for a certain presidential candidate, how closely does this sample percentage represent the real percentage in the actual population of voters?

For all the times we use statistics or quantitative information, most of our personal information is from other sources—for example, experience, tradition, intuition, common sense, or people in authority telling us something. Obviously, statistics represent a very small amount of personal knowledge. But, at the same time, they are frequently used to establish "facts" and in the process seem more important than other types of knowledge. Because we know that statistics summarize other information, it stands to reason that it is the "other" information that is important, not the statistics themselves. So why do this?

The answer lies in *understanding* information. The world around us is very complex and no one is capable of seeing, experiencing, and comprehending everything. As a result, we continually find ways to summarize what we see and "know." This is not only common, it is probably necessary because of the amount of input and stimulation we receive on a continual basis. Some would refer to this as *generalizing* from specific information. This ability to take specific facts and aggregate them into general information is characteristic of sentient (thinking) species and humans do it best. Actually, if we can't do this, living becomes difficult—imagine having to treat everything as unique! Where quantitative information is concerned, the task is complicated by the fact that numbers by themselves are perhaps more difficult to understand than most types of information. Indeed, numbers represent one form of higher thinking capability. A large amount of numbers can make understanding worse, and this is where the use of statistics comes in handy. By summarizing numbers (with other numbers, of course), statistics help in generalizing information. Statistics, then, are merely *one* way of presenting information in a form that is more easily understood than the actual information itself.

THE BASIC TYPES OF STATISTICS

There are three ways that statistics are used to assist us in solving problems of understanding. While we will later discuss each, here is a brief overview of the three basic "families" of statistics.

- *Descriptive*: Sometimes we have too much raw information (data) to make sense of it, or perhaps it is too difficult to determine what it is telling us by just looking at the data. In these instances, we need help in *describing* the data. Descriptive statistics range from graphic pictures of the data to single numbers, such as percentages and averages, that enable us to create pictures in our minds. Most of these descriptive statistics are univariate (meaning they describe a single variable, such as a city's crime rate), but some are used with multiple variables (such as crosstabulations of two variables to see how one variable influences another).

- *Inferential*: Because our ability to measure is not perfect, we need some way of determining if two (or more) numbers are *really* different, or if they are merely the product of our poor measuring abilities (that is, they are really both the same number). These are the statistics used with samples to estimate population information. Sometimes the comparisons are sample numbers to population numbers, other times they are comparisons of various sample numbers (such as opinions of people of different ages) using assumptions about the real numbers in the population. These assumptions are primarily based on sampling distributions, something we will discuss later. Inferential statistics are also known as measures of significance.

- *Predictive*: Relationships are another form of information that statistics can assist with. We often wonder if two variables are related (for example, does gender affect criminality?). Predictive statistics give us information on the degree of relationship between variables. Moreover, they can help us predict what one variable will be by knowing what another variable is (for example, if you know that a person is a female, do you think you might be able to predict the level of criminality as compared to a male's level of criminality?). It is not necessary that one variable be a *cause* of another, just that the two are related. These statistics are also known as measures of associations, or correlations.

Each of these families will be treated in subsequent chapters and in the order presented above.

STATISTICS, KNOWLEDGE, AND EXPLANATION

Why are these types or families grouped in this way? The answer lies primarily in the way we make scientific sense of phenomena. From your research methods class, you should be familiar with the development of methodologies from exploratory to descriptive to explanatory. The early stages of knowing about something are necessarily rough and simple—very exploratory. After satisfying ourselves that the "something" is really there, we want to know more about it and that requires description and, ultimately, accurate description. Once that stage of investigation is completed, we want to know what causes the phenomenon (and what it affects in turn). This final stage of knowledge-gaining requires the accurate description generated by the second stage, particularly the ability to measure the new phenomenon in an accurate and reliable way. Of course, it also means that we have to measure any potential "causes" equally well, so they must have already been accurately described. Let's now look at the sequence in which statistics are used.

What's There?

For our purposes, the exploratory phase and part of the descriptive phase in research methodology are related to descriptive statistics. First, we ask the question "What are we looking at?" This requires a description of the phenomenon, usually ranging from a basic approach to a more definitive approach. The better we can describe the characteristics of something, the more sure we are about what it is. For instance, when we "discover" something, most of the time we are not even certain that it actually exists or is unique. Science is a pretty conservative method of knowledge — the basic position is that whatever is found is either a mistake (an error) or actually something else we already know about. Any first indication of a phenomenon is therefore a basic, or elementary, description.

Quantitatively, this basic description may be nothing more than a smaller or larger degree of some characteristic of another phenomenon we were trying to measure. This fact alone doesn't tell us much, so the next step is to try to better describe what it is we think we found. Characteristics have to be identified and, following that, the degree of these characteristics.

An example of this from the criminal justice field is the "discovery" of serial murderers. Though there was no question that some people had committed multiple murders, it wasn't recognized as a type of murder and there was no "problem" people saw. In the early 1980s, partly as a result of another federal program designed to look for solutions in investigating "serial" violent offenders who committed their offenses in multiple jurisdictions, the FBI recognized there might also be a serial type of murder (and obviously, serial murderers). Their first task was to collect evidence on murders committed in various jurisdictions and then examine the evidence to see if those murders were related — in other words, describe the murders to see if they could be categorized as serial. Following that, the task was to describe the serial murderers. The initial murder evidence and the subsequent attempt to describe unique characteristics is part of the exploratory and descriptive phase of knowledge.

How Is This Different?

Once we have accurately described and characterized a phenomenon, the next question we ask is, "How is this different from other similar phenomena?" An answer requires comparisons with other similar phenomena and some objective criteria by which to determine when differences exist. Moreover, some important variables (gender, race, age) might affect our phenomenon differently. Thus, a method of comparing is needed, along with a method of determining the degree of variability needed to be "different" (for instance, you might find slight differences between two spoons in a set of silverware, but those differences aren't enough to make you say that they represent two different patterns).

The first issue is in the way we make comparisons. Scientifically, such methods need to be systematic, empirical, and reliable. It would help, then, to use already-existing, standard methods so you don't have to create new ones. Just "feeling" something is different is not sufficient to be counted as evidence. Similarly, the criteria for how much difference is needed to declare a true difference should also be a standard one. This way, you don't make a decision that others would not make. Inferential statistics solve both of these problems—they give us standard methods for comparing data and the criteria for deciding when things are different.

Using our serial murderer example, once they are identified, it would make sense to compare them to other murderers. We would want to know if there are characteristics of serial murderers that make them unique. That's precisely what the FBI did—they looked at the serial murderers they had identified and compared them to nonserial murderers. The results led them to believe that serial murderers constituted a different type of murderer and were capable of being identified by certain characteristics. This represents a more complex descriptive phase of knowledge, beyond simple description.

What Causes It?

The final question is, "How do we predict and explain this phenomenon?" In many ways this is the most difficult question because it requires knowledge of other phenomena and an ability to determine cause and effect. The identification of different characteristics is the beginning of the answer to this question and inferential statistics provide much of this evidence.

From this we would want to establish the existence and strength of relationships between other variables and our phenomenon. However, it doesn't help much to have decided that a real difference exists if that difference is rather small. In order to predict that our phenomenon will occur, we need the strongest possible relationships to other variables.

Predictive statistics or measures of association provide indicators of the strength of these relationships. By using them, we can tell which variables best predict the occurrence of other variables. Unfortunately, mere good prediction doesn't mean that a cause is established, although it is common to think so. There may be other variables involved in the relationship that actually act as a cause. Predictive statistics, as a result, tend to be among the most complex and sophisticated of the various types of statistics. They not only have to establish the strength of a relationship between variables, but good ones should have a way of determining whether a relationship continues to be a strong one when several other variables are measured and included.

In our serial murder example, the FBI obviously did not just want to find out how serial murderers were different. They wanted to be able to predict which murders were serial ones and then predict the characteristics of the murderer (now known as "profiling"), thus facilitating their arrest. Further, a last and most difficult task was to explain how people became serial murderers so that they could be recognized in advance. It should make sense, then, that this is the explanatory phase of knowledge.

With this overview of the general types of statistics, we now turn to two essential concepts for both statistics and research methods.

THE FOUNDATION OF STATISTICS

There are *two* foundation concepts that underlie the reason for and the use of statistics. They are *variance* and *error*.

Variance

The way we know about things scientifically is to measure them. But measuring presents problems, and accuracy is always an issue. Imagine that someone asked you to measure the length and width of your classroom. What will you use to measure it? If you use a ruler, a yardstick, or a tape measure, is it possible that you might get different measurements? What if you were given a rubber band and asked how many rubber-band lengths the room was? Would the elasticity in the rubber band affect the result? If other students in the class were asked to make the same measurements, do you think you would all get exactly the same results? Of course not. In part, then, *what* you use to measure with will affect the accuracy of the measurement. The more accurate the measuring instrument, the more accurate the results will normally be. However, there is always the possibility of outside error such as someone recording the wrong number, losing track of the number of ruler lengths, or even reading the tape measure wrong. (We are going to ignore the possibility that the walls in the classroom might be expanding and contracting while you are measuring!)

All of this means that, within reasonable bounds of accuracy, it is virtually impossible to achieve the same measurement twice even when the two measures are actually the *same*. Thus, what appears to be a *constant* (always the same number)

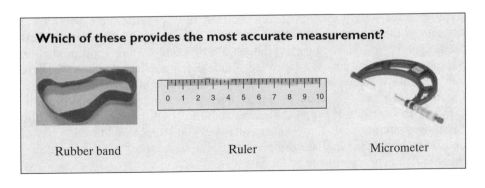

Which of these provides the most accurate measurement?

Rubber band   Ruler   Micrometer

may or may *not* be the same number. Our problem, then, is to determine whether we have measured the same thing, or something different. You can probably see now that there are two basic reasons for variance:

- measurement inaccuracy (the two measures are actually the same) or *error*, and
- true differences between measurements.

Error

Let's now discuss the problem of error. Error is almost always present, even when measurement is very accurate—error is just smaller in that case. But how do we know about error? When we measure, how do we know how much error there is? At what point can we assume that a difference between measurements is error and that the two measurements are really the same?

This is the reason for statistics—they are designed to tell us about error (there are actually many kinds of error, so there are many kinds of statistics). Once we know how much error is present, we can make an informed judgment whether true differences exist or the "differences" we observe are probably just measurement error (therefore, there is *no* difference). Unfortunately, because measurement always has error, so would any estimates we make of the amount of measurement error itself (actually, if you follow this, it never ends—each estimate of the amount of error present in each estimate of error has error). This leaves us in a really thorny dilemma—our estimates of error also have error in them. There is one way out of the problem, however.

If we deal with probabilities of being correct or incorrect in assuming real differences or measurement error, we know that there is always the chance of being wrong, but we can set boundaries that give us a better chance of being right. For instance, isn't it better to know that our estimate may be wrong only 1 in 1,000 times, than 1 in 5 times? We only have to find ways of comparing the differences in our measurements to "guideposts" where we already know the probabilities of error. It should make sense that a very large difference between two measurements is unlikely to be just a result of error. In fact, the larger the difference, the greater the chance that it is a *real* difference. It is small differences that we have to worry the most about. So, in one sense we have just established a couple of "guideposts" to help in our determining why differences occur. Large differences are

---

The Measurement Dilemma

✓ Any two identical measurements may really be the same.

✓ Any two identical measurements may actually be different.

✓ Any two different measurements may really be different.

✓ Any two different measurements may actually be the same.

How do you know which is true?

probably real; small differences are probably error. People have worked long and hard to create statistics that will help us capture the probabilities in between our two guideposts.

GOOD STATISTICS

The final concept to discuss in this chapter is an answer to the question "What makes a good statistic?" As with all things in life, there are good and bad versions of statistics. Obviously from the discussion above, we would prefer the least error possible, but this is complicated by the fact that there are multiple types of error and different degrees of error tolerance. Sometimes a researcher just beginning to examine a potential phenomenon might want quick and easy evidence that the phenomenon is probably there. Other times, a researcher might be exploring nuances and looking for fine details of a phenomenon we know a lot about. In these two cases, the researcher's expectations of error, and how much can be tolerated, differ greatly. In part, the issue is *accuracy* of the statistic and the degree of accuracy needed to answer the question at hand.

Another part of the "good/bad" concept is the image provided by the statistical results. If someone familiar with a statistic is not sure what the results show, the picture provided by the statistic is not too helpful. On the other hand, if the results help to paint a mental picture of a phenomenon or event to an informed person, the statistic would seem to be helpful. Note that this discussion of image uses "someone familiar" and an "informed person." Someone who doesn't know about a statistic and therefore cannot interpret its results would never get a mental picture of any kind and couldn't distinguish between good and bad statistics anyway.

Taking these two pieces of the concept, let's say that *a good statistic is one that provides a quick mental picture of a phenomenon under investigation and has a sufficient degree of accuracy for the task at hand.* In other words, we don't want the picture to be too complex and convoluted (although the statistic can be), nor do we want the degree of accuracy to be insufficient for our task. Perhaps we can now say that a "good" statistic is a relative concept—but the concept can still be applied once we know the detail and accuracy required for research task. In short, the necessity of an accurate and quick picture remains a reasonable criterion for the use of any statistic.

Power and Robustness

This is probably the best time to also mention that the above discussion about accuracy also contains the essence of what statisticians call "power." The *power* of a statistic is an estimation of its ability to find something that is really there. As we discussed, sometimes we need extreme accuracy in that process and other times we don't. When it is needed, though, you can bet that accuracy is critical. When discussing the power of a statistic, a "standard" statistic is frequently used as the benchmark. Assuming everything about the data is precisely what the standard statistic needs, it becomes the 100% power benchmark. Other statistics then are referenced to it with the term "power-efficiency." If, for instance, we say that statistic A is 95% power-efficient, it means statistic A is almost as good as the standard statistic on its proverbial "best day." When the standard statistic is having a "bad data day," statistic A just might even have more power.

Tied to this is the concept of *robustness*. The above statements about "good" and "bad" data days are really analogous to saying that everything comes with its own baggage. Statistics all assume something about the data, primarily because their creators designed them to solve particular problems. Whatever characteristics these problems had, it is a good bet that the statistic uses these characteristics to achieve its maximum power. In other words, statistics make "assumptions" about the data they are given. Give a statistic the wrong kind of data and you usually get results that are full of error. So, one of the things you would like to know about a statistic is its ability to withstand violations of its assumptions. Those with ability to withstand violations are referred to as robust statistics. Be careful here, though. It *does* make a difference how much of a violation, or how many violations, we are talking about. No statistic is robust enough to withstand the violation of *all* of its assumptions.

SUMMARY

If you understood most of this chapter, the probability (our new word) of your successfully making it through a statistics course just went up. Statistics are merely ways to make sense of and understand quantitative information. Whenever we convert real phenomena into numbers (physics does it all the time), it is for the purpose of making our perception of reality more "objective." Once we have the numbers, we need to "ask questions" of them. The various families of statistics partly exist to help answer the various types of questions.

The related concepts of variance and error are the backbone of statistics. Because there are different types of variance and error, different types of statistics have been developed to handle them. Using probability estimates of the existence of "real" variance and the degree of "error" variance enables us to make choices about differences and relationships present in our measurements (the data)—and these are the answers to questions we ask.

The different statistics we use to tell us about variance and error have different capabilities, particularly in regard to their accuracy and ability to withstand problems in the data. The degree of accuracy needed is tied to the critical nature of the research and the kind of answer needed. Certain statistics, given the right data, are very powerful and are best used to answer critical questions. Others provide a quick answer to noncritical questions. If you have one of those critical questions, you need to consider using a statistic that is both powerful and robust.

The next important concept in statistics is also related to measurement. As it turns out, there is more than one way to think about numbers. Some "numbers" are barely recognizable as "real" numbers and others differ in the information they convey. This concept is called "level of measurement" and is the subject of the next chapter.

KEY POINTS OF THE CHAPTER

- Statistics are ways of summarizing quantitative information and making sense of it.
- There are two main concepts that underlie statistics:
  - *Variance*: how things vary.
  - *Error*: the degree of measurement that is not "real"; there is always error—the problem is to estimate how much.
- Different types of statistics exist because of the different types of variance and error.
  - These statistics are at least partly defined by their power and robustness.

CHAPTER 2

Levels of Measurement

Key Concepts

- level of measurement
- nominal
- ordinal
- metric ordinal
- interval
- ratio

Now that you know what statistics are and have a general understanding of the concepts of variance and error, it is time to discuss the issue of measurement. Measurement is the use of numbers to represent things. These "things" are normally referred to as *concepts*. From your research methods class, you probably remember concepts as "symbolic representations of phenomena" (a fancy way of saying that they are names given to ideas we have—and hopefully descriptions of real phenomena). Through the process of operationalization, a variable is developed to represent a concept—and this variable is a way to measure the concept. In short, we take an abstract idea (a concept) and make it concrete (a variable). If a "variable" isn't measurable, it isn't a variable. Concepts can be anything we are able to measure: attitudes, characteristics of people, feelings, crime in a community, and so on. Variables are the actual ways we measure concepts. Unfortunately, most concepts can be measured in several ways.

An example is the concept of intelligence. We all have some idea of what intelligence is, but it is doubtful that all have the same idea or that we would all measure it the same way. Because our concern is about measurement, we won't worry about the different ways we think about intelligence. Let's just say that one measurement of intelligence is to use the Stanford-Binet Intelligence Test. The variable is the score on this test—usually called *intelligence quotient* (IQ).

Another example is age. A way to measure this concept is to ask a question on a survey, "Do you consider yourself young, middle-aged, or elderly?" This is probably not a good way to measure age (imagine the number of people who wouldn't be sure which category they belong to) but it *is* a measurement. A better way would be to ask, "What is your age as of your last birthday?" A response to that question might be "24," which would be more accurate than the three age categories. Now let's look at the number itself.

Though it is easy to see what the number 24 represents (as an age), it is not so easy to interpret the same number if it turns out to be someone's score on an exam or perhaps their fear of crime. An exam score of 24 could be a bad score or a good score. Similarly, someone saying their level of fear of crime is at a 24 doesn't mean anything to us until we know what the scale is. The truth is that numbers do not all mean the same thing. Their meaning is a product of two factors: their relationship to some condition (or set of conditions) and the *level of measurement*.

RELATIONSHIP TO SOME CONDITION

Though this sounds confusing, it is really simple. The idea is that a "24" by itself does not tell us much. For example, knowing that someone scored a 24 on an exam is relatively useless until we know what the possible scores on the exam are. What is the highest possible score? What is the lowest possible score? What did others score? All these questions help us to pinpoint what that "24" means. So, these "conditions" (highest, lowest, relative position) assist in interpreting the meaning of the number. In other words, you always need to know the context in which a particular number was recorded. Sometimes you can assume the context, as in the case of "24 years old," but it is always wise to ask about the context anyway.

LEVEL OF MEASUREMENT

This is a somewhat more confusing issue, and it is not only students who get confused. Sometimes you will find scholars arguing over level of measurement for a particular set of numbers. Worse, it wasn't until 1946 when S. S. Stevens, a British statistician, gave us the current version of levels of measurement that we really began to understand and classify measurement into various levels. The notion is that not all numbers can be treated equally because there are different ways of measuring variables.

For instance, what if we have a questionnaire that asks people about their religious affiliation and places their responses into three categories: Protestant, Catholic, and Other? If we then assign the number "1" to Protestant, "2" to Catholic, and "3" to Other, does it make sense to use these numbers for addition, subtraction, multiplication, and division? Can we add two Protestants (two "1s") and get a Catholic (a "2")? Of course not. But these are numbers, aren't they? And can't you add numbers? The correct answer is, "Of course, you can add numbers"—but only if they represent certain levels of measurement. Obviously, this example is not among those levels of measurement. Worse yet, the issue is not just that we can't *add* the numbers, but a "1" does not mean it is "less than" a "2." That is, a Protestant is neither less than, nor more than, a Catholic (or an "other"). The "1" is just another label for the religion category that we previously called "Protestant." It does, however, mean that the categories are different. *And that is all that it means.*

By looking at numbers in a certain way, we can produce four levels, or categories, of measurement. Beginning with the simplest way of measuring (the example we used earlier) and progressing to the most complex, the four levels are nominal, ordinal, interval, and ratio. We now turn to an explanation of these four levels.

Nominal Level of Measurement

This is measurement in its simplest form. It is the use of numbers to represent categories—nothing more and nothing less. Only one rule is required. Every category must have a different number. This is what we did earlier when we used 1, 2, and 3 to represent Protestant, Catholic, and Other. The numbers themselves are merely labels, or names, for the categories. Indeed, the numbers representing the categories can be changed to other numbers with absolutely no effect (other than calling the categories by different number "names"). Would it make any difference if we changed Protestant, Catholic, and Other to the numbers 27, 5, and 946? Not a bit. You may feel free to substitute any number for any other number (as long as you don't use the same number twice).

The term *nominal* comes from the Latin word *nominalis*, meaning "pertaining to a name." Thus, at this level of measurement we simply *name* the categories, but name each category differently. It hardly seems fair to refer to nominal-level numbers as *real* numbers. Therefore, nominal-level numbers should be used with caution because they lack most of the properties we have come to associate with numbers. Indeed, nominal data exhibit only a single, most basic property of numbers—they categorize (see Box 2.1 for a summary of this level).

This brings up a question: Why even use this level of measurement if it is nothing like what we normally refer to as numbers? The answer is that it is necessary because many of our important variables are usually measured at the nominal level. Think for a moment about the important social variables that describe people, and how we use those variables to predict social events like crime. How would you describe the average person arrested for a crime? A typical description would be a lower-class,

---

BOX 2.1

SUMMARY FOR NOMINAL LEVEL OF MEASUREMENT

Characteristic:

✓ *Categorizes* (assigns values to mutually exclusive and exhaustive groups)

Examples:

| Variable—Gender | 1 = male | 2 = female | |
| Variable—Color | 1 = blue | 2 = green | 3 = yellow |

Note: This is THE basic level of measurement—nothing is less restrictive.

minority male, between the ages of 14 and 29. Of these four variables (class, race, gender, and age), two are nominal-level variables: race and gender. We usually classify race and gender by breaking them down into "named" categories. Thus, they are both nominal concepts. Indeed, many of our most important social variables are nominal in nature. Thus, we are "stuck" with having to use nominal levels of measurement whenever we attempt to characterize people and explain their behavior.

A final note on nominal level measurement: Each "case" (people, cities, or whatever) must be assigned to only one category and all possible categories must be represented. This is referred to as *exclusive* and *exhaustive* classification of cases. If a case can be assigned to more than one category, something is wrong with the way the categories were constructed—when we total up the number of cases, that case is counted twice. In addition, if all categories aren't included, there will be cases that cannot be classified (the usual solution is to include an "other" category).

Ordinal Level of Measurement

This level of measurement begins the first "real" use of numbers. First, numbers at the ordinal level have everything that nominal-level numbers do (they also have categories). To this they add the concept of *order*, or "more than" and "less than." At this point, we can assume that a "1" is less than a "2" (or *any* larger number) and that a "2" is larger than a "1."

The term *ordinal* comes from the Latin word *ordinalis*, meaning "pertaining to order." The basic concept of ordinal-level measurement is that the numbers to be substituted for categories have order implicit in them. If one category is really more (or less) of something than another category, the number used to represent that category would have to be a larger (or smaller) number. For instance if person A is younger than person B and A is assigned the number 5, then B must assigned some number larger than 5. The concept of order, however, does not mean that a *specific* number must be assigned. *Any* number that is larger will suffice.

This leads us to a problem with ordinal-level measurement: Because any number can be used that maintains proper order, the ability to accurately locate any category's position relative to other categories is lost. For instance, suppose you asked people how they felt about prison furloughs and gave them response categories of "not a good idea," "maybe a good idea," and "excellent idea." You then assign values (numbers) to the categories of 1, 2, and 3. It would have also been proper to assign the numbers 5, 31, and 32 to the categories, as long as order is preserved. In short, we don't really know what the true attitude distance is between the categories, so it doesn't make sense to pretend that we do by making more of the numbers than is possible. Keep in mind that you can change the category numbers to anything that maintains the original order (see Box 2.2).

Technically, *anything* with order that cannot be measured accurately enough to establish its exact position is an ordinal-level concept (or variable). Failure to have exact position means that we still can't use the traditional arithmetic procedures (addition, multiplication, etc.). Examples of ordinal-level variables also abound in the social sciences: religiosity, prejudice, punitiveness, fear of crime, and just about any kind of attitude you can name.

BOX 2.2

SUMMARY FOR ORDINAL LEVEL OF MEASUREMENT

Characteristics:

✓ *Categorizes*
✓ *Conveys the concept of rank (or order)*

Examples:

Variable—Fear of crime ("How afraid are you?")

not at all	slightly	moderately	very	extremely
0	1	3	4	5

Variable—Cause of crime ("One of the major reasons for crime is poor parenting.")

strongly disagree	disagree	neutral	agree	strongly agree
0	1	3	4	5

Variable—Crime seriousness

murder	assault	burglary	theft	jaywalking
5	4	3	2	1

Note: Any numbers can be assigned to the values (categories) as long as the correct order is maintained.

Interval Level of Measurement

We discovered that nominal and ordinal levels of measurement do not convey the ideas that numbers normally mean. There is no ability to arithmetically manipulate the numbers. The interval level finally gets us to that point by adding to categorization and order the concept of magnitude. Measurement at the interval level tells us *where* a number is located, what the magnitude of the number is. Or, put another way, we know the actual distance between numbers. Something measured as 47 is really two more than something with a score of 45. Moreover, that difference of 2 is the same distance as *any other* difference of 2, anywhere on the score scale.

The term *interval* comes from the Latin word *intervallum*, meaning "a space between." Thus, the defining characteristic of interval-level measurement is that spaces between numbers are meaningful distances. We are no longer guessing at the distance between categories. We now know the exact distance.

Another way to describe interval-level measurement is to say that it is capable of being continuously subdivided. That is, one does not run a race in 12 seconds but perhaps 12.57 seconds. If our measurement is even more accurate, we may measure 12.574 seconds. If you run the race in 12.573 seconds, you will be faster than I—by a real .001 seconds. This is the essence of interval-level measurement.

Interval-level measures have no *real* zero point. Instead, they have an arbitrary zero, around which other points are scored. The way we measure temperature is a good example of this issue. Celsius temperatures are not really based on hot/cold temperatures, but the three states of water (H_2O). At or below zero degrees water is a solid, from 1 to 99 degrees water is a fluid, and at 100 degrees water is a gas. Zero degrees Celsius is not a *real* zero, it is just a point on the measuring scale defined by something that is not temperature. Every one point on the Celsius scale, however, represents the same distance as any other point. Another example is time. Time obviously is a continuously flowing phenomenon, yet we are able to measure a zero point in a foot race and say how quickly the winner of the race ran the distance. That zero point is simply arbitrary—there was *some* time before and after we started the race. This arbitrary zero point problem also causes problems for arithmetic manipulation. We *should* be able to do mathematical operations with interval-level data and, indeed, we do. However, the lack of a real zero point precludes our really arriving at estimates of relative size (see Box 2.3).

BOX 2.3

SUMMARY FOR INTERVAL LEVEL OF MEASUREMENT

Characteristics:

✓ *Categorizes*

✓ *Ranks*

✓ *Establishes magnitude (actual distance)*

Examples:

Variable—Temperature

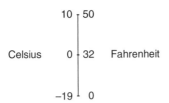

Variable—Time (units are equal—seconds, for example—but where does one begin the zero point?)

Note: At the interval level, one unit of distance is the same no matter where it is on the scale; but there is no real zero.

A final problem is that if we examine our measurement *very* closely for accuracy, we discover that everything is rounded off (for example, 12.57 to 12.6). If this is so, it is also true that what we perceive as an exact position is actually determined by the accuracy of our measurement. No matter how accurately we measure, even more accurate measurement is theoretically possible; thus, we never really know the *exact* position of something. As a result, one can argue that, without exact position, we are simply measuring things at the ordinal level—very exactingly, to be sure—but still ordinal. To overcome this critique, the concept of *metric ordinal* has been introduced. Metric ordinal measurement is measurement that is so close to interval that there is little error involved in treating it as if it *were* interval. When discussing ordinal-level measurement, we normally use the basic version of ordinal—more than, less than—but we are not able to reasonably estimate distance between points. We save the reasonable estimation of distance for the interval level (or call it metric ordinal).

Ratio Level of Measurement

The final level of measurement is aptly termed *ratio*. Having everything that the other levels do, ratio adds the concept of a real zero point. Thus, at the ratio level, a zero point means "nothing," "absence of the thing," "nada," "zilch"—and that point only exists at one place. This means that it is possible not only to establish relative distance (interval level), but also to establish relative size. In other words, something measured at 5.0 is *half* the size of something at 10.0. This can only be done when there is a true zero point.

The term *ratio* is derived from the Latin word *ratio*, meaning "computation or reason." Ratio-level data, then, can finally be used in *any* form of computation. These are the "numbers" that we were exposed to in our early education and these are the numbers that most people think of (see Box 2.4).

Though there are many variables that are capable of being measured at the ratio level, the normal practice in statistics is to stop with the interval level. Our "best" and most sophisticated statistics are interval-level tools, mostly because interval measurement is so close to ratio measurement that there is negligible error in treating ratio data as if they were interval.

LEVEL OF MEASUREMENT AND ERROR

Obviously, the concept of level of measurement must be useful for statisticians. But how? The answer lies in the way we analyze events, conditions, and behaviors. All statistics were originally created (yes, someone "created" each and every one of the statistics you will run across) for special purposes. That is, someone had a problem they need to analyze and developed a statistic to help them in that situation. Once the statistic was created, other analysts began to use it as well, often ignoring the special situation for which the statistic was developed. Though there are many assumptions that one can make about the data for which a statistic will be used, the most basic is level of measurement. For instance, we may have a nominal-level independent variable (gender or race) and want to see its effect on

---

BOX 2.4

SUMMARY FOR RATIO LEVEL
OF MEASUREMENT

Characteristics:

✓ *Categorizes*

✓ *Ranks*

✓ *Establishes magnitude*

✓ *Adds an absolute zero (real zero point)*

Examples:

Variable — Heat (temperature) measured on the Kelvin scale

Variable — Income

       $0 $10,000 $20,000 $100,000

Variable — Prior record (number of crimes previously committed)

       0   1   2   3   4   5   37

Note: At the ratio level the concept of zero is critical — zero must really mean "nothing."

---

some dependent variable (drunken driving, for example). Because one of the variables is nominal, we need to use a statistic that was created for analyzing nominal-level data. If we don't, we introduce *error* into the analysis simply because we chose the wrong statistic.

How does such error develop? Imagine that we used an interval-level statistic to analyze our race and drunken driving data. Race is clearly a nominal-level variable. What would happen if we treated it as if the numbers were interval? The different categories of race would then be perceived as if they were not only more than or less than others, but also as if they were exact distances from the other categories (depending on the numbers we assigned to each race category, of course). The results from our interval-level statistic would be based on these exact distances, which of course don't exist. The effect of this is that we might think that there is a difference between the races and their frequency of drunken driving when, in reality, there is none (or the reverse might be true). This is error, pure and simple, and it might cause us to propose an expensive social program to "cure" drunken driving for some racial group when that group was no different from any other race.

In sum, each statistic "assumes" a certain level of measurement. If you use that statistic with any other level of measurement, you are creating error in your interpretations. How much error depends on how badly you have misjudged the level of measurement. Unfortunately, real data are not exactly represented by the four levels of measurement. Remember the concept of "metric ordinal?" It is

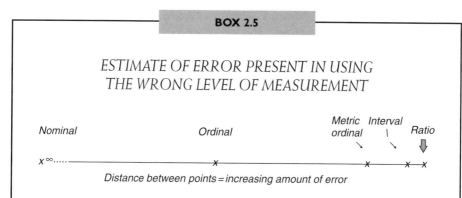

BOX 2.5

ESTIMATE OF ERROR PRESENT IN USING
THE WRONG LEVEL OF MEASUREMENT

Distance between the location of each level of measurement (*x*) represents estimated error in treating the true level as some other level. For instance, interval and ratio levels are at almost the same point so there is little error in treating ratio data as interval. On the other hand, the greatest amount of error, represented by the distance between them, is that of nominal and ratio (note the infinity sign at the nominal end of the chart—this means that the actual level of error is even greater than suggested by the line distance). Metric ordinal data, such as years of age, is pretty close to the interval level and can be treated as interval level without much relative error. Ordinal, on the other hand, represents a lot of error when treated as interval.

actually preferable to treat metric ordinal data as interval data because there is less error in "moving up" the measurement scale than "moving down." The important thing to remember here is that you need to be aware of the level of measurement that each statistic assumes so that you can avoid interjecting error into your interpretations. Box 2.5 presents an estimate of relative error from using a statistic with the wrong level of measurement assumptions. The amount of error represented in this box is not precise, nor does anyone actually know just how much error really takes place. The idea, though, is useful and perhaps you can think of this box as a metric ordinal version of the concept of level of measurement error.

SUMMARY

Level of measurement is one of the most important concepts in statistics. This is because each concept (race, income, victimization, fear of crime) has buried within it a level of measurement. For instance, no one would think of asking "how much" race (a nominal concept) nor would they ask "what kind" of time (a ratio concept). Level of measurement is inherent in concepts. As level of measurement increases from nominal through ratio, the amount of measurement information conveyed by the concept increases. Nominal concepts contain very little information. Ratio concepts contain the greatest amount.

Though you can always measure a concept at a level lower than its real level (unless, of course, it is nominal), this results in throwing away information (a form of error). As a result, it is best to measure concepts and use variables at their true level of measurement.

The next chapter contains what you have probably been waiting for—examples of a type of statistics. But before you get too excited, these are statistics you have seen many times and are graphical versions, or statistical methods using "pictures."

KEY POINTS OF THE CHAPTER

- Nominal—*Categorizes*
- Ordinal—*Ranks* (and *categorizes*)
- Interval—*Establishes magnitude* (and everything above)
- Ratio—*Establishes absolute zero* (and everything above)

There are very few statistics that actually require the ratio level of measurement, so for introductory statistical purposes we can treat interval and ratio as if they were the same.

CHAPTER 3

Graphical Statistics

Key Concepts

- pie charts

- bar charts

- histograms

- line charts

- scatterplots

- discrete data

- continuous data

- extremes

In one sense, all statistics provide an image of data. This image is usually derived from a statistical result, such as calculating an average or probability associated with a *t*-test. The problem is that you have to know something about the statistic before you can form the image in your mind. Some statistics, however, give us a direct image that requires us to know very little about the statistic itself. These images are generically called *graphics*. Most statistical graphics demonstrate the shape of a variable distribution—the way in which the scores (or values) are distributed. These images and shapes give us visual versions of variance present in the data.

Graphical statistics can be very useful in understanding variable distributions so we can make better choices of which inferential or predictive statistics should be used. If we don't use graphic versions, it would be necessary to use tables (numbers and text-based versions) to gain the same understanding.

In this chapter, we will examine five common types of statistical graphics: pie charts, bar charts, histograms, line charts, and scatterplots. In all of them there are at least three parts to be presented:

- labels, so readers know what is being presented
- some type of scale, so readers know the relative size of the graph elements
- the graph elements

A key focus, which is true in the presentation of all statistical results, is not to do something that would mislead people. With graphical statistics, this usually means eliminating distractions or distortions present in the relative size of graph elements, the scale, or too much "labeling."

GRAPHICAL STATISTICS FOR DISCRETE VARIABLES

Data are usually considered to be discrete or continuous. As discussed in Chapter 2, nominal- and ordinal-level data are normally considered to be discrete. A discrete variable is one in which measurement describes categories, regardless of whether they are ranked or not. The numbers used with discrete variables are usually whole numbers (1, 2, 43, etc.). Religion, parole classification levels, or gender are examples of discrete variables. Some graphics are much more useful with *discrete data. Continuous data* are those with interval- or ratio-level measurement. In one sense, these data have unlimited subdivisions (think in terms of values after a decimal point)—so values such as 3.1417 are meaningful. Because continuous variables can have so many potential values, graphics that show each value as a category can become meaningless or very hard to interpret. As a result, some statistical graphics are especially designed for continuous variables. We will first examine those used for discrete variables.

Pie Charts

Pie charts are used for quickly seeing the relative proportions of the categories (values) of a variable. They are at their most useful when there are few categories (perhaps six or fewer). A pie chart is composed of a circle which represents all of some variable. Segments, or pieces of the pie, represent the categories of the variable. Because the entire pie is the "whole," it represents 100% or a proportion of 1.0—all of the scores. Each piece of the pie represents the percentage or proportion of the scores contained in that category.

The pie chart in Figure 3.1 is a basic one, demonstrating the proportion of people who reported ever being called for jury duty. The interpretation is relatively straightforward: Slightly more people have been called for jury duty than those who haven't. In percentage terms, we might estimate that perhaps 55% of those who responded to this survey had been called for jury duty. The exact percentage is, of course, not known from the pie chart—it has to be estimated. While it is possible to have percentages (and raw number of cases) reported in a pie chart, one of the general flaws of a pie chart is that most people find it difficult to estimate how much the various segments actually represent. Indeed, a general rule is that the difficulty of estimating relative amounts increases as the number of segments increases.

Consider the chart in Figure 3.2—an illustration of a variable having too many segments to be presented properly in a pie chart. There are approximately 20 values (categories) in the variable, which is the number of prior arrests for a sample of released prisoners. Even the graph program's automatic identification of separate slices cannot handle the number (there are four "black" slices). Moreover, trying to estimate the percentage of each category is very difficult. For instance, what percent of released prisoners would you estimate have 14 prior

FIGURE 3.1 A Simple Pie Chart

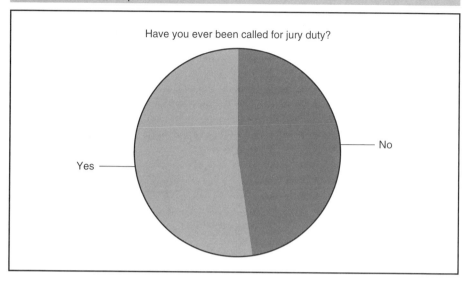

FIGURE 3.2 A Pie Chart with Too Many Slices

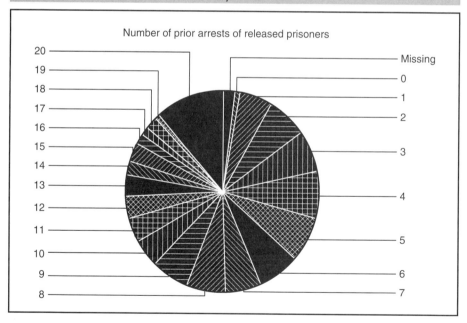

arrests? How different is this from those with 13 and 15 prior arrests? The differences are hard to determine.

It is also possible to use pie charts to compare data, but they are not very good for this purpose. The difficulty of estimating differences between slices within a pie is exacerbated by trying to compare slices between two or more pies.

FIGURE 3.3 Example of Pie Charts Used for Comparison

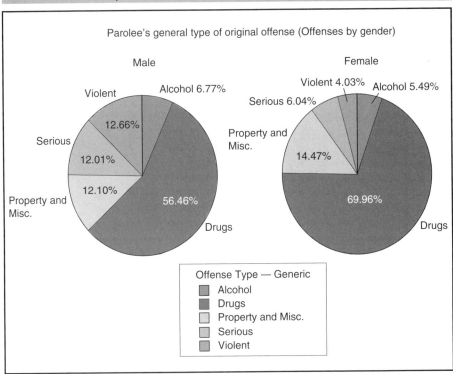

Look at the comparison of male and female offenses in Figure 3.3. A few things are immediately evidently, such as the fact that females are more likely to have been imprisoned for a drug offense. Beyond that, however, the two pies must be closely inspected to find possible differences. In fact, the percentages in the pie charts are more useful than the relative size of the slices. The general lesson here is to stay away from pie charts when you are trying to compare things.

On the whole, data presented in pie charts are probably better represented with bar charts or even tables. Actual category percentages and proportions frequently must accompany pie charts for viewers to make sense of them. If that is the case for the data you intend to present, use better approaches to data visualization and leave pie charts alone.

Bar Charts

Bar charts are also a simple way to view data quickly and in many cases are a highly efficient way to do so. Most people are familiar with them and the bar's approximation to the length of a line is an intuitive approach for establishing the concept of magnitude (number of cases in the category). In bar charts magnitude is usually placed on the Y (vertical) axis and the categories of a variable are placed on the X (horizontal) axis. It is also possible to construct a bar chart with the X and Y axes reversed (the variable on the Y axis) when category labels are too long.

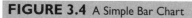

FIGURE 3.4 A Simple Bar Chart

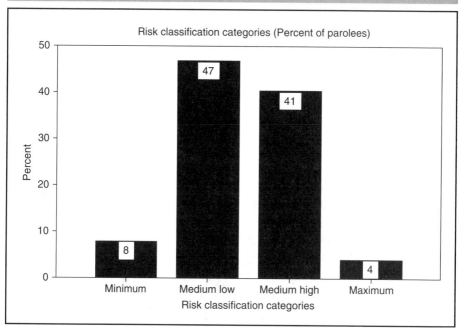

Figure 3.4 is an example of a typical bar chart constructed with the variable on the *X* axis representing parolee risk classification categories. Each bar represents the percent of parolees classified into that risk category. The conclusion one can quickly draw from this bar chart is that there are very few parolees in the minimum and maximum classification categories. The percentages can be found by using percent tick marks on the *Y* axis and looking across (grid lines can be added to make this easier), but in the case of our example, the bars have percentage labels added. If your graphics program will allow it, the best practice is to add labels to the bars.

Bar charts are also useful when there are several categories, something a pie chart can't handle. There is a limit, however, to the number of categories people can visually compare. That limit is somewhere around 15 categories. Beyond that number, it becomes difficult to see differences along the scale (the lowest to the highest categories), particularly when one attempts to compare individual categories. Figure 3.5 has 21 categories of "number of prior arrests" and that is only because the last category of "20" arbitrarily was created to contain all higher numbers of arrests. You can see the overall trend at a glance, however, and that is a decreasing number of parolees who have larger numbers of prior arrests after one to eight arrests. Another problem is evident in Figure 3.5—the "20" and more category is misleading. Parolees with 20 prior arrests appear to be the most common, but the collapse of all numbers above 20 into that category is the cause of the large bar. In reality, the decreasing progression seen in bars representing 9 through 19 prior arrests continues.

A bar chart can also be easily constructed to compare two variables. The second variable results in multiple bars for each category, called a "clustered bar

FIGURE 3.5 Example of a Bar Chart with Many Categories

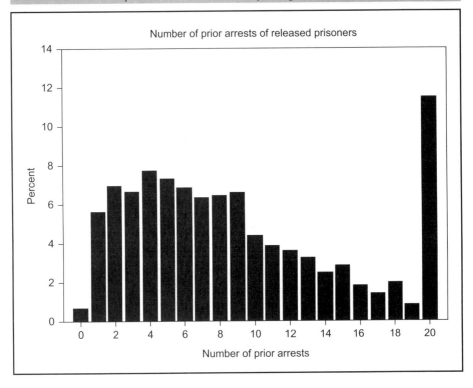

FIGURE 3.6 Example of a Clustered Bar Chart with Two Variables

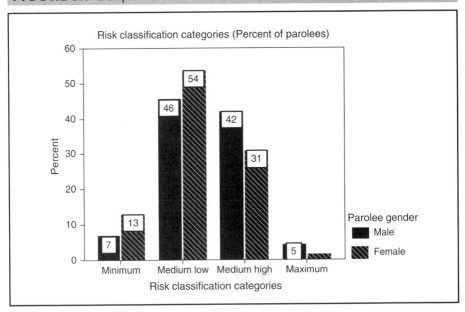

chart," as is Figure 3.6. This allows for an easy comparison of potential differences created by the categories of the second variable. The example depicts the parole risk classification categories we looked at earlier (Figure 3.4) and adds the parolee's gender. Thus, there are now two bars for each risk classification category—one for males and one for females. It seems that females are more likely to be in minimum or medium-low classifications and males in medium-high and maximum classifications. However, the number of bars for the four categories has now doubled to eight and, had there been a third category in the second variable (such as young age, middle age, and old age), the ability to see the data image quickly would become much more difficult.

A second variable can also be added by creating multiple bar charts instead of one clustered bar chart. Figure 3.7 demonstrates what this version would look like using the risk classification variable with a three-category age variable.

FIGURE 3.7 Example of a Second Variable Used with Multiple Bar Charts

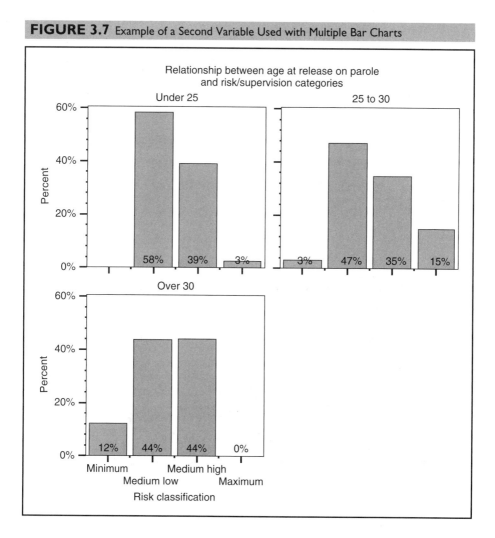

Notice that the comparison of the three age groups now requires the viewer to shift back and forth to compare the charts because the bars are no longer next to each other. This suggests that a clustered bar chart is a better approach than using multiple bar charts. It also takes much less space.

GRAPHICAL STATISTICS FOR CONTINUOUS DATA

Histograms

A histogram is a form of a bar chart used for continuous data rather than for discrete data. So far, our examples have used discrete data (except for the number of prior arrests variable in Figure 3.5). Histograms have bars that touch each other because the continuous numbers are interval- and ratio-level measurement. Each number on the X axis is "whole" unit rather than an actual numeric point and merely serves as a handy location for marking the axis. For instance, the number 3 could be rounded up from a 2.50 or might be as high as a 3.49; thus the sides of bars in a histogram represent the halfway point between whole numbers. Figure 3.8 is an example of a histogram. Because it uses the same variable as Figure 3.5, you can compare the way the two look. One difference is that this chart has the number of cases on the Y axis rather than percent—that frequently makes more sense when there are a large number of values (categories). A second difference is that

FIGURE 3.8 Example of a Histogram

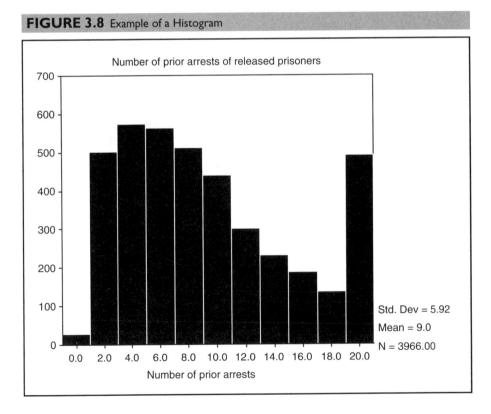

some group statistics are provided: the standard deviation, the mean, and the number of cases. For discrete variables such statistics make no sense, but for continuous variables they add important information (these statistics will be discussed in later chapters). Note also that the X-axis tick marks now have decimal points rather than the whole numbers present in bar graphs.

Line Graphs

Line graphs are potentially the most useful of all graphs. They are designed for continuous data, but are also visually appropriate for discrete data. The graph has an X and Y axis, much like a histogram, but there are no bars—just a line running through what would have been the top of each bar. As a result, line graphs are primarily used when there are two variables to show the relationship between them. They are also useful in showing trends over time.

Figure 3.9 is a simple line graph of a single discrete variable, in this case our risk classification categories as previously pictured by the bar chart in Figure 3.4. The results are the same, suggesting that for a single discrete variable either a line or bar chart could be used. When the variable is continuous, such as our age variable, the line graph is a better choice.

The two-variable line graph is probably one of the most commonly-used graphical techniques in statistics. It excels in demonstrating comparative differences and relationships. For instance, the two variables used in Figure 3.3, original offenses and gender, can quickly show the differences between males and females by using a line graph. Figure 3.10 places the original offenses on the bottom of the graph (X axis), the percentage of parolees in each general type of offense is on the side (Y axis), and the two lines represent the percentage of males and females in each offense type. We might interpret the results as females

FIGURE 3.9 Example of a Simple, One-variable Line Graph

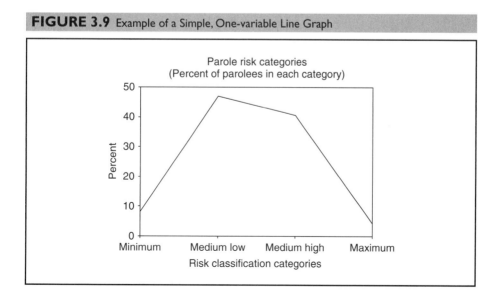

FIGURE 3.10   Example of Two-variable Line Graph with Two Groups in the Second Variable

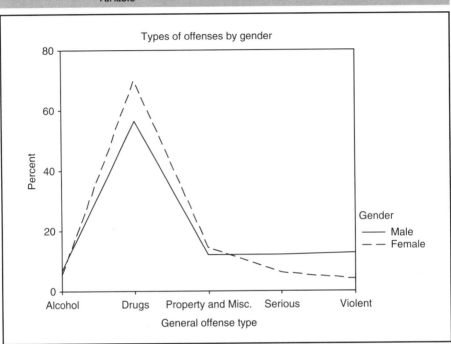

are more likely to have committed a drug offense and males are more likely to have committed serious and violent offenses.

Finally, the use of line graphs for demonstrating trends over time is illustrated in Figure 3.11. Plotting the cumulative parole failure rate over time (each day of the first year on parole), we can see that the failure rate steadily increases until about 100 days when it begins to level out and slowly increase. The total failure rate is about 50%, with most of that happening in the first 200 days. While this is a simple plot, the data image yields important information.

Scatterplots

Another form of graph used with continuous data is a scatterplot. These graphs illustrate relationships between two variables by putting one variable on the Y axis and the other on the X axis and placing a dot at the corresponding values for each case. For instance, a person who is 18 years of age (X axis) with 4 prior arrests (Y axis) would have a dot at the graph junction of $Y = 4$ and $X = 18$. Figure 3.12 shows a scatterplot using these two variables. Because we have not yet reached the point where a discussion of the concept of relationships is appropriate, suffice it to say that there is not much in the way of a relationship present in the data represented in Figure 3.12. What little exists suggests that there is a small relationship in which the number of prior arrests increases with age (but this changes after approximately age 50 or so).

FIGURE 3.11 Example of Using a Line Graph to Demonstrate Trends

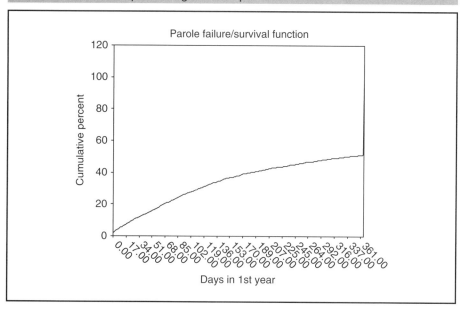

FIGURE 3.12 Example of a Scatterplot

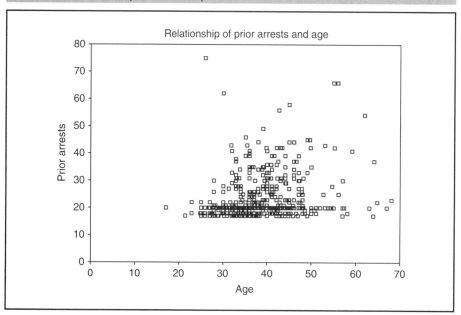

Scatterplots are also useful in locating extremes in the data. For instance, some of the data points in our example show an extremely high number of arrests, 50 or above. At the same time, there are some extreme ages, those 60 or above and one case under 20. Extremes occur when there are very high or low scores for a few cases. These are also referred to as *outliers* and can affect the results of some statistics. Later we will discuss why this is so and how outliers might be handled.

SUMMARY

Graphical statistics are part of what is generally called *exploratory data analysis.* They provide an image of important aspects of data, thus enabling an analyst to grasp the essential details of variable distributions and, in some cases, relationships between variables. One of the most important parts of any analysis is to understand the data at a fundamental level. This means you should never jump in at the very beginning with a sophisticated, complex analytical tool; the chances of making mistakes are great. A better practice is to explore the data at its elementary levels, and graphics are one way to do that. At the same time, you should refrain from using these kinds of graphics for complex issues because the pictures become complex, and difficult to interpret, as well.[1]

KEY POINTS OF THE CHAPTER

Use graphical statistics to simplify the presentation of information.
- For discrete data, use pie charts or bar charts.
- For continuous data, use histograms, line charts, and scatterplots.
- Additional variables can be added to any graphical statistic to compare multiple categories.
- Never let the graphics become too complex to understand at a glance.

---

[1]There are some more complex forms of graphical statistics. For those who are interested, Appendix A describes a "box plot" that provides information on several levels at once. You might want to wait to examine this until you have read through the chapters on both measures of central tendency and dispersion, though.

CHAPTER 4

Measures of Central Tendency

Key Concepts

■ univariate statistics

■ central tendency

■ mode

■ median

■ mean

We are now ready for our first nongraphical statistical techniques, and in the next few chapters we'll discuss what are known as *univariate statistics*. Univariate statistics are designed to give us information on a *single variable*—therefore, they do not tell us about relationships but, instead, about the way the scores in a variable are distributed. The graphical statistics in the previous chapter were primarily univariate in nature, yet they can also accommodate more than one variable (bivariate or multivariate). Some of them, like a scatterplot, are naturally oriented toward multiple variables.

Among the most common of univariate statistics are those called "averages," but their correct term is measures of *central tendency*. In one sense, all statistics assist us in creating a mental picture of the ways data may be distributed (i.e., a picture of the way some characteristic looks). For instance, if we asked the ages of a sample of 100 students, it would be difficult to look at all of the individual ages and make sense of that characteristic. So, we might attempt to determine the *average* age as a way of describing and making sense of the group. In fact, we could use the average age to compare our sample of students to another group. Thus the term measures of *central tendency* refers to the fact that they focus on the *middle* of the data. In other words, they provide us a picture of the entire data set by focusing on the central part, or point, of the group.

If there were only one "average," it would be easy to talk about a central tendency. Indeed, you already know what an average is and you probably have been using one for years—the *mean*. Unfortunately, a mean requires data with certain characteristics and should only be used when these criteria are met. Other averages are used with other forms of data. The three measures of central tendency we will discuss are mode, median, and mean.

THE MODE

The first, and simplest, measure of central tendency is the *mode*. This average makes no arithmetic requirements of data with which it is used. That is, it can be used with data measured at the nominal level. Actually, the mode is considered the nominal level measure of central tendency. A mode is defined as the category with the greatest number of cases. In other words, *any* category, no matter the size of its value, is the mode if more cases occur in it than any other category. For example, if we have 62 cases distributed across three categories (values)—5, 21, and 33—like this:

> 12 fives
> 44 twenty-ones
> 6 thirty-threes

then the category (or the value) 21 is the mode. It has more cases than either of the other two values or categories. Box 4.1 has another example of locating the mode.

When There Is More than One Mode

The mode gets a bit more complicated if *two or more categories* are tied for the largest number of cases. If two categories are tied, we call the distribution *bimodal*. If three are tied, the distribution is called *trimodal*; four or more would be referred to as *multimodal*. Examples of these types of modes (shown as line graph distributions in the figure) are in Figure 4.1.

Usefulness of the Mode

Because the mode only requires nominal-level data, it can be used with any level of data. One way the mode is useful is to tell us the most frequent value—for instance, if we wanted to know the most frequent type of crime, a search for the modal category of index crimes in the UCR would tell us that it is theft (the most frequently occurring crime). As another example, if you had to make a correct guess about the results of throwing a pair of dice (as in the game of craps), the

---

BOX 4.1

AN EXAMPLE OF THE MODE

Locating the mode: If 122 cases were distributed across five values, or categories, as follows

Value:	1	2	3	4	5

and the number of cases with each value is as follows,

Number of cases:	23	22	25	32	20
				▲	

Then the mode would be 4 because it has the *largest number* of cases (32).

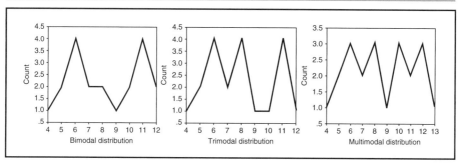

FIGURE 4.1 Example of Distributions with More than One Mode (more than one category with the same number of "highest" cases)

mode would be your best guess. The modal guess for throwing a pair of dice would be "7" because it occurs more times than any other result (there are actually seven ways to get a "7" with a pair of dice).

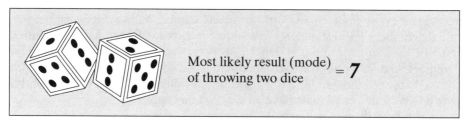

Most likely result (mode) of throwing two dice $= 7$

Therefore, you could say that the mode helps us to predict outcomes or categories—and that's pretty useful for such a simple statistic.

THE MEDIAN

The second measure of central tendency is called the *median* (you will frequently see "*mdn*" used in formulas to represent the median). A median is defined as the midpoint case in an ordered distribution. In other words, if all the values in a distribution are place in order from low to high (like 1–100), the median is the value of the case exactly in the middle of that distribution. For example, with five cases having values of 1, 2, 3, 4, and 5, the distribution is already ordered from low to high scores and the middle case (the median) is 3. (Don't forget to arrange the values in *order*!) As long as there are an odd number of cases (3, 7, 23, 101, etc.), finding the median is easy (as in Box 4.2).

A bit of a "glitch" in the scheme of locating a median comes when there are an *even* number of cases in a data set. For all data with an even numbers of cases, you wind up with two cases in the "middle." For example, a sample of 12 cases would have cases 6 and 7 sharing the middle like this:

case 1 case 2 case 3 case 4 case 5 case 6 case 7 case 8 case 9 case 10 case 11 case 12

└─────── 5 cases ───────┘   ▲   └─────── 5 cases ───────┘

median

BOX 4.2

AN EXAMPLE OF THE MEDIAN WITH AN ODD NUMBER OF CASES

Locating the median: If the following 11 cases, or scores, are in a data set

$$1, 5, 7, 10, 2, 1, 4, 11, 8, 127, 3$$

we would first order them this way:

$$1, 1, 2, 3, 4, \underset{\blacktriangle}{5}, 7, 8, 10, 11, 127$$

With 11 cases, the midpoint case in the ordered distribution is the sixth case, or *5*. That is, there are five cases before the value of 5 and five cases after it. The median is therefore *5*.

In this event, the median is an "artificial" number halfway between the two middle numbers. For instance, if the example in Box 4.2 did not have case with a score of 127 and therefore had only 10 cases, the two middle numbers would be 4 and 5. The number halfway between them is 4.5 and that would be considered the median, even though there is no case with a value of 4.5. As a result, samples with an even number of cases have an *artificial* median.

There is, by the way, a "formula" for determining the median. It is $(n + 1) \div 2$. The *n* represents the number of cases, but this only works well when the actual scores are changed into ordered case numbers (that is, the real scores are substituted with a number that represents their rank among the rest of the scores). With small data sets, it can sometimes be easier to look at the data and locate the median. Save the calculation for larger data sets. Keep in mind that this calculation does not mean that ordinal data can be arithmetically manipulated, it is just a quick way to locate the median case (this is also *not* the median value, but the *case* with the median value—you still have to find that case).

The Median and Extremes

The median requires at least ordinal-level data (that's why the values must be placed in *order*) and is referred to as the *ordinal-level average*. One handy feature of the median is that it is not influenced by the size of extreme values in the data. In Box 4.3 the value of 130 is an extreme value and certainly not characteristic of the rest of the data, which ranges from 1 to 14. If we calculated a mean, the 130 would swing the average higher (to an approximate value of 18.5) than all of the other 11 scores (if the score of 130 were eliminated, the resulting 11 scores would sum to 92, with a more representative mean of 8.36).

The problem comes in the fact that an average (and most other statistics) is meant to draw a *mental picture* of the "usual" scores in the data. If we used the approximate mean of 18.5, most people would get the wrong picture. A mental picture using an average of 9.5, however, would represent everything but the

---

BOX 4.3

AN EXAMPLE OF USING A FORMULA
FOR FINDING A MEDIAN

Original ordered *scores* (even number of cases):

$$1, 4, 5, 6, 7, 9, 10, 11, 12, 13, 14, 130$$

Ranked scores version:

$$1, 2, 3, 4, 5, 6, 7, 8, 9, 10, 11, 12$$

Calculation from formula:

$$\text{mdn} = (n + 1) \div 2$$
$$= (12 + 1) \div 2$$
$$= (13) \div 2 = 6.5 \text{ (i.e., between ranked scores 6 and 7)}$$
$$= 6.5 \text{ ranked score} = \text{between original scores of } \mathbf{9} \text{ and } \mathbf{10} = \mathbf{9.5}$$

Which is better? Would you want to represent the scores in Box 4.3 with

the mean of 18.5? Or,
the median of 9.5?

---

score of 130 fairly well. Where the median statistic is concerned, the 130 score is just "another score" and its size is not important. For this reason, the U.S. Census Bureau reports the *median* income and not the mean income of U.S. citizens because someone like Bill Gates would draw the mean income higher. Any time you see extremes in a data set (or anticipate them) it is a wise idea to use the median when reporting an average.

MEMO **Why It Is Preferable to Discuss *Median* Income Levels**

The U.S. Census Bureau estimates a U.S. income distribution in which people who have annual incomes over $150,000 represent only about 5% of the population. This small group represents extreme high scores (incomes) that will influence the overall mean.

The *mean* household income in 2004 was $60,528, whereas the *median* household income was $43,389.

Using the mean as the average allows a small group of higher-income earners to swing the average household income up by more than $17,000, a not insubstantial amount.

To best characterize the income of *most* of the population, you would want to use the median as the measure of average.

THE MEAN

The final average we will discuss here is the *mean* (the formula symbol for a sample mean is $\bar{x}$—an "*x*" with a bar over it—and the symbol for a population mean is the Greek letter μ). It is defined as the *arithmetic average* of a set of scores. This denotes that it is a calculated score requiring at least interval-level data because it uses magnitudes or "real" values (a score of 127 is just that—127). This average is also the one taught in school as you grew up; therefore, everyone knows about it. The main thing to keep in mind is that you cannot perform arithmetic operations (add, subtract, multiply, or divide) with nominal or ordinal data, so the mean shouldn't be used with such data because it is an arithmetic average. When you have interval or ratio data, the mean is an excellent measure of central tendency. (Just keep in mind the problem of extremes.)

How is the mean calculated? (Sorry, this is an instance where we *must* do some arithmetic.) The formula is simple. It is the sum of the scores divided by the number of scores:

$$\bar{x} = \frac{\Sigma x}{N}$$

Where Σx is the sum of the individual scores and N is the number of cases (individual scores).

For instance, to calculate the mean for three scores of 11, 14, and 20, you would first add them (a total of 45) and then divide by 3 (the number of scores) to get a mean of 15, like this:

$$\Sigma x = 11 + 14 + 20 = 45 \qquad \bar{x} = 45 \div 3 = 15$$

Other than needing interval- or ratio-level data and the problem posed by extreme scores, the mean has no "glitches" and is easily interpreted and popular. You don't even have to order the scores, just perform the calculations directly (see Box 4.4 for an example). Moreover, it is the foundation for most of our more sophisticated and most powerful statistics.

BOX 4.4

AN EXAMPLE OF THE MEAN

Locating a mean: If the following 11 cases, or scores, are in a data set

$$1, 5, 7, 10, 2, 1, 4, 11, 8, 127, 3$$

we would first add them to get 179, then divide by 11 to get 16.27

This is the mean for the set of 11 scores.

Here's the formula again, just in case: $\bar{x} = \dfrac{\Sigma x}{N}$

The mean also has an interesting property because of its arithmetic base—it is the one point that is closest to *all* of the scores in the data. That is, if you were to subtract all scores from the mean and sum the results, the resulting number would be lower than subtracting and summing all scores from any other number. This property will justify using the mean as the standard reference point in the next chapter.

As an information item, there are more types of means, each with their own way of calculation. The one we have been discussing, and the formula above, is called the *arithmetic mean*. Two other less common ones are the geometric mean and the harmonic mean. We won't go into those here because they are only used in the social sciences by advanced statistics.

THE USE OF AVERAGES TO COMPARE GROUPS

One of the major uses of measures of central tendency, especially the mean, is to compare two or more groups of individuals to see if they are different. Admittedly, this is a simple comparison, but it is really common—probably because most people understand a mean. In the foundation terms with which we began our discussion of statistics, this is a form of variance. The issue is whether two averages *vary* from each other. Thus, measures of central tendency for multiple groups can be compared to see if the groups vary from each other by their central points.

For example, if we had a sample of victims and we wanted to see whether males or females were more likely to be victimized by drunk drivers, it would be easy to calculate the mean occurrence of lifetime DWI victimizations for each group. A data set from one of the author's surveys provides this information:

Group	Mean occurrence of lifetime DWI victimization
Males	0.16
Females	0.14

From this information, we could conclude that males are slightly more likely to be a DWI victim in their lifetime than females. The difference is very small, though, and may not be a "real" one. Let's ask a similar question about people with different levels of education, but change the victimization question to any lifetime experience of a violent crime. The results are as follows:

Educational level	Mean occurrence of lifetime violent victimization
Less than high school	0.10
High school graduate	0.20
Some college	0.24

It seems that those with the lowest level of education are less likely to have been a victim of a violent crime and those with high school or above are more likely (but relatively the same). While the interpretation of these results may be questionable,[1] you can see that measures of central tendency can, indeed, be used to compare groups on some characteristic.

SUMMARY

Measures of central tendency are common statistics and we learn about the mean in elementary school. The measures are handy for prediction, splitting up a group for sampling, determining "normal" characteristics of groups, and giving us a standard point of reference when looking for differences when comparing groups. In fact, the latter use is why measures of central tendency are sometimes discussed as *central points* in the data.

While measures of central tendency are informative, as we have seen, they sometimes do not adequately represent a distribution and give misleading results, particularly when two distributions are being compared. Take, for instance, the following two distributions.

Group A	*50*	*75*	*100*	*Mean = 75, Median = 75*
Group B		*60 75 85*		*Mean = 75, Median = 75*

It should be obvious that while the means and medians for both A and B imply that they are similar distributions, they are not. The scores in distribution A are more spread out than those in B; therefore, the two are not the same. How is this problem resolved?

The problem of difference in the way data scores are spread out is specifically answered by measures of dispersion, or variation. These measures are the subject of the next chapter.

KEY POINTS OF THE CHAPTER

There are three major measures of central tendency.
- *Mode*: The nominal-level average can be used with any kind of data, and provides the most frequent score.
- *Median*: The ordinal-level average provides the midpoint of a set of scores, and can be helpful in locating a more characteristic average when there are extreme scores in the data.
- *Mean*: The interval-level average is the arithmetic midpoint in a set of scores, requires the ability to arithmetically calculate, is sensitive to extreme scores in the data, and is used in most sophisticated statistics.

These statistics give us a numeric *point* that can be used to represent a set of data.

---

[1] Just in case, you should know that the sample contained all "adults" aged 17 and older. The younger ones obviously haven't as much chance to increase their educational level and have a limited amount of time to experience victimization.

CHAPTER 5

Measures of Dispersion

Key Concepts

■ measures of dispersion

■ homogeneity

■ heterogeneity

■ range

■ variance

■ standard deviation

Measures of dispersion (or variation) are designed to represent the *spread* in a data distribution by providing a number that gives a picture of the relative amount of spread. (Another way to put this is that they represent a *distance* along a score scale.) There are dispersion statistics for each level of measurement, but we will consider these only for the interval level here.

Because the concepts behind these measures are important to many other statistics, this is the one time we will actually "construct" the statistics involved. The boxes in this chapter will demonstrate the simple mathematics involved in the concepts leading to the dispersion statistics that are actually used. This will be done by starting with the concept of distance (something you have already seen in the mean) and then introducing solutions to various problems that cause errors in interpreting the amount of dispersion. At the end of this chapter, we will have conceptually developed the two major dispersion measures used in contemporary statistics: the *variance* and the *standard deviation*.

ALIKE OR DIFFERENT?

Before we start looking at the statistics, there are two general concepts that are important to dispersion. When we speak of scores that are very close to each other, the scores are referred to as being *homogeneous*. When scores are wide apart, the term is *heterogeneous*. Perfect homogeneity would happen when all scores are the same. That is, there is no distance between the scores. Perfect heterogeneity occurs when all scores are different and are as far apart as possible for the scale on which they are being measured. As a result, perfect heterogeneity is

41

BOX 5.1

EXAMPLES OF HOMOGENEITY
AND HETEROGENEITY

Homogeneity—scores that are "more" alike:

  1 1 1 1 2 2 2 2 2 2 2 2 2 3 3 3 3 3 (Scores are close together)

  1 1 1 1 1 1 1 1 1 1 1 1 1 1   (*Perfect* homogeneity—all scores are the same)

Heterogeneity—scores that are "more" different (unalike):

  1 3 8 9 40 61 67 72 84 106   (Scores are not close together)

  1 200 400 501 690 822 1,009 1,327 (Scores are even more different than the first group above—there is *no perfect* heterogeneity)

Homogeneity and heterogeneity are *relative* terms (except for perfect homogeneity), and we use them to compare groups to each other in terms of which group is *more* homogeneous or heterogeneous.

---

a relative concept, depending on the highest and lowest possible scores. When perfect homogeneity occurs, a measure of dispersion should yield an amount of zero (0). A maximum heterogeneity score depends on the measurement scale. Numbers moving away from zero suggest a decreasing homogeneity in the data and an increasing heterogeneity (Box 5.1).

USING THE EXTREMES TO MEASURE DISPERSION

The Range

The simplest measure of dispersion (at the interval level) is called the *range*. It is a measure of the distance between the highest and lowest scores in a set of data. For instance, in the following set of data

$$95 \quad 100 \quad 105 \quad 106 \quad 107 \quad 110 \quad 112 \quad 215$$

the range is calculated by subtracting the lowest score from the highest score. For the data above this would be

Highest score → 215
Lowest score → 95
Range = (215 − 95) = **120**

| BOX 5.2 | | |

EXAMPLE OF THE RANGE

| *Group A* | 50 | | 75 | | 100 | Mean = 75, Median = 75 |
| *Group B* | | 60 | 75 | 85 | | Mean = 75, Median = 75 |

Group A range calculation: $100 - 50 = \textbf{50}$ ← More disperse than B, more *heterogeneous*

Group B range calculation: $85 - 60 = \textbf{25}$ ← Less disperse than A, more *homogeneous*

The larger the number representing the range, the greater is the amount of dispersion in a set of scores. Because a range of 100 is lower than 120, the above data would represent more dispersion than the data represented by a range of 100.

In the problem presented at the end of Chapter 4 and reproduced here in Box 5.2, the A distribution would have a range of 50 (100 minus 50) and the B distribution would have a range of 25 (85 minus 60). At this point, one could see that the two distributions are not equal because they are spread differently. Thus, A is more heterogeneous than B.

Though the range has the advantage of being extremely simple to calculate, it is *not* a good measure of dispersion because it uses the worst *extremes* in the data and therefore may not be representative of the distance between most of the scores. If, for instance, a set of 14 scores is distributed as follows

$$1\ 1\ 1\ 2\ 2\ 2\ 3\ 4\ 4\ 5\ 5\ 5\ 5\ 100$$

the range would be 99. However, the mental picture that "99" creates is of a widely spread set of data. In truth, all but one of these scores are between 1 and 5, which is a relatively tight spread. The mental picture created by the range would be in error because it would misrepresent the dominant portion of the data. This fact suggests the range can easily misrepresent the distribution of data.

Another major reason for calculating data dispersion is to help us compare one set of data to another. The range is not very helpful for this purpose, either.

THE VARIANCE AND THE STANDARD DEVIATION STATISTICS

Using the Concept of Distance

Instead of using the extremes, a better approach to dispersion would be to use the distance between each score and its central point (the mean) to measure the *total* amount of dispersion. Box 5.3 shows how this would take place and the way it was

BOX 5.3

DEVELOPING THE CONCEPT OF DISTANCE FROM A CENTRAL POINT

If we use the mean for a standard central point, we can develop a "distance" concept by subtracting it from all scores.

For instance, a sample of data with the following scores

$$3 \ 4 \ 5 \ 6 \ 7 \ 8 \ 9$$

would have a mean of 6. (Sum of 42 divided by 7 = 6.)

Subtracting 6 from each score would yield the following score distances from the mean:

$$(3 - 6) + (4 - 6) + (5 - 6) + (6 - 6) + (7 - 6) + (8 - 6) + (9 - 6)$$
$$\text{Or,} \quad (-3) + (-2) + (-1) + 0 + 1 + 2 + 3$$

If these scores were summed, the result would always be zero (actually, this is a good way to check your addition). Therefore, a potential method of resolving this problem is to use the absolute values (remove the negative signs) of the distances before we add them.

$$|3 + 2 + 1 + 0 + 1 + 2 + 3|$$

The summed result is a total of 12. Therefore, the dispersion in the data is **12**.

If we turn what we just did into a formula, the formula for our simple "measure of dispersion" ("D") is

$$D = \Sigma(|x - \bar{x}|)$$

Where x represents a score, and $\bar{x}$ represents the mean.

originally developed. The best approach is to use the mean because of the fact that it will create the minimum possible amount of dispersion. That way, a standard approach to dispersion can be used—the minimum amount—when comparing multiple groups. Doing this will lead us to the two most commonly used dispersion statistics.

Subtracting the mean from a score also produces a new concept—that of *distance*—which can be used as a standard approach to dispersion. Indeed, whenever you see an equation with a term like $x - \bar{x}$, you are seeing the use of distance from some reference point to create variance (the *foundation* term, not the statistic with the same name—which will appear later in this chapter). Indeed, such terms can be called *distancing techniques*.

Now that we have the concept of distance, let's continue our development of measures of dispersion.

The Number of Cases Problem

While the idea behind the use of a distance concept is a good one, there are still problems with our approach. The primary problem at this point is that the number of scores (or cases) could affect the dispersion score. In fact, the number of scores could have a greater effect on the size of the dispersion number than the actual spread in the data—an effect that is very undesirable. This can be demonstrated by the following example comparing two data distributions in Box 5.4 using the ideas and formula developed in Box 5.3.

In comparing the "dispersion scores" of 22.5 and 24, the larger and more disperse distribution would appear to be B. Yet a close look at the two sets of scores clearly indicates distribution A is more disperse than B because the score of 20 is relatively far from the other scores of 5. On the other hand, distribution B is composed of scores that are really only one unit from their mean—a tightly knit group by any standard. So, what has happened to make our dispersion score "wrong"? The answer is simple: The discrepancy exists because A has 4 cases and B has 25 cases. When the individual distances from the mean are added, the *number* of distances generated by the number of cases (scores) becomes a factor in the size of the dispersion score. In our example in the box, group A distances totaled 22.5 with four scores and group B distances totaled 24 with 25 scores.

Fortunately, this problem can be easily resolved by *dividing by the number of cases*. In the case of distribution A we divide 22.5 by its number of cases (4) and get 5.625. The dispersion score for distribution B (24) would be divided by its number of cases (25), thus yielding 0.96.

> *Group A = 22.5 ÷ 4 = 5.625*
> *Group B = 24 ÷ 25 = 0.96*

These results match our expectations (the picture we get from looking at the scores of the two groups), because A is indeed more disperse/heterogeneous than B. The

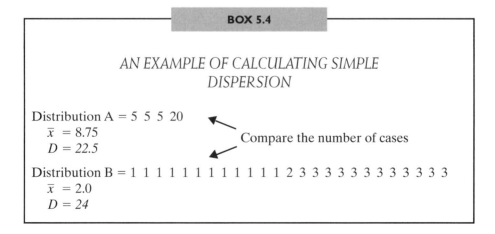

BOX 5.4

AN EXAMPLE OF CALCULATING SIMPLE DISPERSION

Distribution A = 5 5 5 20
  $\bar{x}$ = 8.75
  $D = 22.5$

Compare the number of cases

Distribution B = 1 1 1 1 1 1 1 1 1 1 1 1 1 2 3 3 3 3 3 3 3 3 3 3 3 3
  $\bar{x}$ = 2.0
  $D = 24$

number of cases problem is resolved. The new, but temporary, equation (with this problem resolution included) is now[1]

$$D = \frac{\Sigma(|x - \bar{x}|)}{N}$$

Solving the Absolute Value Problem—Creating the Variance Statistic

As you might have guessed by now, there is another general problem. Absolute numbers are mathematically undesirable and we want to avoid this technique. Therefore, we must find another method of generating the same results. The most obvious choice is to eliminate negative numbers by *squaring* the distances. This yields the same essential result but leaves us with a larger dispersion number. As long as all groups have dispersion calculated the same way, the fact that the dispersion numbers will be larger is no hindrance—they will still be in the same relative positions. The final formula (introducing squared distances and changing the "D" to a "V") gives us the commonly used measure of dispersion called the *Variance*:

$$V = \frac{\Sigma(x - \bar{x})^2}{N}$$

Let's put into words what we have done in creating this formula. The *variance* is actually the average squared distance of each score from its mean. Put another way, the statistic represents the average amount of dispersion present in a data set for some variable. We could be referring to age, income, crime rates, or anything at the interval/ratio levels. Box 5.5 illustrates the use of the variance for comparison purposes, using the two groups you have already seen in prior examples.

BOX 5.5

EXAMPLE OF THE VARIANCE STATISTIC

Distribution A = 5 5 5 20
  $\bar{x} = 8.75$
  $V = \Sigma(x - \bar{x})^2 \div N$
   $= [(5 - 8.75)^2 + (5 - 8.75)^2 + (5 - 8.75)^2 + (20 - 8.75)^2] \div 4 = \textbf{42.187}$

Distribution B = 1 1 1 1 1 1 1 1 1 1 1 1 1 2 3 3 3 3 3 3 3 3 3 3 3
  $\bar{x} - 2.0$
  $V = [(1 - 2)^2 + (1 - 2)^2 \dots \text{etc.} + (3 - 2)^2] \div 25 = \textbf{0.96}$

---

[1]This formula actually represents a real, but old, statistic called the mean deviation. It is rarely used today because of the next problem. The only reason it is included here is to show the development of the variance and standard deviation statistics.

Comparing A with B, it is obvious that a variance score of 0.96 shows that A has scores that average much more alike than B, with a variance score of 42. In fact, because a perfectly homogeneous variance score would be 0.0, A has a very small amount of dispersion. Relative to A, B has a large amount of dispersion; indeed, we might say that B has 42 times more average dispersion than A (42 ÷ 0.96).

Solving the Squared Units Problem—Creating the Standard Deviation Statistic

Even the variance has a problem remaining: All of the original units are now in squared units. For instance, if we started with scores representing ages, we would now have squared ages—and that doesn't make sense in the real world. (This is not a problem for computer calculations, however, only for *understanding* the results.) To get back to the original units (so we can talk in terms of age rather than squared age), we need to take the square root of the variance. The formula is now (adding the square root and changing the "V" to "S"):

$$S = \sqrt{\frac{\Sigma(x - \bar{x})^2}{N}}$$

The "V" is changed to an "S" because this is the formula for a common measure of dispersion called the *Standard Deviation* (the population symbol for the standard deviation is the Greek lowercase letter σ, or *sigma*). Actually, the standard deviation is just the square root of the variance. In words, *the standard deviation is the square root of the average amount of deviation of all scores from their mean.* The reason we can refer to it as the *standard* deviation is that it is standardized for both sample sizes (the "N" in the formula) and the minimum distance of all scores from a common point (the mean). No matter what size a sample may be, you can compare the standard deviation with another sample. This means we don't have to have two groups, say males and females, of the same size to make a comparison of their crime rate deviations.

Sometimes you will see either the variance or the standard deviation formula written with "$N - 1$" rather than just "N" in the denominator. This is done to produce a more "conservative" estimate of the statistic. And, perhaps this is a good time to say that scientists—the people who created statistics—prefer to make conservative estimates of virtually anything they study. The most conservative estimate possible, of course, is that nothing is really there—it's just measurement error. We'll discuss this in detail in Chapter 9.

You can find the concept of the standard deviation in other instances. If we were comparing samples of means, for instance, rather than individual scores, the same formula could be used by substituting individual means for x (the score term) and the grand mean of all of the samples for $\bar{x}$, and then calling the new formula the *standard error of the mean*. This is a term you will frequently see in computer output from statistics programs.

FURTHER USES OF MEASURES OF DISPERSION

In addition to comparing the distributions of different groups to see if they are different, measures of dispersion are used in many other statistics. The variance statistic is used in most of the interval-level measures of inference and correlation. The idea is to see if the *way* the scores in one distribution vary (another way of saying "a variable") is related to the way other variables vary and, if so, how. Because of this, we will see the variance in the formula of other common statistics. The standard deviation is usually not used in these formulas because a computer doesn't have the problem of interpreting "squared variables." On the other hand, the standard deviation becomes a handy measure when placed into the concept of a normal curve, so you will see it again there.

One final comment may be useful. There is actually a problem in comparing the standard deviations of different groups. If the means of the two groups are not essentially the same, the size of the mean will affect the size of the standard deviation. This is a *magnitude* issue and would result in a misinterpretation of the dispersion levels for two groups with really different means. For example, a group with an average score of 100 and a standard deviation of 4 would actually have a relative dispersion equal to that of a group with an average score of 50 and a standard deviation of 2. They both represent the same relative spread around the mean.

The solution is to divide the standard deviation by the mean of its group—a measure called the *Coefficient of Relative Variation* (CRV). Not many people use the CRV today because the comparison of group dispersions is a relatively elementary statistical procedure. There are better ways to compare groups. Nonetheless, there is value to simple comparisons because they provide an understanding of the shape of variable distributions necessary for choosing among the different types of more sophisticated statistics.

SUMMARY

Measures of dispersion add to our ability to characterize and compare variables. In addition to a variable's average, we now know that it is helpful to ask about its dispersion, or spread. The two main statistics here are the variance and the standard deviation, which are almost the same measures. They are frequently used and reported in research, although the standard deviation is the more common in these instances. These measures are also used in the formulas of inferential and predictive statistics to help determine the amount of variation present, and whether that variation corresponds (covaries) with other variables. Even where the data are nominal or ordinal and these two measures don't apply, the use of the general distancing approach developed in this chapter is frequently found in other statistics.

Now that we have explored the basic univariate descriptive statistics, it is time to put these statistics to use in statistical distributions and frequency distributions. The next chapter does this by exploring the types of distributions, particularly the normal curve, and the way information about a variable can be displayed in a frequency distribution.

KEY POINTS OF THE CHAPTER

 Measures of dispersion are ways to measure the spread of data in a distribution. There are two common statistics for this purpose:

- The *Variance*, which is an interval-level approach to developing average amounts of spread in data, is used in the formulas of many inferential and predictive statistics.
- The *Standard Deviation*, which is the square root of the variance statistic, is used for describing the amount of spread in terms of the original measuring units of the data.
- Any mathematical operation like $(x - \bar{x})$ is a way of creating variation or distance to be used in a statistic.

CHAPTER 6

Curves and Distributions

Key Concepts

■ distribution

■ normal distribution

■ curve peak

■ curve tails

■ symmetry

■ asymptotic

■ Z-score

Now that we know about both graphical statistics and what, for the moment, we will call *quantitative statistics* (central tendency and dispersion), we can put them together to examine the shapes displayed by variables. Each variable has a shape, or *distribution*. Most of these distributions are relatively similar, but there are a few odd ones. Because many variables have similar shapes, this makes it easier to develop statistics to match those distributions—that is, create a statistic specifically for variables with a certain distribution. If this can be done, the estimates from that statistic will be more accurate. Even better, one of these distributions, the *normal distribution*, has a relationship with the standard deviation that produces uniform results. Because of this, a simple statistic, called a *Z-score*, was developed long ago that allows comparison of the relative positions of individual scores.

STATISTICAL DISTRIBUTIONS

The Normal Curve

Many statistics assume that the distribution (shape) of data is a normal curve. A normal curve is sometimes referred to as a *bell-shaped* curve because of the way it looks. The illustration in Figure 6.1 shows what that curve looks like. If you would like to see the actual building of a normal curve, check out a Web site that uses a "pinball" concept to create one (www.dirhody.com/home.html—click on "For Parents" and then "The Normal Distribution Curve in Action!").

50

FIGURE 6.1 The Normal Distribution Curve

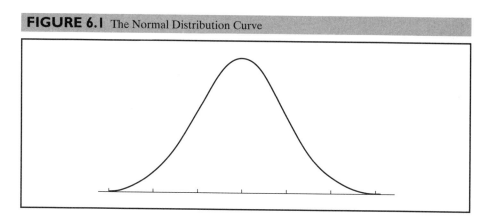

Each distribution has at least three important parts:

- the *peak*, or the highest point
- the *tails*, or the ends of the curve
- the *baseline*, or the zero cases location

These parts are displayed in Figure 6.2, using the normal curve as an illustration.

The normal curve is actually a theoretical concept—a real-world distribution can only approximate it—and is formally called the *unit normal distribution* or *standard normal distribution* (it is also called a *Gaussian* distribution, after mathematician Karl Gauss). In reality, every type of curve represents a probability distribution. Each point in a distribution corresponds to the probability (or likelihood) of that point occurring. For instance, the ends of the normal curve almost touch the baseline of zero. This means that the probability of a score occurring near the ends of a normal curve is fairly low. On the other hand, a score occurring near the peak of a normal curve is relatively high (actually, the peak itself represents the score most likely to occur). If you know the actual

FIGURE 6.2 Components of a Curve

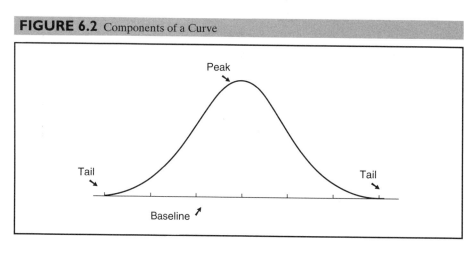

distance of each point on a curve above the baseline, you can calculate the probability of its occurrence.

These score probabilities are as follows:

- The peak of a normal curve has the highest probability of a score occurring
- Each end of a normal curve has a low probability of a score occurring
- Scores between the ends and the peak of a normal curve have an increasing probability of occurring as the point on the curve moves toward the peak

Now that these generalities are in place, let's discuss some other features of the normal curve.

Uniform Features of the Normal Curve

The normal distribution has some features that are helpful in statistics. It is symmetrical and asymptotic. *Symmetrical* means that both sides are identical. Put another way, if the curve is folded at its peak (actually, that would also be its mean), you would not be able to tell that it was folded—it would appear as if it were one-sided. As illustrated in Figure 6.3, this means that each "side" of the curve has 50% of the data in the curve. The numbers under the curve represent standard deviations, the number ".50" being the proportion of scores in the curve from the end of the tail to the midpoint.

Asymptotic means that tails of the curve never touch the baseline (remember, this is a theoretical concept) and continue to infinity. Thus, there is always a probability (no matter how unlikely) of a more extreme score in the tails. These features yield some interesting probability facts. When the standard deviation statistic (s) is calculated for a normal distribution, the percentage of scores under the curve always fall into the same locations. The numbers under the curve are actually standard deviations. Note that the numbers under the right tail are positive, the one in the middle is zero, and those under the left tail are negative. This is because we relate the numbers to the mean of the curve. If scores are higher than the mean, they are positive, and if the scores are lower

FIGURE 6.3 Symmetrical Sides of the Normal Curve

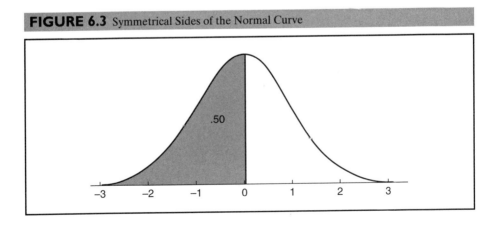

FIGURE 6.4 Percentage of Scores under the Curve at 1 and 2 Standard Deviations

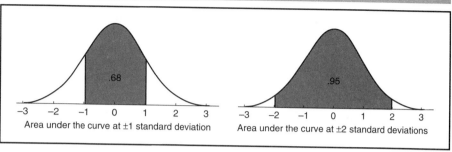

than the mean, they are negative. Also note that the same number is at the same relative location on each tail (−2 s is the same distance from the mean as +2 s), a product of the curve's symmetry.

Finally, this utility for the standard deviation statistic means we can assign probabilities of occurrence (Figure 6.4). Looking at the entire distribution, scores between the mean and one standard deviation occur 68% of the time (note that these percentages are rounded off). Those between the mean and two standard deviations occur about 95% of the time (the actual value is 95.44%). Thus, if you had a score that was 2.1 s from the mean, you would know that it was relatively rare—slightly more than 95% of the scores would be less extreme. At ±3 s more than 99% of all scores are included.

We can also talk about extremes from the vantage point of being higher or lower than the mean. For instance, if someone scored −2.0 s from the mean (note that is a *negative* 2.0), they would have scored *lower* than 97.5% of all other scores. How did we determine this? Fifty percent of the scores were *above* the mean (the top half of the curve), plus the 47.5% (¹⁄₂ of 95%) below the mean. Figure 6.5 shows these areas under the curve for 1 and 2 s.

These handy percentages (or probabilities, if we talk about a range from 0 to 1.0) allow us to discuss how common or rare scores are and make

FIGURE 6.5 Proportions Representing Standard Deviation Distances from the Mean

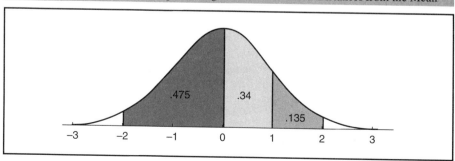

comparisons between them. Later, we will see the concept used in inferential statistics (measures of significance) to determine if an observed difference between two scores is "real" or not. In fact, this is a good point to bring up one more percentage related to the standard deviation. You will see something called the *95% confidence interval* associated with inferential statistics. This, in a nutshell, means that we are reasonably certain that our results are likely to be due to random error only 5% of the time $(100 - 95 = 5)$. Thus, we are "95% confident" that results are "real." This 95% point on the normal curve is located at 1.96 standard deviations—slightly inside of 2.0 standard deviations (remember, the 2 s point is really 95.44%).

So much work has been done on the properties of the normal distribution that it is the basis of many of our commonly-used statistics. In fact, if data are not normally distributed, we try to see if they are "close enough" to be treated as if they were normal. One of the reasons we want to look at the statistics we have described already (univariate statistics) is to see if a variable's distribution is reasonably normal.

BOX 6.1

PERCENTAGES ASSOCIATED WITH SCORES AND STANDARD DEVIATIONS IN THE NORMAL CURVE

 Also referred to as "area under the curve," the approximate percentage of scores associated with standard deviations in the normal curve are worth memorizing:

✓ *Each half* of the normal curve has 50% of the data

✓ *One standard deviation* (1 s) from the mean on *each* side has about 34% of the data
  • **±1 s** (both sides) encompasses about **68%** of the data (the actual number is 68.26%)

✓ *Two standard deviations* (2 s) from the mean on *each* side have about 47.5% of the data
  • **±2 s** (both sides) encompass about **95%** of the data (the actual number is 99.44%)

✓ *Three standard deviations* (3 s) from the mean on *each* side have about 49.5% of the data
  • **±3 s** (both sides) encompass more than **99%** of the data (the actual number is 99.74%)

Scores beyond three standard deviations are, obviously, *very* rare.

Sampling and the Normal Curve

As long as a variable has a normal distribution in the population and you have a good sample, you can expect these numbers to hold up. If the real variable distribution varies from the normal one, the percentages will change, introducing error if you assume the normal distribution. There are two theorems that give us a degree of assurance that it is reasonable to assume the normal distribution for variables.

First, the *Central Limit Theorem* holds that, as long as the data are drawn from a simple random sample out of a normally-distributed population, even a relatively small sample size will produce a normal distribution. This means you don't have to have large sample sizes to use normal distribution assumptions. Even if the population is somewhat skewed (discussed below) and therefore not exactly normal, large sample sizes will tend to produce a normal sampling distribution.

Second, what about an instance where the population distribution is *really* outside of normal? How bad can things be? A Russian statistician, Tchebychev (*Tchebychev's Inequality Theorem*), found that in the worst-case scenario of tails that did not behave like a normal curve (really badly skewed), 75% of the data will still fall within ± 2 s and 90% of the data will still fall within ± 3 s. In other words, the error is substantial, but not as bad as you might think. Therefore, assuming a normal distribution is a fairly common statistical criterion.

SOME NONNORMAL CURVES

Normal curves are obviously not the only distributions possible. There are several curves that are relatively common among real-world phenomena — you might even be familiar with some of them. We'll take a quick look at three of these curves just to see how they appear.

Uniform Distribution

The uniform distribution is one in which each score occurs exactly the same number of times. This happens when a sample (or population) is composed of an equal number of cases for each score. For instance, if we wanted to know how frequently people commit crimes of different types, the following would produce a uniform distribution with these numbers of cases and with a shape as in Figure 6.6.

FIGURE 6.6 Uniform Distribution

Type of crime	Number of crimes
Burglary	25
Robbery	25
Embezzlement	25
Illegal pollution	25

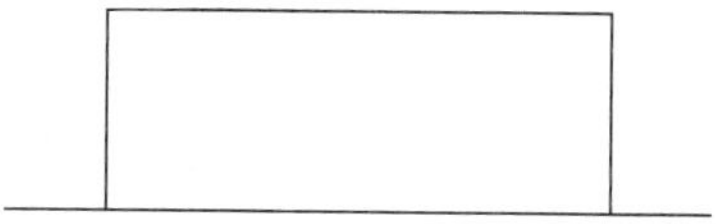

FIGURE 6.7 Negative Exponential Distribution

Type of crime	Number of crimes
Burglary	50
Robbery	40
Embezzlement	25
Illegal pollution	5

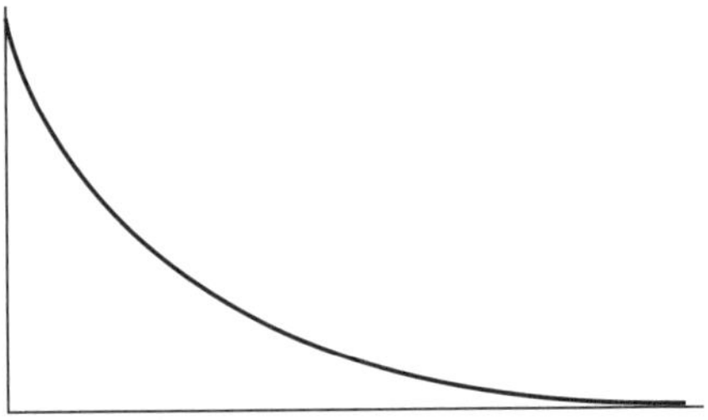

Negative Exponential Distribution

A negative exponential distribution has an increasing rarity of scores as they increase in size. In other words, smaller scores are common and large scores are rare. Therefore, the curve slopes downward, but on a curve rather than on a straight line. An example is presented in Figure 6.7.

Logarithmic Distribution

A logarithmic distribution shows an initial quick increase in the number of scores as it increases in size and then it tapers off in the rate of increase. These distributions can be used to demonstrate explosions and even match the rise of rockets into the atmosphere. The data in Figure 6.8 demonstrate this distribution.

FIGURE 6.8 Logarithmic Distribution

Type of crime	Number of crimes
Burglary	5
Robbery	25
Embezzlement	40
Illegal pollution	50

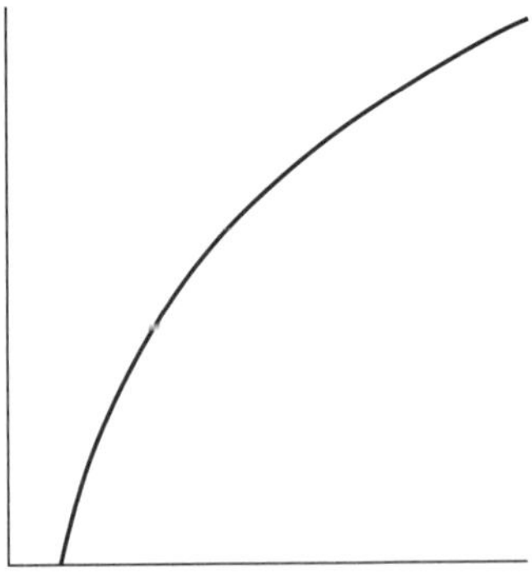

How Curves Differ

While there are many forms of curves that do not resemble the normal curve (actually there are an infinite number of curves and the normal curve is merely one family of those), there are two major ways in which a curve can differ from the normal:

- the lengths of the two tails are unequal (or asymmetry)—called *skewness*, and
- the relative height (or peakedness) of the curve is higher or lower than normal—called *kurtosis*.

These two concepts of variation are useful in describing both the way in which a distribution differs from the normal curve and the amount of that difference. The first approach, the way a curve differs, is based on the graphic image of a normal curve—in this case you can actually see the difference and we describe that difference as a form of skewness or kurtosis. The second approach, the degree of difference, compares a distribution to the theoretical normal distribution (based on setting the normal curve to a value of zero) and uses a formula to create a measure of the difference (a statistic). You can find information on skewness and kurtosis in Appendix B if you want to see how this works.

THE RELATIVE POSITION OF SCORES—Z-SCORES

As is suggested earlier, combining the normal distribution and the standard deviation allows us to make estimates of the location of a score relative to other scores. A simple statistic, called *standard scores* or *Z-scores* is created for this purpose. You have seen these scores before, most likely on standardized tests you took in elementary through high school. Many psychological tests also provide results as standard scores. This statistic uses a score in a group, the mean of that group, and the standard deviation to locate the relative position. The end result is a the creation of a new score, "standardized" for its position in relation to its group mean—which is why it is called a *standard* score (or Z-score). Let's look at how this is done.

First, we need to examine the formula for a Z-score. It is

$$Z = \frac{x - \bar{x}}{s}$$

Where x is the individual score,
$\bar{x}$ is the group mean, and
s is the group standard deviation.

Now let's see how this works. Assuming we have one student from each of five different sections of a statistics class, we would like to compare their grades on a recent exam to see how well each did. We'll also say that the exams for each class are different. We could, of course, just compare the scores directly to see who did best in comparison with their peers. However, that would require each exam to have the same grading scale and we would want to know how others in that class did as well. For instance, a score of 90 might look pretty good, until you found out that everyone else in the class scored 100—then you realize that 90 was the worst grade in the class.

For this example, we'll arbitrarily assign a class mean, an exam score, and a standard deviation for each student. The information is below. For instance, student A has a grade of 90, the class had an average of 80, and the standard deviation was 5.

Student	Raw Grade	$\bar{x}$	s
A	90.0	80.0	5.0
B	90.0	60.0	10.0
C	75.0	80.0	10.0
D	60.0	75.0	15.0
E	50.0	20.0	20.0

Just looking at the scores themselves, A and B scored the highest and E scored the worst. But, relative to their peers, that quick impression might change. We already know that central points (averages) only tell part of the story when looking for differences—spread needs to be considered as well. So, let's combine central point with spread and see what happens.

Beginning with student A's score of 90, we subtract the class mean of 80 to get a difference of 10. Then we divide this difference (10) by the class standard deviation of 5 (this is a pretty tight-scoring class) to get a Z-score of +2.0. But what does this mean? Considering that we have just changed differences into standard deviations, student A scored 2 s above the class mean. Because we know exactly where 2 s is on a normal curve, we can now estimate that student A scored *better* than 97.5% of her fellow students. How do we know this? Look at these calculations:

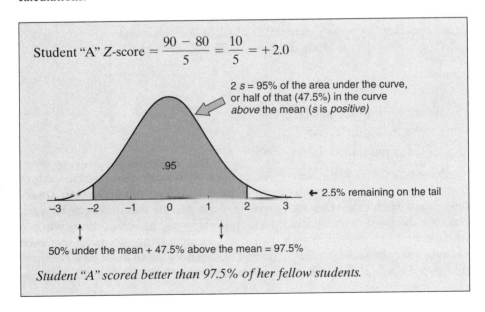

$$\text{Student "A" Z-score} = \frac{90 - 80}{5} = \frac{10}{5} = +2.0$$

2 s = 95% of the area under the curve, or half of that (47.5%) in the curve *above* the mean (s is *positive*)

.95

← 2.5% remaining on the tail

50% under the mean + 47.5% above the mean = 97.5%

Student "A" scored better than 97.5% of her fellow students.

Now we're ready to look at the entire group of five students. We need to calculate the Z-score for each, so the information below has this column added (far-right column).

Student	Raw Grade	$\bar{x}$	s	Z_i
A	90.0	80.0	5.0	2.0
B	90.0	60.0	10.0	3.0
C	75.0	80.0	10.0	0.5
D	60.0	75.0	15.0	−1.0
E	50.0	20.0	20.0	1.5

As you can now see, looking at the Z-scores, student B at 3.0 scored higher, relative to the rest of his class, than any of the other students (at 3 s that's higher than about 99% of the rest of the class). Here are some other things we can say

- student A scored high, but not as high as student B.
- student E, whose score looked pretty bad initially, actually scored okay (1.5 s would put her at about the 93rd percentile)
- student D had relatively the worst score at −1.0 (about the 16th percentile)

Z-scores, then, can tell us about the relative position of an individual score and that can be helpful.

SUMMARY

Curves and distributions are at the heart of many statistics. They not only tell us the way a variable is shaped but provide handy assumptions by which to create probability statistics. When paired with random sampling, the normal curve is the most important distribution in statistics. Because so much is known about its properties, particularly the percentages or proportions of scores at different points in the curve, it is the basis for determining how much error is likely to be present in our estimation of differences between phenomena. As we will see later, this becomes the basis for creating the probability distributions for an entire family of statistics (the probability tables you frequently see in the back of statistics texts). The normal curve also is common enough to justify assuming most variables are normally distributed. Other curves exist and, if you can identify them, they can be useful as well.

One of the important uses of the normal curve, when random samples are present, is to match it with the standard deviation to locate the relative position of a score. Because standard deviations are always located at the same place on a normal curve, they can be used to judge whether a score is different from other scores, its rarity compared to other scores, and even to compare scores in different groups. This final use is called standard scores or Z-scores.

The next chapter explores a simple statistical technique that shares the term *distribution*—frequency distributions. These numerical versions of a variable's distribution are based on the number of cases in each category (or score) of a variable.

KEY POINTS OF THE CHAPTER

 Every variable has a shape, or distribution. These shapes are worth knowing because we can use them to establish position and rarity of scores (and error).

- The normal curve is the most commonly-used shape in statistics.
- When the normal curve is combined with the standard deviation, a fixed set of points emerges that provide us with probabilities of a score occurring.
- Certain percentages (or probabilities) are associated with certain points on the normal curve. These can be used, via Z-scores, to translate any score into a position relative to all other scores.

CHAPTER 7

Frequency Distributions

Key Concepts

■ frequency

■ frequency distribution

■ valid percent

■ cumulative percent

■ missing data

■ grouped frequency distributions

There are more ways to think about the concept of a distribution than graphics. One alternative is to create a numerical distribution. Actually, we have already done that by combining measures of central tendency and deviation. With numbers representing the two measures, a "mental picture" of a group of scores can be created. True, all you would have would be a line with a middle point and the spread of that line, but it's still a distribution picture (okay, it's not a very *good* one). This chapter will provide you with a way to create almost the same mental picture you had with graphic versions of distributions, but with numbers in frequency distributions.

WHAT IS A FREQUENCY DISTRIBUTION?

A *frequency distribution* is a tabulation of the number of cases in each value (or category) of a variable. It is a very useful way to see quickly how subjects (groups, neighborhood, cities, or whatever your unit of measurement is) distribute themselves across the categories of an item. Let's take the example of asking people how much of a problem crime is in their community. We'll have them respond on a scale of 0–10, with 0 being "not a problem" and 10 being "biggest problem." If the responses of 20 people were observed directly, they might look something like this:

> 5 7 4 9 5 5 5 4 4 1 5 9 2 8 3 10 0 6 5 8 4

It is difficult to summarize what people are telling you, even with such a small number of cases. Making the problem even worse, a survey commonly has around 1,000 respondents. Imagine trying to make sense of that many responses. It would be almost impossible to tell anything from a quick look at the raw responses (here are about 350 of them in Box 7.1).

On the other hand, with those responses presented in a frequency distribution like the one in Table 7.1, it is much easier to see the results. If you don't see it right away, don't worry—we're about to go through the parts of this table.

BOX 7.1

RAW RESPONSES TO THE COMMUNITY CRIME PROBLEM QUESTION

5 7 4 9 5 5 4 4 1 5 9 2 8 3 10 0 6 5 8 4 4 3 6 3 7 5 5 5 3 8 5 6 7
6 6 1 4 6 6 5 5 5 8 7 8 2 5 9 7 4 6 2 1 4 9 6 4 8 10 6 8 5 7 10 6 5
9 9 7 2 2 6 4 10 5 4 7 8 7 6 5 2 5 4 6 9 9 6 8 6 8 6 3 6 5 5 3 2 10
2 3 5 6 8 9 8 10 8 10 4 5 7 7 6 10 1 5 3 5 5 8 7 7 3 4 6 5 10 1 8 7
5 8 3 6 7 6 9 5 3 6 7 6 6 7 10 7 6 3 7 8 3 4 3 6 10 3 6 6 2 10 10 6
4 6 3 9 3 6 2 5 7 7 4 6 8 10 6 7 5 7 8 10 6 4 8 5 10 6 8 7 8 7 5 6
4 7 7 10 10 8 5 9 8 7 1 8 4 5 3 7 4 8 8 6 8 3 7 2 8 10 8 3 5 8 9 3
6 1 8 4 6 6 7 2 7 7 7 7 6 8 5 3 7 5 7 1 6 8 7 6 8 6 8 6 10 4 2 3 8
5 7 5 8 4 10 7 9 4 5 8 5 5 1 2 5 3 6 2 3 7 3 8 8 4 7 6 5 1 7 4 0 7
4 5 4 2 3 5 4 3 7 4 10 4 3 2 3 5 7 6 6 6 4 8 2 5 6 3 3 3 7 7 2 4 5
4 7 2 5 6 1 4 6 7 6 7

Can you determine at a glance the most frequent numbers?
What did the average person respond?

TABLE 7.1 Example of a Frequency Distribution

How Much of a Problem is Crime in Your Community?

		Frequency	*Percent*
Valid	0 Not a problem	17	1.4
	1	34	2.9
	2	53	4.5
	3	94	8.0
	4	90	7.6
	5	139	11.8
	6	112	9.5
	7	140	11.8
	8	103	8.7
	9	46	3.9
	10 Biggest problem	69	5.8
	Total	897	75.9
Missing	−9	285	24.1
Total		1182	100.0

TABLE 7.2 The Basic Parts of a Frequency Distribution

How Much of a Problem is Crime in Your Community?

			Frequency	*Percent*	
	Valid	0 Not a problem	17	1.4	Number of cases in each value
		1	34	2.9	
Categories or values		2	53	4.5	
		3	94	8.0	
		4	90	7.6	
		5	139	11.8	Percent of cases in each value
		6	112	9.5	
		7	140	11.8	
Total line with number of non-missing cases		8	103	8.7	
		9	46	3.9	
		10 Biggest problem	69	5.8	
		Total	897	75.9	
	Missing	−9	285	24.1	
	Total		1182	100.0	

In this frequency distribution it is clear that most of the responses are in the middle. However, before we proceed further, let's look at the same frequency distribution in Table 7.2 to discuss its components.

The numbers in the left column are the categories or values of the variable (responses to "How much of a problem is crime in your community?"). Only the first value (zero) and the last category (10) are labeled. All other values are points that make sense once you know the range of the scale and its low and high values. Also in the value column you will find the words "valid," "missing," and "total" (twice). "Valid" is sometimes found on statistical output to designate the values with at least one case (at least one respondent gave that answer)—think of it as a reminder that some values may not appear. The term *missing* beside an arbitrary number, in this case –9, is used to represent those respondents who are missing from this question—that is, they didn't answer. The "total" under the value labels (right under "Biggest problem") tells us that the number in the next column is the sum of all the valid responses. The other "total," on the bottom of the table, gives us the number of respondents in the survey.

The column "frequency" is the number of cases (or respondents in this example) who gave an answer corresponding to each value. For instance, 139 people gave an answer of "5" to the question; similarly, 69 people said "10."

The last column, "percent," is the percent of responses for each value, based on the final total of all people who responded to the survey. For the 139 people who answered "5," the percent is 11.8 of the total (percentage figures are normally rounded off or truncated at the first decimal digit, so the sum may not equal 100%). Notice that these percentages *include* those who did not respond to this question (the "missing" category). While this is technically all that is necessary for a frequency distribution, most computer statistical programs add another column or two with more helpful information.

While you are still familiar with this frequency distribution, let's quickly look to see what our respondents were telling us. Notice that, for each response from 3 to 8, at least 90 people responded. Fewer people responded at each of the two ends of the distribution. Thus, we can say that most people felt that crime was slightly above the middle score in our scale (5 represents the "average" on the *scale* but not necessarily the average *case*) and crime is slightly more than an "average" community problem. The "percent" column is handy for getting a feel for the relative size of the number of responses in each category and can be used rather than the frequencies to say the same thing.

Now let's return to the issue of missing cases. Any time there are more than a few missing cases, percentages are difficult to interpret because the missing cases are included in the "percent" column. Put another way, in generalizing to the population we can't say that those who would answer "1" represent 2.9% of the population. This would be true only if the 285 missing people would have answered exactly the same as those who did respond to the question. However, we don't know how they would have responded and cannot assume they are the same as those who responded. Thus, we need to compare our results to those we know about. To interpret our results, we would have to create another column of percentages based on the number of questionnaire respondents who actually responded to this question ("valid" responses = 897). We can usually get this information, and more, from statistical programs when we ask for frequency distributions. Table 7.3 shows the routine frequency distribution output from SPSS, a common statistical analysis program.

TABLE 7.3 Frequency Distribution with Missing Values Removed from Percentages

How Much of a Problem is Crime in Your Community?

		Frequency	Percent	Valid Percent	Cumulative Percent
Valid	0 Not a problem	17	1.4	1.9	1.9
	1	34	2.9	3.8	5.7
	2	53	4.5	5.9	11.6
	3	94	8.0	10.5	22.1
	4	90	7.6	10.0	32.1
	5	139	11.8	15.5	47.6
	6	112	9.5	12.5	60.1
	7	140	11.8	15.6	75.7
	8	103	8.7	11.5	87.2
	9	46	3.9	5.1	92.3
	10 Biggest problem	69	5.8	7.7	100.0
	Total	897	75.9	100.0	
Missing	−9	285	24.1		
Total		1182	100.0		

> *Question: What percent of the respondents in Table 7.3 felt that crime was a "more than an average problem" in their community?*
>
> Hint: Use the cumulative percent column and look for answers above the midscale point of 5.
>
> On the basis of your answer, would you say about neighborhood crime attitudes for the entire group of respondents?

Not only is there a new column based on the number of valid responses (*valid percent*), but there is also a column labeled *cumulative percent*. The first new column is the percent of responses based on only those who responded to the question. It is called *valid* percent because those are the only responses we know. Those who responded 1, for example, are 34 of 897 responding or 3.8% (rounded off). Now we can express these respondents as the correct percentage of the total who responded to the question. Whenever there are missing cases, it is best to use valid percentages rather than total percentages.

Further, the cumulative percent column gives us a running total of the percent of people who responded to a value *plus all of those who responded to a lower value* (the values above it). For example, people who said that crime was a problem at the level of "1" or "0" are 5.7% of all valid respondents (1.9 + 3.8%). Thus, we might estimate that around 6% of the population do not think crime is a problem in their community. About one-third of our respondents (32.1%) tell us that crime is less than an average problem for their community—or, all responses from 0 to 4.

Let's try another example of interpreting a frequency distribution. This time, we'll examine a more specific type of neighborhood crime problem: burglary. Table 7.4 is from the full output of the SPSS statistical program, with markups to add explanation.

The first thing we need to do is to establish where the "average" point is on the response scale for the question. This one is easy, because we already know from the previous example that 5 is the midpoint of a 0–10 scale. Therefore, a response of "5" is saying that burglary is an average problem in their neighborhood (see Box 7.2).

WHAT TO DO WHEN THERE ARE TOO MANY CATEGORIES: GROUPED FREQUENCY DISTRIBUTIONS

Sometimes a variable has so many values that it is of little help to list them all in a frequency distribution. Age, for instance, can have a wide range of values—say 18 years old to 90 years old. You couldn't present a helpful picture of the data by listing

TABLE 7.4 Interpreting a Frequency Distribution

How Much of a Problem is Burglary in Your Community?

		Frequency	Percent	Valid Percent	Cumulative Percent	
Valid	0 Not a problem	39	3.3	3.3	3.3	Fewer than 30% feel that burglary is *less* than an average problem
	1	37	3.1	3.2	6.5	
	2	68	5.8	5.8	12.3	
	3	93	7.9	8.0	20.3	
	4 Average	99	8.4	8.5	28.7	
	5 ⟸ crime	159	13.5	13.6	42.3	
	6 problem	132	11.2	11.3	53.6	More than 57% (100 − 42.3%) feel that burglary is *more* than an average problem
	7	163	13.8	13.9	67.6	
	8	142	12.0	12.1	79.7	
	9	97	8.2	8.3	88.0	
	10 Biggest problem	140	11.8	12.0	100.0	
	Total	1169	98.9	100.0		
Missing	−9	13	1.1			
Total		1182	100.0			

all of the ages at once. Take a look at Table 7.5. With all the different age categories, from 18 to 87, it is very difficult to draw a good picture of the variable distribution.

When this happens, we sometimes use "grouped" frequency distributions. In other words, we place some of the values into groups or categories. In the case of age, we might group everyone from 10 to 19 years old into one category, those from 20 to 29 in another, and so forth. This would help us to "make sense" of the

---

BOX 7.2

INTERPRETING FREQUENCY DISTRIBUTIONS

Here are some hints to help you interpret a frequency distribution.

✓ Look at the column labeled "cumulative percent"—this is the accumulated percentage from the first value to the last.

✓ Determine where the middle of the values might be. This can be done from the "cumulative percent" (look for the value with the 50% point) or by using the mean and median, if they are available.

✓ Determine where the majority of values lie—this will be in a low/high range of values and can be located using the "cumulative percent."
- Try using the bottom/top 10% or 25% to eliminate extremes.
- Express the majority range by using those values at the majority low/high point.

✓ State what the "average" person looks like, but in *words*, not numbers (i.e., *describe* the average person).

TABLE 7.5 Example of Too Many Values

What Is Your Age?

		Frequency	Percent	Valid Percent	Cumulative Percent
Valid	18	1	.1	.1	.1
	20	3	.3	.3	.3
	21	2	.2	.2	.5
	22	22	1.9	1.9	2.4
	23	30	2.5	2.6	5.0
	24	22	1.9	1.9	6.9
	25	34	2.9	2.9	9.8
	26	28	2.4	2.4	12.2
	27	50	4.2	4.3	16.5
	28	43	3.6	3.7	20.2
	29	33	2.8	2.8	23.0
	30	43	3.6	3.7	26.7
	31	25	2.1	2.1	28.8
	32	35	3.0	3.0	31.8
	33	21	1.8	1.8	33.6
	34	61	5.2	5.2	38.9
	35	27	2.3	2.3	41.2
	36	27	2.3	2.3	43.5
	37	19	1.6	1.6	45.1
	38	34	2.9	2.9	48.0
	39	20	1.7	1.7	49.7
	40	24	2.0	2.1	51.8
	41	30	2.5	2.6	54.4
	42	31	2.6	2.7	57.0
	43	21	1.8	1.8	58.8
	44	21	1.8	1.8	60.6
	45	27	2.3	2.3	63.0
	46	16	1.4	1.4	64.3
	47	19	1.6	1.6	66.0
	48	20	1.7	1.7	67.7
	49	22	1.9	1.9	69.6
	50	17	1.4	1.5	71.0
	51	18	1.5	1.5	72.6
	52	13	1.1	1.1	73.7
	53	13	1.1	1.1	74.8
	54	12	1.0	1.0	75.8
	55	18	1.5	1.5	77.4
	56	13	1.1	1.1	78.5
	57	20	1.7	1.7	80.2
	58	9	.8	.8	81.0
	59	15	1.3	1.3	82.2
	60	20	1.7	1.7	84.0
	61	19	1.6	1.6	85.6
	62	13	1.1	1.1	86.7
	63	8	.7	.7	87.4
	64	11	.9	.9	88.3
	65	11	.9	.9	89.3
	66	9	.8	.8	90.1
	67	7	.6	.6	90.7
	68	13	1.1	1.1	91.8
	69	10	.8	.9	92.6
	70	12	1.0	1.0	93.7
	71	9	.8	.8	94.4
	72	14	1.2	1.2	95.6
	73	7	.6	.6	96.2
	74	5	.4	.4	96.7
	75	7	.6	.6	97.3
	76	5	.4	.4	97.7
	77	4	.3	.3	98.0
	78	3	.3	.3	98.3
	79	5	.4	.4	98.7
	80	4	.3	.3	99.1
	81	4	.3	.3	99.4
	82	1	.1	.1	99.5
	83	2	.2	.2	99.7
	85	1	.1	.1	99.7
	87	3	.3	.3	100.0
	Total	1166	98.6	100.0	
Missing	−9	16	1.4		
Total		1182	100.0		

TABLE 7.6 Example of a Collapsed Interval-level Variable

Collapsed Age Categories

		Frequency	*Percent*	*Valid Percent*	*Cumulative Percent*
Valid	20 and under	20	1.7	1.7	1.7
	21 to 30	307	26.0	26.0	27.7
	31 to 40	293	24.8	24.8	52.5
	41 to 50	224	19.0	19.0	71.4
	51 to 60	151	12.8	12.8	84.2
	61 to 70	113	9.6	9.6	93.7
	71 and older	74	6.3	6.3	100.0
	Total	1182	100.0	100.0	

age distribution (see Table 7.6). Now you can see that 50% of the respondents are aged 21–40, only 15.8% are over 60, and that there are very few people in the extreme young and elderly categories.

Note that collapsing the values works as long as we don't construct our groups so that they present a picture that is not really present in the original distribution. To prevent this, we need to follow a few simple rules for grouping data (Box 7.3).

BOX 7.3

"RULES" FOR GROUPED FREQUENCY DISTRIBUTIONS
(Okay, they're more like guidelines)

✓ *Use at least 6 and not more than 15 categories (or groups).* Too few categories and you run the risk of creating an erroneous picture of the original distribution.

✓ *Define categories (group data) so that all cases are included.* One way to do this at the ends of a distribution is to have an open-ended category. For instance with ages you might begin with a first category "under 10" and end with a category of "75 and over." Just be careful not to create one of these categories with a large number of cases. If that happens, you should create a few more categories before the final one.

✓ *Each case should only fit into one category.* Don't use something like "ages 20 to 30" and follow it with "ages 30 to 40." In this instance, age 30 is in two categories and that can't happen.

✓ *Whenever possible, the category intervals (the beginning and end values) should be of equal size.* For instance, every category could contain three values or five values, as in 12–14 or 10–14.
  • Don't make the intervals too large because this practice tends to complicate your ability to get a good picture of the data distribution.
  • On the other hand, having equal size intervals doesn't mean that if

(continued)

(continued)

you have a break in the data, say ages run from 20 to 67 and then there is a gap until 72, that you have to have categories with zero or few cases.

- It is possible, and even desirable, to have categories like the ones at an end of the distribution (where you expect very few cases) with a different-sized interval, just don't

create categories that would be misleading.

✓ Finally, to reiterate the most important rule, *don't do anything in creating your groups that would change the "picture" of the underlying raw distribution*—that would be misleading.

Remember, the goal is to create *a reasonably accurate "picture" of the way people respond (or the characteristics of an average group).*

STATISTICS USEFUL WITH FREQUENCY DISTRIBUTIONS

Any of the univariate statistics, those dealing with central tendency or variation, are used with frequency distributions. For instance, and assuming interval-level data, it is helpful to know the mean age and standard deviation and relate that to the other ages of a distribution. One can also usually request bar charts and other graphs of the variable's distribution in most common statistical packages. In combination, many of these statistics and the frequency distribution can be used to better understand the shape of a variable's distribution—an important ingredient in choosing correct statistics for more sophisticated analyses of both difference and relationship.

SUMMARY

Frequency distributions are essentially a count of cases in each category of a variable but, of course, after the categories have been ordered if the variable is ordinal level or higher. They are very useful in interpreting the distribution of a variable without having to see actual graphics. They also are a good way to determine what people are collectively telling us by their responses to survey questions. More formally, this is a way to interpret public opinion (or whatever you are measuring).

The addition of valid and cumulative percentages to a frequency distribution provides additional valuable information. When coupled with univariate statistics, frequency distributions provide a quick picture of the way cases are grouped and spread around the distribution. With these we can remove the potential effect of missing cases and quickly estimate the percentages of respondents in different areas of the distribution. In other words, frequency distributions meet our criteria of a good statistic because they provide a quick and reasonably accurate picture of the data.

Finally, grouped frequency distributions are commonly used with interval- and ratio-level data. Their purpose is to help us get a good picture of the variable's distribution without too much distortion. That's why there are rules about how to group the data so we don't lose the general picture or distort it too much.

This is the last chapter on univariate statistics. The truth of the matter is that we are not very interested in single variables. After describing them, we want to know what affects those variables—what relationships they have with other variables. Ultimately, the question will become: What causes this variable or, even perhaps, what does this variable cause? The next chapter begins the slightly more complex presentation of two variable relationships.

KEY POINTS OF THE CHAPTER

 Frequency distributions provide us with a count of the number of cases in each category of a variable and, from that, we can get a good picture of the variable's distribution.

- Use frequency distributions to interpret opinions derived from surveys or otherwise describe variables.
- Draw "mental" pictures by describing the distributions so that others can see their dominant features.
- Group the data whenever there are too many categories to quickly view a frequency distribution and construct a good picture of it.

CHAPTER 8

Elementary Relationships: Crosstabulation Tables

Key Concepts

- crosstabulate
- 2×2 Table
- cell
- row
- column
- marginal
- diagonal
- bivariate statistics

One of the most elementary ways to determine the effect of one variable on another is to *crosstabulate* the two variables. Crosstabulation means to present two (or more) variables in one table, with the values of one representing the rows of the table and the values of the other representing the columns. While many representations of statistical results are presented as "tables," crosstabulations are referred to in statistical shorthand as *tables*. So, don't confuse tables created to present statistical results with crosstabulation tables. By looking at the combination of rows and columns, it is relatively easy to see potential relationships between variables. This chapter will examine the concept of crosstabulation and relationships. Thus, this begins the discussion of *bivariate* analyses through statistical approaches—that is, the focus will be on the relationship between *two* variables.

BASIC TABLES AND RELATIONSHIPS

The basic idea behind crosstabulations is to show the joint distribution of two variables. Think of this as two frequency distributions joined together. The simplest

TABLE 8.1 Example of a Crosstabulation Table

		Fear of Crime	
		Low	High
Gender	Male	35	25
	Female	20	40

table showing the relationship between two variables is called a *2 × 2 table* because there are two variables, each with two values. It looks like this

		Variable 1	
		value 1	value 2
Variable 2	value 1	cell 1	cell 2
	value 2	cell 3	cell 4

An example of such a table, with data, is in Table 8.1. The two variables are gender, with male and female values, and fear of crime, with low and high values. Note that it is easy to see the joint relationship in a table of this size, mostly because the comparisons are limited. If you focus on the high fear of crime column, the two numbers there can be compared.

One of the findings would be that males are not as afraid of crime as females. This is the case because the number of females with "high" fear of crime is greater than the number of males with "high" fear of crime. If you don't see this immediately, that's okay. We'll repeat the table below and make the critical information easier to find.

Look at the male and female rows under the high fear of crime column in Table 8.2. The boldfaced and italicized numbers illustrate our discussion. Forty females are in the high fear of crime column, as compared to 25 males. Therefore, females are more afraid of crime than males. Conversely, there are 35 males in the low fear of crime column, compared to 20 females. Be careful in applying this example to other tables, though—there is a critical ingredient that makes the direct comparison of these numbers possible.

TABLE 8.2 Locating a Relationship in a Table

		Fear of Crime	
		Low	High
Gender	Male	35	*25*
	Female	20	*40*

INTERPRETING MORE COMPLEX TABLES

While a 2 × 2 table is easy to interpret, the ability to look at a table with a quick glance and tell what's going on becomes more difficult when there are more than four cells. Table 8.3 has a new column added (medium fear of crime) and now has six cells and is a 2 × 3 table.

We can still see that females are more afraid of crime than males because the new "medium fear" category is equal for both males and females. However, if the numbers are unequal, the relationship gets harder to see and interpretation becomes more difficult.

TABLE 8.3 An Example of a More Complex Table

		Fear of Crime		
		Low	*Medium*	*High*
Gender	*Male*	35	**30**	25
	Female	20	**30**	40

Adding Percentages

Another problem in interpreting tables is having a *different number of cases* for the categories (or values) of the independent variable. In the examples so far, we have been careful to use the same numbers of males and females (the independent variable) so that the numbers in the cells can be directly compared. If the total number of males and females differ, direct comparison is not possible. Table 8.4 has the numbers of males and females changed to 90 males and 60 females. If you just looked at the raw numbers in the cells, you might think that males were as likely as females to have high fear of crime. The *percentages*, though, correct for the unequal number in the two groups and tell a different story. Having percentages in each cell makes it easier to see the relationship, even though the numbers of males and females are different. This is why we calculate percentages.

TABLE 8.4 Using Percentages in a Table

		Fear of Crime		
		Low	*High*	*Total*
Gender	*Male*	50	40	90
		55.6%	**44.4%**	100%
	Female	20	40	60
		33.3%	**66.7%**	100%

Calculating Percentages Incorrectly

When you are calculating percentages for the cells, remember to calculate across the independent variable (that is, make the percentages across the categories of the independent variable each add to 100%). In the above example, gender is the independent variable (it doesn't make sense to use fear of crime as the independent

TABLE 8.5 Calculating Percentages the Wrong Way in a Table

| | | Fear of Crime | | Total |
		Low	High	
Gender	Male	50	40	90
		71.4%	**50.0%**	
	Female	20	40	60
		28.6%	**50.0%**	

variable because it cannot affect gender). Otherwise, you end up discussing the sample size differences instead of talking about the relationship between the variables. This is a common problem that people fail to catch and it can lead to wrong conclusions. Take a look at Table 8.5 to see how that can happen.

In this example, the percentages are based on the columns rather than the rows—that is, percentages were calculated *down* and not across. Because our focus is on gender, if you just looked at the percentages in the cells without paying attention to which way they were calculated, your conclusion would be that males had the lowest fear of crime. This is obviously wrong (and, yes, the high fear of crime column percentages result in a "weird" interpretation). What happens is that the percentages, when calculated the wrong way, become more sensitive to the number of cases in each of the row categories rather than the distribution of cases *within* a category.

Just in case you think this "wrong-percentaging" problem is unlikely, let me share a brief story with you. Years ago a master's student had just finished the final draft of her thesis, complete with conclusions and recommendations on the topic. The analysis contained more than three dozen crosstabulations. She had worked primarily with her chair, who was not known as a methodologist. The committee members were not given the thesis materials until the very end. One of them, reading the analysis for the very first time, noticed that the data in first table did not match the conclusions because the table was percentaged incorrectly. This led to a check of the next table and, sure enough, it had the same problem. In fact, all tables were percentaged incorrectly and, as it turned out, the conclusions to be drawn from the data were virtually the opposite of those the student had come to, based on the wrong percentages. The entire thesis had to be rewritten, and four months of work was wasted. Such problems are much more common than you might think. The lesson is *always look to make sure the percentages are calculated on the categories of your independent variable.* If you don't have an independent variable, you will surely have one you intend to focus on—calculate percentages based on it.

The final point to note about the direction of percentaging is that it should be done the same way when you are presenting multiple tables. For instance, in a report with several tables, if the first table has the independent variable on the side (the rows), all other tables in the report should have independent variables in the same location. Some textbooks specify that "in the social sciences tables always have their independent variables in the columns." Others will tell you they are supposed to be in the rows. It actually doesn't make any difference whether the independent or dependent variable is in the rows or the columns. Just do it the same way every time to keep from confusing readers. In this book, a consistent effort has been made to use this format:

		Dependent Variable	
		value 1	value 2
Independent Variable	value 1	cell 1	cell 2
	value 2	cell 3	cell 4

RELATIONSHIPS AND THE DIAGONAL

There is one other important concept to discuss about table relationships: the *diagonal*. When you look in a table to locate a relationship, you are actually looking at the diagonal line across the cells even if you just compare the percentages or numbers in a single row or column (and that's okay because it's quick and easy). In tables with an even number of cells (2×2, 3×3, 4×4) the diagonal line is real, whereas in tables with an odd number of cells (2×3, 3×6, etc.) it is an imaginary line. Table 8.6 has a diagonal line so that you can see what is meant by this.

For instance, if we hypothesize that females have a higher fear of crime, we expect females to have their highest percentage in *high* fear and males to have their largest percentage in *low* fear. That's what the table shows—on the diagonal cells. It doesn't make any difference which diagonal you use because, especially in a 2×2 table, one hypothesized direction is the opposite of the other. So, the opposite of the earlier hypothesis would be "females are less likely to have a low fear of crime" (and its corollary, "males are less likely to have a high fear of crime"). Looking at this opposite diagonal, the percentages are 33.3% of females in the low fear category and males with 44.4% in the low fear category. Both genders have their lowest percentages in fear of crime categories exactly where we expected. If you remember to calculate percentages across the categories of independent variable and check the diagonal, you should be able to interpret relationships in tables easily.

TABLE 8.6 Relationships on the Diagonal

		Fear of Crime		
		Low	High	Total
Gender	Male	50	40	90
		55.6%	44.4%	100%
	Female	20	40	60
		33.3%	66.7%	100%

As a word of caution, there are times the diagonal concept won't work. Almost universally the problem will be a product of nominal-level variables. If you remember from our earlier discussion of nominal-level measurement, the values or categories of those variables can take on any number you want. In a 2 × 2 table, nominal-level variables work okay because changing the categories around essentially results in a reverse version of the same relationship. Once a table gets larger than that, changing the position of categories changes everything else and your relationship results become a product of where you put the categories. But, again, you don't *have* to focus on the diagonal, you can compare the percentages directly within a column or row, wherever your focus lies—and that's usually the easiest way to check for relationships.

Many relationship statistics (particularly measures of association) are designed to do exactly the same thing we just did—look for and analyze the diagonal cells. If you remember this when we begin the discussion of these statistics in later chapters, you will already be ahead of the game.

An Example of a Typical Relationship Test

Before leaving the crosstabulation/relationship subject, let's examine one more table. This time, we'll look at the kind of table that might be part of a real research project. A survey asked a random sample of adults about their attitudes on a typical criminal justice myth—that the police and the courts are too easy on crime. We could make several hypotheses[1] about why some people believe this. For instance, we might assume that watching television affects the perception of this issue, or perhaps even that conservative/liberal political positions are involved.

For this example, though, we will hypothesize that groups who have more direct contact with the police and courts will be less likely to agree with the "leniency" position. From long-term research evidence and official statistics, we know that minorities are overrepresented in the criminal justice system. Therefore, using a racial self-identification variable present in the survey data, we will assume that whites will be more likely to agree that police and courts are too easy on crime and that minorities (African Americans, Hispanics, and "others") will be more likely to disagree. Let's use a crosstabulation to see if our proposed relationship exists.

Table 8.7 presents the results of crosstabulating our two variables, race/ethnicity and "leniency," as part of the output from a computer statistical program.

There are two variables, each with four values, making up a 4 × 4 table. The race/ethnicity variable (just called "race" henceforth) is measured at the nominal level. For simplicity, the category of "white" was placed at the top of the list so that we can more easily compare all "minority" categories below it. This is also a good time to reiterate that the concept of a diagonal will only loosely apply to these

---

[1]The next chapter will discuss hypotheses in detail. The usage of the term here is a general one.

TABLE 8.7 Crosstabulation of Race/Ethnicity and CJS Leniency

			Police and Courts are Too Easy on Crime				
			Strongly disagree	*Disagree*	*Agree*	*Strongly agree*	*Total*
Respondent's Race	White	Count	210	116	234	285	845
		%	24.9%	13.7%	27.7%	33.7%	100.0%
	African American	Count	39	14	32	31	116
		%	33.6%	12.1%	27.6%	26.7%	100.0%
	Hispanic	Count	59	25	52	43	179
		%	33.0%	14.0%	29.1%	24.0%	100.0%
	Other	Count	13	3	5	9	30
		%	43.3%	10.0%	16.7%	30.0%	100.0%
Total		Count	321	158	323	368	1170
		%	27.4%	13.5%	27.6%	31.5%	100.0%

variables. That's because, as a nominal variable, we have no real way to establish any priority of one race over another (other than majority/minority status), even if we wanted to "guess" at how much each race would agree with the leniency position.

Making this even more difficult, as you can see in the table, is the four-value leniency variable. How could you predict a smooth diagonal movement across the races in their agreement/disagreement, particularly when the order of the race categories can be changed at a whim? So, with a "real-life" research dilemma before us, let's resolve the problem by saying that "on the whole" we expect to find a greater percentage of whites more frequently in the "agree" cells and other races (the "minorities") more frequently in the "disagree" cells. Even this resolution of the problem has problems because there are two "disagree" cells and two "agree" cells (imagine the difficulty presented by a variable with 10 or more values!). Let's try two approaches to this: comparing only the *strongly* agree/disagree cells and then collapsing the two agree/disagree cells into one each. We will also compare whites to all other race categories.

Using the first approach, the comparison of the strongly agree/disagree cells, it appears that whites at 24.9% in strongly disagree have the lowest amount of strong disagreement. Our minority groups range from 33.6 to 43.3%, all of which evidence a higher percentage of strong disagreement than whites. So far, our "hypothesis" of minorities being less convinced of CJS leniency is holding up. But, to raise an issue, what you say if *one* of the three minority categories was the same or slightly lower than whites (the opposite of what you expected)? Would that be enough to discard your hypothesis?

Looking now at the strongly agree column, the expectation is that minorities will have lower percentages here. That appears to be so, but not by much. Whites are highest with 33.7% and minorities range from 26.7 to 30.0% in the strongly disagree column. So, you could say that our expectation continues to be supported. On the basis of this version of our test, the "hypothesis" looks good—whites are more apt to buy into the CJS leniency myth.

Now let's take the second approach to testing our expectation. We'll need to combine the percentages in the "strongly disagree" and "disagree" cells and those in the "strongly agree" and "agree" cells. Here are the results:

Race	Combined Disagree (%)	Combined Agree (%)
White	38.6	61.4
African American	45.7	54.3
Hispanic	47.0	53.1
Other	53.3	46.7

Note: Not all groups will total to 100% because of rounding.

We might be led to look at these results and say that "three of four racial groups have a majority who believe in the leniency myth," and therefore, minorities really don't feel that the CJS is less lenient. Some people will actually do that and stop there. That, however, was not our expectation. The hypothesis we made was that "whites will be *more likely* to agree that police and courts are too easy on crime." We didn't say anything about majorities or absolute percentages, just that whites will be more likely to agree. Comparing the combined agree percentages, whites are indeed more likely to be in that column than any other group (61.4% compared to a range of 54.3–46.7%). Conversely, whites have a lower percentage in the combined disagree column (38.6%) than any of the minority groups (45.7–53.3%).

Apparently, no matter which of our relationship tests we rely on, our hypothesis is supported—whites are more likely to believe that police and courts are too easy on crime. But, you might say, "The difference is not a large one." If so, you would be correct—but that would also not change our conclusion. The criterion of "more likely" doesn't have absolute numbers, it just requires whites to have a higher percentage of belief. Now if you are concerned about the possibilities of error, that's a *real* concern and one we can't handle here. The next chapter, though, begins the discussion of this problem—and that is deep in the heart of statistics.

SUMMARY

The use of crosstabulations to examine relationships is a valuable tool. Not all relationships can be examined in this manner though (interval-level variables fare poorly), but those amenable to the technique yield a good, intuitive interpretation. To use these tables, make sure you have calculated percentages for the cells and that those percentages are based on the "independent" variable. If feasible, examining the table diagonal is also a good way to check for relationships.

The results of crosstabulations can sometimes be difficult to interpret. This is particularly the case with multiple-category nominal-level variables, but it can also happen when you have any variable with more than three or four categories.

The problem, of course, is that crosstabulations by themselves rely on your looking at the table to make sense of it. That's why there are statistics designed for such tables—to give us a summary of what is in a table in much the same way that averages and standard deviations describe distributions. The next chapter introduces the primary concepts needed to understand these statistics. There are even crosstabulations that combine three or more variables for a form of "multivariate" analysis and these will be the subject of our final statistical discussion.

KEY POINTS OF THE CHAPTER

Crosstabulations present the combined distributions of two (or more) variables. They rely primarily on percentages in the cells for interpretation of relationships.

- Crosstabulations should have a percentage, not just the number of cases, in each cell.
- Percentages should be based on the variable of interest (the independent variable).
- As long as it is feasible for the type of variables involved, the table diagonal can be used to view relationships.
- Crosstabulations work best for variables with a few categories; larger numbers of categories make interpretation difficult.

CHAPTER 9

Hypotheses and Sampling Distributions

Key Concepts

- hypothesis

- null hypothesis

- alternative hypothesis

- two-tailed hypothesis

- one-tailed hypothesis

- sampling distribution

- random sampling error

This chapter presents the essential concepts necessary for testing for relationships and differences. When little is known about a phenomenon, combinations of variables are examined to see if there are any relationships and then those relationships are used to construct theory. This is essentially the exploratory part of science. There is even a form of theory called "grounded theory" that is essentially like the exploratory form in putting preference on exploring relationships among variables in a data set and creating hypotheses *ex post facto*. Most of the time, however, we have already have some evidence about a phenomenon and scientific inquiry uses that to construct theory and, from that, make hypotheses about relationships. For the sake of convenience, we'll focus on the latter form. Once hypotheses are discussed, we'll go on to see how error and real differences relate to statistical distributions. This will require a discussion of the use of error to create statistical distributions.

HYPOTHESES

Hypotheses are used to "test" for relationships. In fact, one way to define a *hypothesis* is to say that it is *a statement of a relationship between two (or more) variables*. Hypotheses are important to us because

- they provide a very specific statement for us to test, and
- they form the logical basis of inferential statistics.

The issue of having a specific statement to test is very important. Without specificity, a researcher might accidentally test something that is not what he or she intended. Or, two researchers might test some issue, like crime prevention, get different results, and ultimately discover that they were testing two different things. Or, time and effort could be put into testing some critical program, or proposed policy, and only after testing would they realize that the measurement was too general and conclusions can't be drawn. If you remember that hypotheses (as we use them in statistics) are *measurable* statements, the entire issue of letting the hypothesis focus your measurement and your statistical tests makes sense.

On the issue of a logical basis for inferential statistics, every concept, tool, or technique has some kind of underlying foundation. For inferential statistics that foundation is the null hypothesis, which is itself based on empirical sampling distributions. We'll discuss how and why this is so later in this chapter.

Kinds of Hypotheses

There are two basic, or general, forms of hypotheses: the *null hypothesis* and the *alternative hypothesis*. Though both forms are important, researchers spend more time phrasing alternative hypotheses because that's what they will be testing.

Null Hypotheses

A *null hypothesis* is used as a foundation by inferential statistics (measures of significance) and it represents the "fallback" position for a test of an anticipated effect. A null hypothesis *always* says that there is *no relationship* between the two variables. The reason it is used by inferential statistics is that the probability distributions used by these statistics (discussed later in this chapter) tell us the likelihood that any difference is a result of random error. Thus, it is easier, and a more scientifically conservative approach, to say that a difference is *not real*; then we don't have to explain the difference, it is just "error." If the difference is likely to be "real," we have the problem of trying to explain the difference. As a result, all inferential statistics "assume" the null hypothesis is true—one variable does not affect the other.

 Null Hypothesis Example

The number of police officers in a patrol vehicle does not affect *the amount of crime in a patrol district.*

In discussing the null hypothesis, we will frequently use the terms "the same" or "no difference" for simplicity. However, the null hypothesis really means that the likelihood of a result being due to random error *cannot be "rejected at the moment."* Put another way, saying that two or more measurements are the "same" is tantamount to saying that we do not have enough evidence to justify treating them as different measurements. Of course, there is always the possibility that they may indeed be the same.

Alternative Hypotheses

Any alternative hypothesis represents an attempt to explain real differences. They are required to state which variable affects which other variable. If we get really specific, they even say *how* one variable affects the other. So, in a sense, there are both nonspecific and specific alternative hypotheses. We prefer to use other terms for this, though.

Two-Tailed Hypotheses

A nonspecific alternative hypothesis is called a *two-tailed* (or *nondirectional*) *hypothesis*. These hypotheses cannot specify the way in which the independent variable affects the dependent variable—they just say that there is an effect of some kind. For example, if you think income is related to religiosity, but don't know whether higher income will increase or decrease religiosity, you should propose a two-tailed hypothesis. It would be stated as follows:

 Alternative Two-Tailed Hypothesis Example
Income affects *religiosity*.

The reason it is called a two-tailed hypothesis is based on the concept of the normal curve. Because the curve has two tails, a lower tail (low scores) and an upper one (high scores), we have to use both tail directions to test the relationship. No difference would essentially be scores right around the mean (pretty much all the same). The tails represent extremes or scores that are *really* different from the others. Put another way, you are neither predicting an outcome that is lower or higher—but you are predicting a difference. So, the difference can be represented by scores on either tail.

One-Tailed Hypotheses

If you think you know the direction of a relationship, or some theory proposes a direction, you should use a directional or *one-tailed hypothesis*. These are based on the concept that extremes at only one end of the curve will be needed (and we are referring *only* to the dependent variable here). For instance, if you say that males have higher crime rates than females, you are only interested in the extremes at the upper end of the crime rate curve. That is, males must be higher, or larger, or on the upper extremes, compared to females. If males turn out to have *lower* crime rates than females (the extremes at the other end of the curve), you are wrong and it doesn't matter if you are *significantly* wrong (there is actually no such thing in statistics!).

Because there are two possible directions in any relationship, there are both positive and negative one-tailed alternative hypotheses. *Positive* one-tailed hypotheses are stated as follows:

 Alternative One-Tailed Hypothesis Example (Positive relationship)
Higher *levels of education* increase *success on parole*.

Note that this hypothesis says that more education is related to more success on parole. Its corollary statement is that lower levels of education decrease success on parole. The two statements represent the same thing—when you specify one, the other is implied. The key is that the two variables have to travel in the same direction. If one increases, the other has to increase; if one decreases, the other has to decrease. Either way, if the results match our hypothesis, we're correct about the direction. However, if more education results in *less* parole success (or if less education results in more success), we're wrong.

The *negative* one-tailed hypotheses are stated as follows:

 Alternative One-Tailed Hypothesis Example (Negative relationship)
Higher *education* decreases *criminality.*

Notice that in order to be correct in this instance we need a relationship in which education is inversely (negatively) related to criminality. The two variables must travel in opposite directions. Here, education must increase while criminality is decreasing (or education must decrease while criminality is increasing). Because the expected tail is dictated by the direction hypothesized of the *dependent* variable, we need criminality scores on the *lower* end of the curve. Even if you find a huge difference on the extreme high end (upper tail) of the curve, you hypothesis is incorrect. The prediction was that a difference would occur on the lower end.

More About Hypotheses and "Tails"

Why are we interested in extremes at the end (tails) of the curve? If you remember the discussion about error, recall that big differences are more likely to be real than are small ones. Thus for an independent variable to have an effect, we need the differences between the independent variable's categories to be "large" ones. Because we normally use some average point to compare categories, this means that we expect true differences to be well above, or well below, the "average." Since the middle of a curve is the average

---

A case of *"don't"* look before you leap!

Unless you are doing initial, exploratory research, always propose an alternative hypothesis *before* you look at your test results. If you look at the test results first, it is pretty difficult to get the direction of a relationship wrong. Put another way, how can you be wrong when you already know the answer? This is why most of our tests are informed by theory or existing research literature. For instance, data indicating that youthfulness is related to higher crime rates has been around for decades. If you want to test this relationship, you propose the hypothesis first and then conduct your tests. This is not to say, however, that you won't find some researchers conducting tests, looking at the outcomes and then writing the research report as if they had proposed hypotheses in advance.

point, the most distant point is at the ends of the curve, or the tails. Thus, the further out on the tails you get, the bigger the difference is from the average and the less likely it is to be an accidental (random sampling error) score right around the average.

The idea of averages and tails in a curve has already been introduced in our discussion of the normal distribution. It also plays an integral part in the testing of hypotheses. In order to discuss this, let's look at random samples, random error, and the way that statistical probability distributions are created.

STATISTICAL PROBABILITY DISTRIBUTIONS

Random (sampling) error distributions really represent calculations of the amount of random error likely to occur under various random sampling circumstances. The reason "random sampling" error is used is because of our ability to reproduce that type of error. Any other type of error is too idiosyncratic and has too many unknown factors; thus, it can't be reproduced with any degree of accuracy. Choosing subjects in a sample by conveniently using people we know, for example, depends on who does the choosing. You would likely choose different people than I would, precisely because we know different people. As a result, the difference in our choices would be governed by a large number of factors influencing the process of how each of us gets to know people. If you have had a research methodology course that included sampling, these concepts are elementary. If not, then please take my word that humans cannot choose subjects for a sample in a true random manner—we just have too many biases (which produce systematic error). As a result, we normally use computer programs to create random samples for us. You can check the Web for random number generators. Two good ones are located at www.fourmilab.ch/hotbits and www.random.org.

So why are random samples so useful? In an ideal world, a sample from a population ought to have the same characteristics as the population itself. Of course, this almost never happens—most good samples are slightly different from the population, although some can have quite large differences. Because the population has no differences, any differences found in the sample would be a product of the sampling process, not the population. Another way to put this is that any difference between the sample and the population would be a *product of sampling error* and not real differences. The diagram below illustrates this problem.

Population with no difference	→	*Random sampling*	→	*Random sample with differences*	=	*Differences are sampling error*

It should occur to you that most research uses a sample as an efficient means of representing the population of interest (police officers, victims, potential juvenile delinquents, etc.). And, in most cases, we don't know the true characteristics of the population—so, we use the sample to estimate the population characteristics. Therefore, sampling error is a real concern in research.

Fortunately, true random samples (actually called "simple random sampling" or "random sampling with replacement") give us the ability to estimate the likelihood (probability) of error created by the sampling process. On the other hand, we also know that there will *always* be error in sampling—the only question is how much. That's where the ability to estimate the amount and size of error becomes important and random sampling is the only sampling process that allows us to do that. Because random sampling tends to average out differences, these types of sampling processes generate a sample that has only random error present in the selection of subjects.

Why is this random error important? The reason is mostly that estimating the size and amount of random error gives us a way to determine whether an observed difference is real. If these error estimates are uniform and standard (and they are), it is possible to use them in making a decision about sample differences. These standard estimates are used to create statistical sampling distributions. Let's see how they are created.

First, imagine that we can create a true random sample from a population. Further, imagine that in this population there are no differences between people.[1] In this event, with a reasonably large enough random sample, theoretically there also would be no differences in the sample and thus no sampling error. To illustrate this, let's say that males and females in our population have the same average incomes. This means that, if we compared male and female average incomes in our sample, the true result would be a zero difference. Knowing that random sampling error exists, we expect a result other than zero. Because the *true* result is actually zero, it makes sense that any sample differences we find are mostly likely to be small ones, spread randomly around the zero position. On the other hand, you can get a large difference from a "bad" random sample—but that rarely happens. So, the task is to find out how frequently various amounts of difference occur. In general, the frequency of random error is as summarized in Box 9.1.

The frequency of random error differences is actually easy to determine, but it takes some time to do it. You begin with a "no-difference" population (an artificial one is okay) and then create a random sample from it (we'll also use a population with a normal distribution). Let's continue with our male/female income example. We'll want to subtract mean female incomes from mean male incomes in the sample (remember, the result *should* be zero) and save the result, which for these purposes we will hypothetically say was a difference between the two mean incomes of 0.1538.[2] Now we create another random sample and we once again

---

[1]Technically, all we need is a population with no difference between certain characteristics of interest. This "no difference" can be precisely that, or it may mean that the differences in the population "average out" to no difference.
[2]A positive number in this example means that male incomes were higher.

BOX 9.1

THE LOGIC OF RANDOM SAMPLING ERROR

Any random sample yields random sampling differences from its population with these results:

✓ small errors occur frequently

✓ large errors occur infrequently

Therefore, most differences caused by random error will be close to zero (the no difference point).

---

subtract the incomes and save the result (hypothetically an income difference of –0.849, where female incomes were higher). If we continue to do this 100,000 times,[3] the final results will create an error distribution around the zero point. The distribution will have a few very large differences from the zero point, more medium-sized differences, and a huge number of small differences. And, that distribution would provide an estimate of the probability that a difference of any size is merely a random error difference. Such a distribution might look like the one in Figure 9.1.

A sampling distribution such as the one we created above, when combined with the concept of standard deviations, actually has a name. Because we calculated sample means and subtracted them from the population mean, the error

FIGURE 9.1 Creating a Sampling Distribution

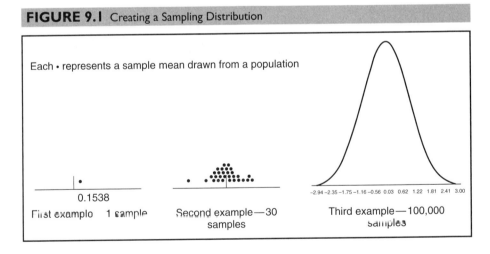

Each • represents a sample mean drawn from a population

0.1538

First example   1 sample

Second example—30 samples

−2.94 −2.35 −1.75 −1.16 −0.56 0.03 0.62 1.22 1.81 2.41 3.00

Third example—100,000 samples

---

[3]Obviously, we don't want to do this because it would take a long time. A computer program can be created to do the sampling and calculations, though, and the job is much easier. Several of the Web-based random number generator sites can do this for you while you watch the distribution build.

differences represent random error from the population mean and the standard deviations (which use *scores* not means) are called *standard errors*. Our statistical distribution yields random error estimates that are known as the *standard error of the mean*. All we would need to do to find the probability of any size error difference is to count the number of times that difference occurred (and divide by 100,000 for this example).

This can be done for any statistic. We simply random sample, calculate the statistic, create a difference from zero, and continue the process enough times. Of course, saying we "simply" do this belies the effort involved. Before computers were available, statisticians might spend years creating such a statistical standard error distribution using hand calculations and selecting random samples. This is why you will find many statistics using the same standard error distributions—it wasn't worth the effort if there was evidence that an existing one was close enough.

It is these statistical error distributions that determine what the results mean for any inferential statistic we might use. To relate this to the earlier discussion of hypotheses, these distributions are the tools used to determine whether a hypothesis is accepted or rejected.

SUMMARY

Hypotheses are the key to most types of research. These statements of expected relationships are used to guide tests of data to see if we are correct. Because of this, hypotheses need to be as specific as possible or the results of our tests become questionable.

There are two general forms of hypotheses: null and alternative. The null is a statement that there is no difference or no effect, that is, nothing is expected to happen. The alternative is the statement we make for testing—a proposal that a specific relationship or difference will occur. Because there are a couple of possibilities in proposing something will happen, alternative hypotheses can be very basic (*A* affects *B*) or more complicated (as *A* increases *B* increases). The latter form can predict a positive relationship (as *A* increases *B* increases) or a negative relationship (as *A* increases *B* decreases).

To test these hypotheses, we use random sampling to establish error distributions for the statistics used. By sampling from a no-difference population a sufficient number of times and calculating a statistic where population results are zero, all nonzero results create a distribution based on random sampling error. Once that exists, it can be used to determine the "rarity" of any statistical result happening merely by chance. The task is to match this random error against a statistical test of a hypothesis to determine if an observed difference is big enough to support the hypothesis.

In the next chapter we turn to the way statisticians determine when a difference or effect is "large enough" to be real. That is the realm of statistical significance.

KEY POINTS OF THE CHAPTER

Hypotheses are the key to doing research. They tell us what to test and how to test it. There are two basic forms of hypotheses.

- Null hypotheses are statements that there is no difference, or no effect.
- Alternative hypotheses state a difference or effect.
    - ♦ Two-tailed versions accept any kind of effect.
    - ♦ One-tailed versions provide the direction of effect.

Statistical error distributions are the foundation for statistical probability. They are

- based on random sampling;
- created by empirical distributions of random sampling error distributions;
- used to determine if alternative hypotheses should be accepted or rejected.

CHAPTER 10

Statistical Significance

Key Concepts

- significance

- alpha level

- confidence level

tatistical significance is a technical term used to describe a reasonable level of certainty that results are not due to chance (random error). This "reasonable level of certainty" is defined in terms of probability—specifically, the probability that an observed event or relationship is strictly a random occurrence. We use the concept of *significance* for multiple purposes, but one major use is to determine whether two or more measurements are different or the same. The "same" is our default—if we are not comfortable that measures are different, we say that they are automatically the "same." In the terminology of hypotheses, this result is equivalent to the null hypothesis. This is done to keep us from thinking that small differences are real ones. On the whole, it is a more conservative decision to reject difference than to accept it—that is, it is "safer" to say that nothing is occurring. The reason this is a conservative/safe decision is that no special explanation is required for a no-difference finding (the automatic rationale is that any "difference" is merely a product of random error). If you find a "true" difference, you have to attempt an explanation—and that can be difficult.

Thus, the search for difference is a search for true variation, or real variation without error. Because this is virtually impossible, we use probability to determine the *likely* amount of error in our measurement of variation. Here's the way it works:

 If the likely error (the probability of error) is relatively small, it makes sense to conclude that variation is real (that is, there is a small probability of error).

 If the likely error is large, we conclude that the variation is not real (there is a high probability of error).

Knowing what constitutes small and large amounts of error is the key to the process. We can achieve this through a logical sequence.

THE LOGICAL SEQUENCE OF DETERMINING SIGNIFICANCE

Though it may not seem so, finding difference or statistical significance is actually easy. There is a series of logical steps involved, but they are relatively routine and you rarely have to know anything about the statistic itself to go through the steps and arrive at an interpretation. We will use a series of questions to demonstrate the logic involved and show the steps leading to the use of probability in statistical tests. They begin with the concept of difference.

How Do We Infer Difference or Effect?

You already know from the discussion in Chapter 1 that measurement error always exists. As long as we can mostly restrict this error to random error, we are in good shape. That means random error distributions can be used to help estimate the amount of error *likely* to occur. Notice the word "likely" in the previous sentence. That suggests we won't know for sure how much of any difference we find is error, but we can work with probabilities to guess how likely it is. Let's recap one of the Chapter 1 maxims about error as our logical beginning point and then add the random error postulate:

 Any two numbers representing groups may be same, but appear different because of measurement error.

 If random samples are used, statistical error distributions can establish the probability of different amounts of random error.

Now we simply have to calculate differences between measurements (frequently referred to in statistics as "observations") and compare the size of those differences to the same amount of random error. This is equivalent to calculating a difference between two measurements of 2.7 and then looking at an appropriate sampling error distribution to see where 2.7 is under that curve. Once we know where our number is, there is an associated probability of that number occurring by random error alone. Pretty simple concept, isn't it? But, where do the difference calculations come from? Those calculations are the province of inferential statistics, or measures of significance. Each member of this statistical family is actually nothing more than a difference measure. They just measure different types of differences. When we discuss the Chi-square statistic, you will see how it defines difference and then sums up all the differences in a table. This leads us to our next statement:

 We find measurement differences by using statistical tests of inference (tests of significance).

How Much Difference Is Necessary?

Using these inferential tests is really not difficult, particularly when you have a computer program calculating the results for you, because most of them produce very similar results. This means their interpretation is virtually the same. The problem is to know when to use each one, not necessarily how to use it. This being the case, there is a critical ingredient remaining before the tests can be used. How do we know *how much difference is required* before we can call it *real* and not random error?

You could say, that's easy too—just choose an appropriate large amount of difference you feel comfortable with. The obvious problem is that you might choose one amount, someone else another amount, and so on. All of you would potentially come to different conclusions about whether the differences are real or error. While we're discussing this problem, keep in mind that we would like to substitute the *probability* of a difference being random error for the actual amount of difference. This way, various types of difference and different calculations can all be discussed on the same terms—probability of error.

The solution to people selecting an arbitrary error probability as their "comfort" level is to standardize the criteria for difference.[1] So, let's do that. At least theoretically we could choose a probability of error at .49 (or 49% chance of being wrong—remember probabilities are expressed as *proportions*). I don't know about you, but if there was an assurance of going to Las Vegas with 51% odds in my favor, you would not be reading *this* book! I would lose a lot, but I would win more—I'd just have to stay at the gambling tables long enough. Unfortunately, .49 is not a good probability for error. For most purposes that's way too much. And remember, science is famously conservative about such things as making mistakes. Obviously, we don't want much error as a routine matter. When we say something is different (or a variable affects another variable), we would like to have a good chance of being correct. This "good chance" of being correct is a criterion we call the *alpha level*—the criterion for pronouncing something to be a real effect. This leads to our next statement:

 The statistical criterion for a real difference or effect is the alpha level.

What, then, would be a good chance of being correct (the opposite proportion of being wrong—the random error probability)? Or, what should you choose as the alpha level? If you think back to the normal curve and standard deviations (or *standard error* as we later called it), plus and minus one standard deviation represented 68% of the data. This means, on both tails, there is 32% left. This equates to an error probability of .32, or slightly less than a one-in-three chance of a larger difference from the mean being the same as the mean. Would this be

---

[1]Actually, it *is* possible for individuals to choose their own "comfort" level of error probability. Moreover, it might even be desirable. The issue is *justifying* the chosen probability level. Different types of problems lead to different tolerances for error. If a larger amount of error can be tolerated (i.e., if you make a mistake, it's not so important), your error probability could be higher. If a mistake would be critical (i.e., dangerous criminals would be released from prison if you are wrong), you have a lower tolerance for error and want to choose a lower level of error probability.

safe enough? Not for science! Okay, let's go to plus and minus two standard deviations. That was close to 95% with only 5% (probability of .05) being left over on the tails. If we use that as our criterion, only 5 in 100 or 1 in 20 cases where we call a difference real will be wrong (random error). That sounds reasonable, and pretty conservative—a .05 probability of being wrong and a .95 probability of being correct. The .05 level is the one researchers commonly use as the alpha level. The reverse of the error probability, .95 probability of being correct, is frequently referred to as the *confidence level.*

 The most commonly used alpha level is an error probability of .05.

What Is "Significance"?

The alpha level, as an acceptable probability criterion, determines the point at which we say the statistical results demonstrate a difference or effect among variables, categories, or groups. When we meet the alpha level, the result is termed *statistical significance.* At this point, you have to be careful, though. The word "significance" is a commonly used term. What it suggests are thoughts like "meaningful," "important," "strongly implied," and so on. This is NOT what significance means in statistical language. It simply means that the probability of random error is equal to or smaller than your chosen criterion, the alpha level. In other words, if .05 is used as the alpha level, any statistical difference with a random error probability that meets that alpha level is "significant." This leads to our next statement:

 Statistical significance is a matter of meeting your chosen alpha level.

Now let's discuss the idea of "meeting" the alpha level. With a choice of .05 (researchers commonly write this as "$p \leq .05$" or, "a probability of equal to or less than .05"), you are saying that you will accept error up to a level of 5 times in 100. Therefore, anything lower than .05 is even better. But, *all you have to do is to get to .05*—you don't have to have a smaller probability to be "significant" (although it will be). At the same time, .05 is also saying that your level is NOT .051. If you agree to 0.5 as the alpha level, anything other than zeros after the "5" digit is too much error. Yes, you are correct—that's a very small difference; but you can't start fudging the criterion. If you say .05, then .05 it is. Here's the rule:

 To be significant, your statistical result must be at least as small as a standard probability level of .05. If it is larger than .05, the result is not significant.

The resulting interpretations are pretty straightforward. If a result is not significant, there is no difference (or one variable does not affect the other). If a result is significant, there *is* a difference (or one variable affects another).

Combining Significance with Hypotheses

Now let's tie all this together with hypotheses. The statistical test is designed to determine if the hypothesis you propose (a one- or two-tailed alternative hypothesis) is accepted or rejected. We accept alternative hypotheses when error is low and reject them when error is high. It should make sense that when an alternative hypothesis is accepted, the null hypothesis is rejected. Similarly, when an alternative hypothesis is rejected, the null hypothesis is accepted. Box 10.1 summarizes the decisions from construction of a hypothesis to the acceptance or rejection of a difference/effect.

Only one issue remains: Where do you find the correct probability level for a calculated statistic value? When a computer statistics program (like SPSS, SAS, Minitab, or OpenStat) is available, a probability level will automatically be provided for the statistical results. That makes it easy; in fact, you can pretty much ignore the statistical results (unless they are being used to determine whether the direction of an observed relationship matches the alternative hypothesis) and just use the probability to make your decisions.

An Example of Testing Hypotheses

Here's a demonstration of how this works. Our hypothesis will be: "Income affects crime reporting." There is no direction to this alternative hypothesis so it is two-tailed (the computer results may call the probability *2-sided*). We'll use the standard alpha level of .05 to determine significance. Look at Table 10.1 to see how easy this is, even when you don't know what the statistics are.

For the moment, we don't care what Chi-square is (or its calculated value or "*df*"). Probability is the information we want. The table contents represent

---

BOX 10.1

STEPS IN USING AN INFERENTIAL STATISTIC TO DETERMINE IF AN EFFECT EXISTS

✓ Make an appropriate alternative hypothesis.

✓ If the hypothesis is one-tailed, make sure the data have the correct direction. If not, stop here.

✓ Calculate an inferential test statistic and get the resulting value.

✓ Look up the probability of getting the calculated value.

✓ Compare the probability level of the "calculated value" to your alpha level, usually .05.

✓ If the probability is *larger than .05, REJECT our alternative hypothesis and ACCEPT the NULL hypothesis.*

✓ If the probability is *equal to or smaller than .05, ACCEPT the ALTERNATIVE hypothesis and REJECT the NULL hypothesis.*

TABLE 10.1 Example of Statistical Results with Probability

	Value	*df*	*Probability (Two-Sided)*
Chi-square	19.756	6	.003 ◄────

an inferential test of a possible relationship between income and reporting of crime. Looking at the probability value, we see .003 reported. This is the direct probability level for a two-tailed test, which ours is. Our only question is whether .003 is equal to or smaller than .05. And, of course it is. Therefore, *our results are significant and we accept the alternative hypothesis* (and reject the null hypothesis). Income does affect crime reporting.

What If The Computer Doesn't Give You a Probability Value?
(Or, worse yet, you had to calculate the statistic by hand ...)

Not all statistical results come with an attached probability level. In that case, you have to determine what the approximate probability is. There are two approaches to this. Both require using the statistic's sampling error distribution (the ones you find in the back of most statistics texts).

✓ The easiest way is to use or find a value for our statistic that is *equivalent to a probability of .05.*
  • Look in the correct table, say the *t*-test table, for the .05 value.
  • Compare the .05 table value to your calculated statistic value.
  • If your *statistic value is equal to or higher* than the .05 table value, accept the alternative hypothesis.
  • Some of these values are so commonly used that they are worth memorizing:
    ◆ For the *z*-distribution or *t*-test with a sample size of 120 or larger: a two-tailed $p_{.05}$ is 1.96 and a one-tailed $p_{.05}$ is 1.64.
    ◆ For the Chi-square test with 1 degree of freedom: a two-tailed $p_{.05}$ is 3.841 and a one-tailed $p_{.05}$ is 5.024.

✓ The other way is to look in the same tables to find your calculated statistic value or as close to it as you can get. Then locate the approximate probability level for that value.

Here is something to remember that will sound confusing at first. The necessary statistic value is always the *opposite* of probability.

✓ "Significant" **probabilities** are *equal to or SMALLER than the critical value of .05.*

✓ "Significant" **statistic values** are *equal to or HIGHER than the critical statistic value at the .05 level.*

More than You Wanted to Know: "Tails," Hypotheses, and Probability

The tails of a distribution and two- or one-tailed hypotheses refer to the same thing. Because probability also refers to the same tails, we can translate significance into both types of hypotheses. In doing so, we will assume an alpha level of .05 for significance.

Here's what you need to know:

✓ Two-Tailed Hypotheses:
- Must use *both* tails of the distribution.
- Have a probability of .025 on each tail, for .05 total.
- Use the computed probability level directly.

✓ One-Tailed Hypotheses:
- Use only *one* tail of the distribution.
- Have a probability of .05, *all* on one tail.
- Divide the computed probability level by two (unless it already says "one-tailed").
- BUT, make sure the direction of the data matches the direction of your hypothesis or else the hypothesis must be rejected.

Because you can cut a two-tailed computed probability level in half, a one-tailed hypothesis gives you a better chance of accepting the hypothesis.

SUMMARY

Statistical significance is a very specific concept and does NOT mean "important" as it does in normal language. It simply means achieving a result that meets your probability criterion. That probability criterion is called the alpha level and is usually set at a .05 level.

Hypotheses are tested by using a statistical test and comparing the result, with its associated probability, to the alpha level. If the resulting probability is equal to or smaller than the alpha level, the result is statistically significant and the alternative hypothesis is accepted. If the resulting probability is greater than the alpha level, there is no difference or effect and the null hypothesis is accepted.

KEY POINTS OF THE CHAPTER

Finding significance is a way to determine whether differences and effects are real or likely due to error.
- The probability of random sampling error is used to determine significance.
- The criterion for deciding when a statistical result is not random error is the alpha level, which is normally set at a probability of .05.
- Significance is when a statistical result is at the alpha level or below.
- Hypotheses are used with statistical tests.
  - When the results are at a probability of .05 or below, the alternative hypothesis is accepted.
  - When the results are at a probability larger than .05, the null hypothesis is accepted.

CHAPTER 11

Testing for Significance: The Chi-Square Test

Key Concepts

■ Chi-square

■ observed frequencies

■ expected frequencies

■ degrees of freedom

■ unequal marginals

■ statistical independence

■ nonparametric statistics

■ Fisher's exact test

This chapter begins the process of testing for significant differences (or significant effects) between variables. These tests are referred to as *inferential tests*, or *measures of significance*. "Inference" comes from the verb "to infer" so we use the tests to determine whether an observed difference between two or more categories or variables can be "inferred" to be a "real" difference. We will begin with a *bivariate* approach, or an analysis of a two-variable relationship. The simplest version is, as you might expect, also a nominal-level test. At the nominal level of measurement, if you think back to earlier chapters, there is little information other than which category a score represents. So, nominal-level inferential tests compare categories for differences. You can use ordinal level or higher data with them, but they won't use the extra information. The measure we will examine here is the Chi-square test. And, just in case, it is pronounced "kai"-square.

WHAT IS CHI-SQUARE?

Chi-square can be used to compare categories in a single variable (when compared to a hypothetical distribution) or the cells in a crosstabulation created by two variables. In its most common table version, Chi-square is a test for a relationship between two nominal-level variables. Sometimes known as Pearson's

Chi-square, after the late statistician Karl Pearson, you can find it in almost any statistical program. The statistic is an old one and is quite popular. There are even calculating versions on the Internet if you don't own or have access to a statistical program. As with most measures of significance, larger values of Chi-square indicate bigger differences—and bigger differences are more unlikely to occur by random error alone. The formula is:

$$\chi^2 = \sum \frac{(O - E)^2}{E}$$

Where: O = the observed frequency of a cell
E = the expected frequency of a cell

With: degrees of freedom $(df) = (r - 1)(c - 1)$ for a table
$= (k - 1)$ for a single group

(df represents a control for the number of cells in the table)

Before we leave this formula, let's look at two parts of it. First, in the formula itself there is the $(O - E)$ term. This is what we called a *differencing technique* when discussing the variance and standard deviation. This part of the formula establishes difference from E. Then there is the $(O - E)^2$ term. Similar to our "creation" of the variance statistic, this resolves a potential problem of positive differences cancelling out negative differences, resulting in zero. Actually, if you just change the letters in the formula, it looks a lot like the variance formula. Instead of summing the squared differences and then dividing by the number of cases like the variance does, Chi-square divides by the "expected" number and then sums the results.

We also need to discuss the *degrees of freedom* (df) concept. The name comes from the idea of the number of scores that are free to vary before the remaining scores are fixed. I know, that's confusing. Try it this way. If you had a 2 × 2 crosstabulation, there would be four cells. This means there are, at least theoretically, four cell scores "free to vary," the maximum possible df. Now imagine that you know the sample size and the number of cases in each category—from this you try to guess what the scores in the cells would be. How about if one of the cells already had a score in it—if you can guess the other three then they are "fixed." Only one score, the first one, was "free to vary" and df is 1. If you still can't guess the remaining scores, then we have to add at least one more "free to vary" score and the df would be at least 2. Actually, in a 2 × 2 table, the df is 1. Look at Box 11.1 to see why.

Instead of trying to puzzle our way through each different-size table like this, the df formula is $[(r - 1)(c - 1)]$, or the number of rows (r) minus 1 times the number of columns (c) minus 1. The answer for a 2 × 2 table equals 1 df. For a 5 × 4 table, it would be $[(5 - 1)(4 - 1)]$ equals 4 times 3, or a df of 12. But, here's the good news—you don't need to memorize this, the computer program will do it for you! Knowing the df is only necessary if you have to calculate the statistic and find a tabled probability level (or somehow get a computer result without probability).

Now let's discuss the Chi-square statistic itself.

BOX 11.1

DEGREES OF FREEDOM

 How many cell scores do you have to know to guess the scores for the remaining cells?

Scores on the bottom and right side of each table are the marginals (the total number of cases in each column and row), and the large score is the total number of cases in the table.

Number of unknown cell scores

No cell scores

?	?	20
?	?	20
15	25	40

Result:
No cells guessed

1 cell score

12	?	20
?	?	20
15	25	40

Result:
All remaining cells are known

Because only one score has to be known to guess the remaining scores, the degrees of freedom are 1.

THE MAGICAL WORKINGS OF CHI-SQUARE

Conceiving of a Null Relationship

The statistic itself is conceptually quite simple. As with all inferential statistics (those used to infer whether a difference, if any, is real), there has to be a way to conceive of what would be a "no relationship" (or independent[1]) baseline between the variables. For Chi-square, the concept is that of all categories being distributed equally—for example, 5 categories with 25 cases each or 3 categories with 10 cases each. In a table, however, that concept gets more complex. If the values of the variables have different total numbers of cases, then equality is based on the number of cases in the rows and columns. We'll discuss this problem in more detail a bit later. For now, let's focus on the expectation of all groups being equal.

Determining Differences—A Simple Chi-Square Example

The easiest demonstration of the way it works is to use a "single sample" (that's statistical talk for a single variable) and compare it with a hypothetical distribution. Imagine that you have three cubes all exactly equal in weight. Each cube is colored differently: yellow, blue, and green. Thirty people are told that the cubes have

---

[1]Independence means that things are not related. For instance, independent samples would be two groups that have no relationship with each other. That is, what happens with one has no bearing on what happens to another. Statisticians sometimes refer to this as *orthogonal*.

FIGURE II.I Choices of "Heaviest" Cube

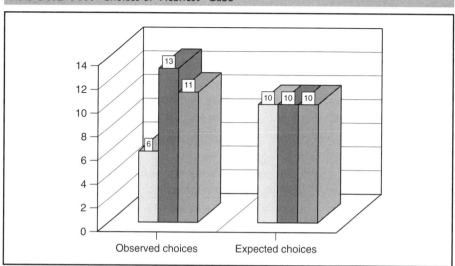

different weights and are asked to choose the one cube that they believe is the heaviest. Because the cubes are actually equal in weight, the choice *should* be a random one and that means any particular cube shouldn't be chosen more than any other. Therefore, the *expected* choices would be 10 yellow, 10 blue, and 10 green.

If we hypothesize that color will influence the perception of weight, then the test is to see whether the actual choices are different from those expected. If so, then we could argue that color influences perception of weight. Figure 11.1 illustrates these expected and observed choices.

Our 30 people made the following choices of a "heaviest" cube: 6 yellow, 13 blue, and 11 green.

Is this *different enough* from the expected values of 10, 10, and 10 to suggest that color might have made a difference in weight perception? Let's calculate the Chi-square statistic and find out.

First, we will set our alpha level at .05 (the probability level at which we will declare a "significant" difference). Now we need to begin the calculation. Look at the Chi-square formula above. First, we need to locate the O and E scores.

- Because O is the observed score, these are the actual choices our 30 people made. There are three O scores: 6, 13, and 11.
- The E scores are the expected scores of 10, 10, and 10.
- Following the formula, we subtract 10 from 6 ($= -4$), 10 from 13 ($= 3$), and 10 from 11 ($= 1$).
- Then we square each difference (-4 squared is 16), (3 squared is 9), (1 squared is 1).
- Each squared difference is then divided by its E score, which in each case is 10 ($16 \div 10 = 1.6$), ($9 \div 10 = 0.9$), ($1 \div 10 = 0.1$).
- These are then added to get the Chi-square value of 2.6 ($1.6 + 0.9 + 0.1 = 2.6$).

The Chi-square value of 2.6 would normally be compared to a table of Chi-square values, but you don't have to do that because the table value is reported below.

- A Chi-square value of 5.991 or larger[2] is the necessary figure for a probability of .05.
- The value of our calculated Chi-square (2.6) must be *equal to or larger than* this table value (5.991) to be statistically significant.
- Because it is smaller, it is not significant and we conclude that the choices of colored cubes made by our 30 people do not differ from the expected distribution.

Therefore, these three colors do not affect perceptions of weight. The result has a probability larger than .05, though we do not know at this point how much larger (there are calculators on the Internet where you can plug in a Chi-square value and *df* and get the probability level).

Chi-Square and Difference

Now let's revisit what we did in the formula as related to the concept of difference. When you see some standard score (in this case the "expected" choices) subtracted from another score (in this case the "observed" choices), the product is called a *difference*—therefore, we have referred to this one-score-subtracted-from-another approach as a *differencing* technique. It should be obvious that had all observed scores been the same, as we expected them to be (in this case, each group with 10 choices), then there would be zero total difference ($10 - 10 = 0$). The moral here is that the larger the cumulative difference between the observed choices and the expected choices, the greater is the likelihood that the difference is real.

 Chi-square is a measure of the cumulative differences between what we expect to get and what we really get.

Chi-square, Tables, and Marginals

Now we turn to the problem of having *different* expected scores. This is frequently the case in a Chi-square calculated on a 2×2 table (or any other size table). For instance, we may have different numbers of males and females and we want to see if crime victimization (whether they have been crime victims—"yes" or "no") is affected by gender. In such a case, we no longer have equal expected values and we have to find a way to calculate what would be expected in each cell of the table. We can do this by using the total numbers in the categories of each variable. These category totals are called the row and column "marginals" and are used to determine the expected values. Figure 11.2 illustrates the cells and marginals concept.

---

[2]Just a reminder, the size of statistic values (like Chi-square) is the *reverse* of the size of probability. Small statistic values happen frequently (have large probabilities); large statistic values happen rarely (have small probabilities).

FIGURE 11.2 Row and Column Marginals

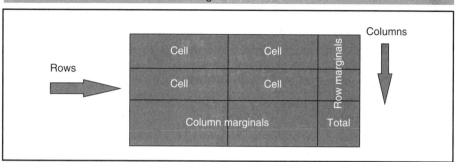

Now let's put the variables and numbers in the table. Table 11.1 shows there are 200 males and 110 females (the row marginals). There are also 115 people who have never been a crime victim and 195 who have been a crime victim (the column marginals). The total number of people is 310.

TABLE 11.1 Table with Marginal Columns and Rows

	Never Been a Crime Victim	*Have Been a Crime Victim*	*(Row Marginals)*
Males	70	130	*200*
Females	45	65	*110*
(Column Marginals)	*115*	*195*	*310*

We can use these marginal totals to determine what numbers would be expected in each cell if gender is *not* related to victimization. We multiply each cell's row marginal number by its column marginal number and divide that result by the total number of cases. To demonstrate this, Table 11.2 duplicates the information but with each cell designated by a letter.

TABLE 11.2 Table with Cell Designations

	Never Been a Crime Victim	*Have Been a Crime Victim*	*(Row Marginals)*
Males	70 A	130 B	*200*
Females	45 C	65 D	*110*
(Column Marginals)	*115*	*195*	*310*

Cell A has a row marginal of 200 and a column marginal of 115, so we would multiply 200 by 115 and get 23,000. Then we divide 23,000 by the total number of 310 resulting in an expected number of 74.19 cases in cell A. The process is repeated for each cell, giving us expected numbers of 74.19, 125.81, 40.81, and 69.19 (cells A, B, C, and D, respectively). Now let's put those numbers in each cell as the expected values (you don't actually need to put the numbers in the cells to calculate Chi-square, this is just for illustration purposes). Table 11.3 below adds these numbers to the crosstabulation.

TABLE 11.3 Table with Expected Values

	Never Been a Crime Victim	Have Been a Crime Victim	(Row Marginals)
Males	O = 70 A E = 74.19	O = 130 B E = 125.81	200
Females	O = 45 C E = 40.81	O = 65 D E = 69.19	110
(Column Marginals)	115	195	310

As you can see, the observed or actual number of 70 in cell A is not too different from the expected number of 74.19. In fact, you might have already noted that each cell's observed and expected numbers are relatively close. With that being the case, how much difference do you think is really in this table—enough to be statistically significant?

What is the reason for using this "expected" value in each cell? The answer is that by calculating expected values from their marginals, we compensate for the *unequal* row and column totals. Think of this as a type of sample-size correction, just as we did in creating the variance statistic. Now let's look at a Chi-square calculated from a table.

An Example of a Table Version of the Chi-Square Test

In order to use the Chi-square test, we need a hypothesis. How about this *one-tailed* alternative hypothesis?

> **Female parolees are more successful on parole than male parolees.**

This particular hypothesis requires that female parolees have a larger percentage[3] of successful cases than male parolees. Table 11.4 below contains real data on this

TABLE 11.4 Example of a Chi-Square Test

Crosstabulation of the Relationship Between Parolee's Gender and Success on Parole

			Success on Parole		
			Failure	Success	Total
Parolee gender	male	Count	2116	1412	3528
		%	60.0%	40.0%	100.0%
	female	Count	171	192	363
		%	47.1%	52.9%	100.0%
Total		Count	2287	1604	3891
		%	58.8%	41.2%	100.0%

---

[3]It is unwise to phrase a hypothesis using "the number of," as in "A larger number of females will succeed on parole than male parolees." The reason for this is that, instead of testing the relative value of each group, you end up testing the size of the group samples. If females have a much smaller number of cases than males (a common situation in criminal justice data), even a much larger proportion of successes will likely be a smaller *number of cases* than males. In short, stay away from using numbers in making hypotheses and discuss proportions or percentages. Better yet, try "are more likely to" or some such phrase.

issue, so we'll examine it to see if the direction of our hypothesis is correct. (Don't forget that a test of any directional hypothesis first looks to see if the direction is correct and, if so, then continues with a test of significance.)

We first look at the crosstabulation table and determine that the direction of our hypothesis is correct—females have the highest rate of success (52.9% compared to 40.0% for males). Therefore the direction of the hypothesis is supported. Now we need to determine whether the difference between the two percentages is statistically significant, or if this is merely a chance difference.

We need to set our alpha level (the level at which we will call a result "significant"), so we'll use the traditional .05 level. This means the calculated probability level must be .05 or smaller in order to be significant. Table 11.5 reports the Chi-square results for this crosstabulation.

TABLE 11.5 Chi-Square Results for Crosstabulation Table

Chi-Square Test

	Value	*df*	*Probability (Two-Tailed)*	Note: Probability is all you really need to interpret this table
Chi-Square	22.500	1	.000 ◁	

The Chi-square value of 22.500, with 1 *df*, has a probability value of .000,[4] which is *smaller* than .05. True, this is a one-tailed test and the probability is two-tailed, so we need to divide the two-tailed value. In this case, there is no reason to do so because it would still be some probability value less than .0004. The key here is the size of the probability; that's what you need to arrive at a conclusion. Therefore, the result is *significant* and we have already determined the direction is correct. We conclude that female parolees are more successful on parole. The alternative hypothesis is accepted (and, if you want to, you can say that "the null hypothesis is rejected").

BASIC ASSUMPTIONS OF CHI-SQUARE

Having seen how Chi-square works, a bit more statistical detail is in order. Every statistic has "assumptions." These are the premises made by the person who created the statistic. Keep in mind that any statistic was originally created to

---

[4]Just in case, whenever you see a probability of .000 it doesn't mean the level is actually *zero*. There are nonzero digits to the right of the last zero—they just don't appear because the program is written to provide only three digits. Assuming rounding has taken place, the only thing you know about the next digit is that it isn't a 5 or larger.

"solve" a problem, so Chi-square is a product of the original problem it was meant to resolve.

Chi-square is part of a family of statistics generally called *nonparametric* statistics. These are frequently referred to as distribution-free statistics. This means that they don't make assumptions requiring a specific data distribution as *parametric* statistics do (these statistics require normal distributions and linear relationships). Actually, when you think about it, it would be pretty dumb to assume a normal curve for nominal- and even ordinal-level data. However, this distribution-free term is sometimes misleading because some people think it means assumption free. While the Chi-square statistic is a very simple nonparametric statistic, it is not entirely free of assumptions (none of them really are). Here are some of the assumptions you must meet to use this statistic:

- *Random sampling* has been used to create the data you are analyzing. Otherwise, there is no random sampling error and no sampling distribution that can be used to establish the probability error. But, this is nothing special—*all* inferential statistics require random samples.
- Observations on all variables are *independent*. This means you cannot calculate a Chi-square with related variables, such as experimental pre-test and post-test groups, matched samples, or time-series data (samples drawn from subsequent periods of time).
- *Large samples* have been used. In statistics, this usually means 30 or more cases, but Chi-square really works best with even larger samples. All other things being equal, Chi-square's ability to identify a real difference in the data increases with the size of the sample.
- Finally, as originally constructed, Chi-square assumes *equal marginals*. Minimally, this means that the categories of the independent variable should have the same number of cases (for instance, the same number of males as females). Because this requirement is not usually met with real data, a general guideline for 2×2 tables is that any category marginal exceeding more than 80% of the total number of cases probably has too much error. This "80/20 split" rule should be used with caution in small sample sizes (see Box 11.2 for the rationale behind this).
- No *cell has an expected value less than 5*. That is, calculated *E*s all have values of 5 or higher (*not* the observed values!). This assumption can be violated with little effect in tables with many cells because the error will be small. Moreover, when the marginals are equal, the *E*s can be smaller than 5 and the statistic will still be able to achieve a probability value of .05 or lower.

There are other "assumptions" sometimes listed by authors of statistics texts. All of these additional assumptions, however, are a product of the requirements for equal marginals and large sample size, so they aren't really new assumptions.

BOX 11.2

WHY ARE UNEQUAL MARGINALS SO IMPORTANT TO CHI-SQUARE?

In a nutshell: Unequal marginals "mess" with estimations of probability when we are trying to determine if one variable has an effect on another.

Here's why.

✓ All numbers are estimates (remember the problem with measurement error?) so we use error estimates (yes, I know, there are *two* estimates in this sentence) to try to pin down their real position.

✓ If two rows (like males and females) in a table have the same number of cases, or equal marginals, then their error estimates should be the same (assuming random sampling) and comparing their numbers (like a Chi-square $O-E$ difference in a cell) is not too difficult.

✓ If the rows have different numbers of cases, or unequal marginals, then the numbers in each row will have different amounts of error. The smaller of the rows will have a larger amount of error in their numbers. Really big differences in marginals produce really big differences in error estimates and big mistakes in making comparisons.

✓ As long as a statistic makes separate error estimates for each comparison group, this problem can be handled. Unfortunately, Chi-square bases its entire error estimate on the total sample size and assumes that all groups are of equal size.

✓ Marginal inequality, for a 2×2 table, worse than approximately 80% in one group and 20% in the other can produce a highly misleading estimate of probability.

On the whole, Chi-square is a fairly *robust* statistic—that is, it handles violations of cell size, sample size, and equality of marginals relatively well. However, you have to be careful when these violations come together in a data set: One problem can be handled, two or more is a much worse issue. When these problems occur, caution should be used in interpreting Chi-square results with probabilities close to the alpha level (.05). Error could move the results to the low side of the .05 level making the Chi-square probability smaller than it should be. This means you will pronounce something significant when it isn't.[5]

CHI-SQUARE AND SAMPLE SIZE

Chi-square probability values are a product of not only the presence of a relationship, but also sample size. Thus, the larger the sample size (all other things equal), the larger the Chi-square value (and the smaller the probability level).

---

[5]This problem is actually known as a Type I error—rejecting a true null hypothesis. Other than this footnote, the book avoids the "Type I" and "Type II" error terminology because it tends to be confusing to students. If your professor wants you to know this, ask her or him about it.

More than You Wanted to Know—Error and Power Curves

One of the reasons statisticians get concerned about error is that it doesn't increase in a straight-line fashion. In other words, the more error the worse the problem gets.

Here's a general error curve—virtually all error operates in a similar distribution. As you can see, low amounts of error don't increment too fast. The further you move along on the error curve (increasing error), the faster the curve increments.

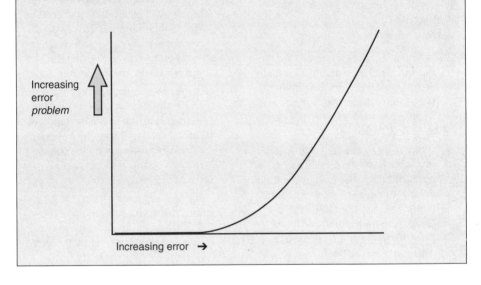

Increasing error *problem* ↑

Increasing error →

With a large sample size, even tiny differences (relationships) can be statistically significant. Strength of a relationship is the province of another family of statistics called *measures of association*. The following three 2 × 2 tables in Table 11.6 demonstrate the sample-size issue. Note in each case the relationship in the table remains constant; the size of the sample is merely doubled each time. Also, you may remember that these tables would have a *df* of 1 and at a .05 probability level, a Chi-square value of 3.841 or larger is needed. The first table is not significant because the Chi-square value is less than 3.841. The second table, with the sample

TABLE 11.6 The Effect of Sample Size on Chi-Square and Probability

Original table			2 × original			4 × original		
7	3	10	14	6	20	28	12	40
5	10	15	10	20	30	20	40	60
12	13	25	24	26	50	48	52	100

$\chi^2 = 1.93$ $\chi^2 = 5.08$ $\chi^2 = 11.50$
$p = .164$ $p = .024$ $p = .0007$

size doubled, is now significant. The third table with the sample size doubled again easily meets the required value.

You can frequently find "significant" Chi-square values for variables in larger samples and very few significant relationships in smaller samples. When you find a relationship, the result is best interpreted as being "just" a relationship, after all significance means you met your alpha level, not that the results are meaningful. A common mistake that researchers make is to treat significance as "importance"— you can actually see the terms "highly significant" used in published articles when they refer to probabilities lower than .01 or so. In fact, this leads us to a rule:

> *Because sample size affects probability levels, never use a measure of significance to mean strength of relationship.*

What If You Can't Use Chi-Square?

There are two likely choices when there are problems with meeting Chi-square assumptions (unless the issue is independent samples).[6] The first only applies to 2×2 tables and is, in fact, made specifically for them. The statistic is the *Fisher's Exact Test*. This statistic doesn't make assumptions about sample size, cell size, or equality of marginals—actually, it was designed for small samples and small cell sizes. Even better, it's calculated value can be directly interpreted as probability. In short, if you can use Fisher's Exact Test, you should, because it is superior to Chi-square. We don't need to discuss it further because you can already interpret it—just treat it as a probability level and compare to your alpha level.

The second choice is to use a more specialized version of Chi-square called a *maximum likelihood Chi-square*. This version is worthwhile when the problem is unequal marginals in a table of any size other than 2×2. Calculation of likelihood ratios[7] contains no assumptions about marginal equality. Therefore, when you are using a statistics program that provides the probability associated with a maximum likelihood version of Chi-square, use it. The resulting approximation will be better than that provided by the traditional Pearson's Chi-square.

Finally, we made an exception above in instances where the data are from related samples rather than independent samples. That is, Chi-square simply can't be used. Should you have these kinds of data, the McNemar and Cochran Q tests are both specifically designed for nominal-level *related* samples. Those, too, are not discussed here, but keep in mind that related samples have their own family of statistics and you should use them whenever you see data of that type (not that we expect you to rush out and start doing research!).

---

[6]There is an older method of dealing with small sample sizes and Chi-square called *Yates Correction for Continuity*. That method is not discussed here because statisticians have found that its effect is minimal at best and largely discarded it. The two methods mentioned here are now the ones to be used in a majority of cases.

[7]A discussion of maximum likelihood and likelihood ratios is beyond our scope at this point. You can find information in several textbooks and even on the Internet.

SUMMARY

The Chi-square statistic is a frequently-used, nominal-level, inferential test for statistical independence when used in crosstabulations. It uses the marginal frequencies in a table to create the expected scores in each cell and then compares the observed scores to the expected ones. If the score differences are relatively large, a relationship probably exists between the two variables in the table. Conversely, small differences are likely to be a product of random error with no relationship.

Though Chi-square is a nonparametric statistic, there are at least four critical assumptions it makes about data. These are as follows: the sampling process used to create the data was a random one, the variables are independent of each other, sample size is sufficiently large, and the marginals are approximately equal. The first two will be true of every inferential statistic we discuss.

Many statistics also require larger sample sizes, particularly those using the normal distribution. The marginal equality requirement is frequently true of statistics used with tables, and this is probably Chi-square's biggest problem.

What can you do with data that really don't work with Chi-square? That would be, in particular, interval-level information. It would create way too many cells for Chi-square to handle with most sample sizes. A better answer is to use a statistic especially designed to handle such data, and that is where we will turn in the next chapter with a discussion of the *t*-test.

KEY POINTS OF THE CHAPTER

Chi-square is a good inferential statistic for nominal-level data. It uses probability distributions to estimate the likelihood that differences among categories are either a product of random error or some effect.

Chi-square can be used to compare single variables to some hypothetical distribution or to compare variables in crosstabulation tables.

It assumes:

- random sampling
- independent samples (variables)
- large sample sizes for accuracy
- equal marginal distributions

CHAPTER 12

Testing for Significance in Two Groups: The t-Test

Key Concepts

■ *t*-test

■ between-group variation

■ within-group variation

■ Levene's test

■ *F*-ratio

■ unequal variance

Now that you have seen how a nominal-level significance test works, let's look at an interval-level test. This time, the data are capable of much more than just determining which category a case belongs to. At the interval level, the issue will be how much more or less one group or category is different from another. As a result, these tests all use the concept of the mean. Rather than saying that one group has more cases in one category than does another, we will now say that one group's *average* is different from that of another. One of the most common of these tests is the *t*-test.

PARAMETRIC INFERENTIAL STATISTICS

Interval-level tests of significance focus on comparisons using the interval-level measure of central tendency, the mean. Most of the analytical work at this level will use one of two measures: the *t*-test or the analysis of variance (ANOVA). Both the *t*-test and ANOVA are called *parametric* statistics. Statisticians refer to them this way because the tests make assumptions about the underlying data distribution, or the "parameters" of the data. Both tests are extremely popular and are frequently used in criminal justice research. This chapter focuses on the *t*-test as it is actually a precursor to the ANOVA. The latter test will be the subject of the next chapter.

THE *t*-TEST STATISTIC

The *t*-test is an *interval-level* test of significance for *two groups* and *one* interval-level dependent variable. This means it can be used to determine potential differences between any two groups (such as males and females) on a dependent variable measured at the interval level (such as income). A sample one-tailed hypothesis would be phrased as follows for this test:

> *Males have higher incomes than females.*

Because the *t*-test uses the mean of each group to make the comparison, the above hypothesis actually requires that the mean male income be higher than the mean female income.

Types of *t*-Tests

A version of the *t*-test is available for both *related* and *independent* data (or samples). In the related samples version, the test examines the means of two paired groups, or compares a "before" and "after" group (the same as a pretest and posttest in an experimental design). The independent samples version is more common in the social sciences and uses data typically found in surveys, such as differences between two groups defined by gender, high and low socioeconomic status, or victimization.

Two Versions of the Independent Samples *t*-Test

The independent samples *t*-test has two different versions because of the possible sources of variation in the data. We are interested in the variation between the *means* of the two groups; therefore, we want a finding of a difference between the two groups, if one exists, to be a product of variation between the two means and nothing else. Let's call this the *between-group variation*. An example of this is found in our gender/income hypothesis above: "The mean male income is higher than the mean female income." Thus, we test to see if a difference exists between the two group means, with a requirement (to support our hypothesis) that the male mean income be higher. If there is any other source of variation acting to create a difference between the income levels of two groups, we might make a mistake in attributing the difference to gender.

Unfortunately, there is a second source of variation created by the difference between the individual scores and their group means. Previously, we referred to

---

Basic Types of *t*-Tests

✓ Related samples *t*-test: For sampling that produces matched or related pairs, or pre- and posttest comparisons.

✓ Independent samples *t*-test: For groups that have no *sampling* reason to be related.

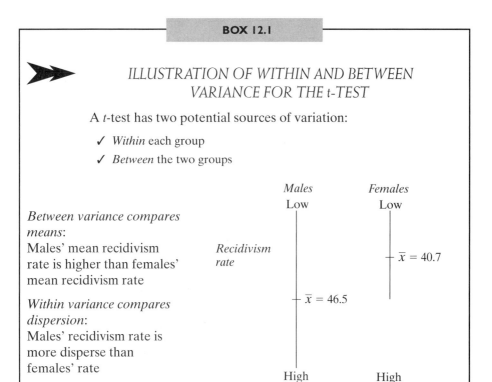

this as *dispersion* in a group. Assuming each score in a group (males, for instance) is not the same as its mean, each score varies from its mean and contributes to variation within its group. We call this *within-group variation.* Any test of differences *between* the groups should not be complicated by different amounts of dispersion *within* each of the groups. (Box 12.1 contains an illustration of the issue.) The two *t*-tests for independent samples therefore are concerned with this within-group variation. There are two tests because different within-group variations either exist or don't exist.

The Equal Variance *t*-Test (or Pooled Variance *t*-Test)

This version is used when the two groups have the *same*, or essentially the same, amount of dispersion. We determine that by calculating the variance statistic for each of the two groups and comparing them. If they are approximately equal, the equal variance *t*-test is used. Of course, we don't just "look" at the two variances, but conduct a statistical test just as you would do to determine if any two numbers are the same.

This version of the independent *t*-test is the more powerful of the two. If the within-group variation (the dispersion) is the same for both groups, there is only one remaining potential source of variation—the *between*-group comparison of means—and that is precisely what the test examines. Further, the estimates of within variance for both groups can be pooled into one estimate,[1] making the calculations easier and the test more powerful (better able to find a real difference).

The Unequal Variance *t*-Test (or Separate Variance *t*-Test)

If the within-group variation differs in the two groups (the variances are different), the second source of variation must be incorporated into the test to make sure the variation doesn't affect conclusions about a difference between the groups. For this purpose the equal variance *t*-test won't do us any good. We need a version of the *t*-test that controls for the within variance of both groups, thus the name *unequal variance t-test*. This means that the formula must account for both variances, making the calculations more complicated. The end result is that the unequal variance *t*-test is less powerful than the equal variance *t*-test.

How Do We Determine Which t-Test to Use?

It would be nice if we could just "eyeball" and compare the variances of our two groups but, of course, we can't.[2] The appropriate approach is to use a separate test of significance to determine whether they are different. This test is the "*F*-ratio test for equality of variances" and tells us which of the two independent samples *t*-tests should be used. In the output from the SPSS statistical program, which will be shown here, the test is called *Levene's test for equality of variances*. Regardless of name, it is essentially a traditional *F*-test[3] comparing the two variances, based on the standard error of the variances (think in terms of looking for differences that are equal to or larger than the size of two standard errors). Table 12.1 contains an example. Note that there are just two numbers in the table: the *F*-ratio value and "Sig.," which is the probability.

If the result of the *F*-test is *not significant*, the variances are essentially the same and can be "pooled" into one variance—so the *equal variance t-test* is appropriate. If the result of the *F*-test is *significant*, the variances are not the same and can't be treated as if they were—so the *unequal variance t-test* would be appropriate. Just in case, though, don't make and test a hypothesis with the Levene's Test and *never* divide the probability as if you were using a one-tailed hypothesis. This would be

TABLE 12.1 Example of Levene's Test

Levene's Test for Equality of Variances	
F	*Sig.*
7.461	.006

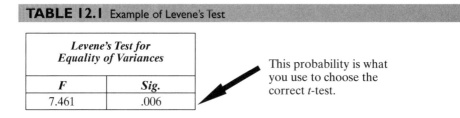

This probability is what you use to choose the correct *t*-test.

---

[1]Pooling the estimates means that they can be treated as *one* estimate. Fewer estimates result in better estimates.

[2]If you want to compare the variances of the two groups to get an idea of their differences, the *t*-test output of most statistical programs provides the standard deviations (SD) of each group. Remember that squaring SD gives you the variance, so any SD difference you see will be even larger when squared.

[3]*F*-tests are all pretty much the same and very simple. They use two numbers and divide one by the other (unless, of course, they are both the same size). In most cases, the largest number (one group's variance) is divided by the smallest number (the other group's variance). The resulting number is the "*F*-ratio."

BOX 12.2

 ## HOW TO DETERMINE WHICH *t*-TEST TO USE

The two possible choices derived from applying the *F*-test (Levene's Test) to the variances are:

✓ *F* probability is *larger than .05*, use the *equal variance t*-test

✓ *F* probability is *smaller than .05*, use the *unequal variance t*-test

---

equivalent to your trying to justify an expectation that one variance is more spread out than another—it just doesn't make sense. Remember, you are merely deciding which *t*-test to use (summarized in Box 12.2).

Sometimes a computer program merely gives the probability, or sometimes only the *F*-ratio. If the latter occurs, you will have to use an *F*-table (found in the back of many statistics textbooks and available on the Internet, as well). Because the *t*-test has three basic decisions (direction, which *t*-test, and significance), it can sometimes be confusing. Try following the logic in Box 12.3, which summarizes the decision steps for using an independent samples *t*-test.

BOX 12.3

GUIDELINES FOR USING A *t*-TEST

1. Propose a hypothesis (either one- or two-tailed).

  a. If you have a two-tailed hypothesis you *must* continue on to the *F*-value probability because your test does not require a specific direction.

  b. If you have a one-tailed hypothesis, examine the means of the two groups. Determine the apparent *direction* of the relationship. Does it match your hypothesis?

  c. If the direction is *not* what you stated, *stop and reject your hypothesis.*

  d. If the direction is *correct*, continue on to determine which *t*-test to use.

2. Look at the *F*-value (Levene's Test) probability (*p*).

  a. If it is equal to or smaller than .05, use the unequal variance *t*-test

(SPSS refers to this as "equal variances not assumed").

  b. If it is larger than .05, use the equal variance *t*-test (SPSS refers to this as "equal variances assumed").

3. Look at the correct *t*-test.

  a. If the probability level (*p*) is *equal to or smaller than your alpha level*, accept your alternative hypothesis (the means of the two groups are significantly different, and in the direction you proposed).

  b. If *p* is *larger than your alpha level*, reject your hypothesis and accept the null hypothesis (there is no difference in the means of the two groups).

BOX 12.4

WHAT ARE THE REQUIREMENTS FOR A t-TEST?

There are three critical assumptions for a *t*-test. They are:

✓ Independent variable is made up of *two groups* (or capable of being split into to "natural" groups).

✓ Dependent variable is *interval level.*

✓ Dependent variable is *normally distributed.*

Like all inferential tests, the data must be from a *random sample.*

Assumptions of the *t*-Test

The *t*-test makes a critical assumption about the data: The dependent variable (the interval measure—income in our earlier example) must be *normally distributed.* Fortunately, the test is also relatively robust and can withstand a "reasonable" departure from this assumption. Keep in mind the other two requirements of the *t*-test: an interval-level dependent variable and an independent variable that can be broken into two groups. If the dependent variable distribution isn't normal, the *t*-test shouldn't be used. The best alternative (for independent—unrelated—samples) is the Mann–Whitney *U*-test and information on that statistic can be found in Appendix C. We should also add the standard requirement that the sample be random. These assumptions are summarized in Box 12.4.

A SAMPLE *t*-TEST PROBLEM

Let's look at a typical independent samples *t*-test analysis. Gender is frequently tested using a *t*-test (as long as the dependent variable is interval level), so we'll use this variable and make a hypothesis.

> ***Male parolees have a higher propensity for violence than female parolees.***

Following the logic in the hypothesis, our *t*-test analysis must indicate that the mean violence propensity is higher for males than for females. If this direction is correct, we decide which *t*-test to use and, finally, we look to see if the associated *t*-test probability is significant. Keep in mind that, unless the direction of the means supports the hypothesis, a significant probability is moot. If the direction is wrong, stop there—your hypothesis is already incorrect.

Now let's turn to the data analysis. First, we need to examine the violence propensity means for males and females to determine whether our hypothesized direction is correct. In our example the measure of violence propensity produced scores ranging from 1 to 5, with higher scores designating greater propensity for violence. We will use two pieces of output from the SPSS statistical package to test our hypothesis.

TABLE 12.2 Descriptive Information for the t-Test

Group Statistics

	Gender-Parolee	N	Mean	Std. Deviation	Std. Error Mean
Parolee propensity for violence	male	3542	2.18	1.24	2.09E-02
	female	360	1.19	1.09	5.73E-02

Compare these means ↗

Because the hypothesis requires that males have a higher mean, we look at the information showing the means in Table 12.2. Males have a mean of 2.18 and females have a mean of 1.19. Because the mean for males is higher, the hypothesis is correct and we continue to the t-test results.

Our second step is to determine which t-test to use. Table 12.3 contains the information necessary for this step. The F-ratio under the "Levene's Test" shows a corresponding probability (sig.) of .000.[4] We compare this to .05 and conclude the variances are significantly different. Therefore, the variances are unequal and we use the unequal variance t-test (the line with "equal variances not assumed").

Following across the line of information beside "equal variances not assumed," we look for the t-test results. The unequal variance t-test value is 16.346, with a probability of .000;[5] the result is indeed statistically significant. The hypothesis is accepted—male parolees have a higher propensity for violence than female parolees.

Note that, in this instance, both t-test probabilities are the same at three digits (.000), so both t-tests lead to the same results. The unequal variances, however, do affect the results—the two t-test values are different (14.636 compared to 16.346).

TABLE 12.3 The t-Test Information to Test a Hypothesis

Independent Samples Test

		Levene's Test for Equality of Variances		t-Test for Equality of Means		
		F	Sig.	t	df	Sig (Two-Tailed)
Parolee propensity for violence	Equal variances assumed	25.191	(.000)	14.636	3899	.000
	Equal variances not assumed			16.346	460.002	(.000)

Look here to choose the correct t-test

Look here to test the hypothesis

---

[4]The probability here is two-tailed, but that is all we require. It doesn't make sense to try and predict which group will have the higher variance (a one-tailed test). A difference between the groups, in any direction, is enough to be concerned about the effect of within-group error.
[5]There is no need to divide this probability by 2 to get a one-tailed version. A probability of .000 (the fourth digit is not printed and would be less than 5) is already lower than .05.

ADDITIONAL INFORMATION ON THE t-TEST

Although the *t*-test is usually discussed as if there is a single distribution, in fact, there is actually a family of *t*-distributions, each one based on the number of cases. Because of this, the *t*-test itself is not sensitive to sample size—an advantage over many other statistics—and can be used with both large and small samples. An example of three of the *t*-distributions is below, with "*df*" (degrees of freedom) referring to the total sample size[6] and the numbers under the curve referring to the critical values of *t* necessary to achieve a .05 probability at each *df*.

Note that the smallest *df* (*df* = 3, the flattest line) in the graph produces a curve that is lower in the middle (more platykurtic) and the tails are higher off the baseline. This means that small sample sizes accommodate more extreme scores than would be expected in a normal curve. Thus, a *t*-distribution for small sample sizes is more conservative, or more cautious, in estimating how much "difference" is required to be a real difference between two groups. Because of this, a larger *t*-value is required. That is, the critical .05 *t*-score is ± 3.18, which is the largest value of the three distributions in the graph.

Larger samples more closely approximate the normal curve and the test becomes less conservative and is better able to find a true difference. As a result, critical values get smaller as the sample gets larger (less error is expected and the *t*-values to determine differences can be smaller). By the time the degrees of freedom are at 120, there is no meaningful difference between the *t*-test distribution and the normal distribution (*df* = ∞, the highest line at the peak in the graph). At that point, the critical .05 *t*-score is ±1.96—the approximate 2-standard deviation (or *Z*-score) distance from the mean in a normal curve.

When you use a *t*-test, don't forget to check the level of measurement for the dependent variable. It should be interval or metric ordinal.[7] A *t*-test conducted with typical ordinal data (such as a Likert scale of "strongly agree" to "strongly disagree") is inappropriate and you should use an ordinal-level test instead. Also, don't forget the requirement for normally-distributed data. If the dependent

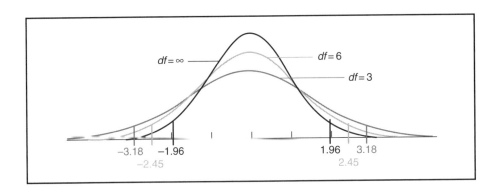

---

[6]Actually, the "total sample size" is [(*n* of group1 + *n* of group 2)−2].
[7]If you have forgotten what metric ordinal is, return to Chapter 2 to refresh your memory.

variable is not distributed approximately as a normal curve for each of the two groups being used for the *t*-test, enough error might be present to make the results meaningless. Again, drop down to an ordinal test if this problem occurs.

SUMMARY

The *t*-test is a commonly-used statistic in criminal justice and criminological research. It requires interval-level data, so it must be used with dependent variables capable of being measured at that level. Remember, also, that the *t*-test is used to compare two groups[8]—any more than that and you must find another statistic. Of the two basic versions, the independent samples *t*-test is the one frequently used for analyzing survey data and secondary data. The related samples version is used in experiments or evaluation research, but is not as commonly found in our field.

The statistic also introduces two types of variance: within and between. The between variance is the critical component of the testing procedure—or put another way, you really want to know if there is a difference *between* the two groups. Within variance is essentially error and different group dispersions can cause problems. That's why there are two versions of the independent samples *t*-test and why a secondary test is required to determine which version to use.

The *t*-test also has some stringent assumptions that must be met, chief among these being the assumption of normality in the dependent variable. It can handle some deviation from these assumptions but, as with all error issues, too much deviation from assumptions results in bad estimates. If that happens, the correct choice of statistic would be an ordinal-level version. Finally, the problem of being able to compare only two groups is a serious limitation. The next chapter explores a multigroup statistic, the Analysis of Variance, that otherwise does much the same comparisons as the *t*-test.

KEY POINTS OF THE CHAPTER

The *t*-test is the "odds-on" favorite for comparing possible differences in two groups—as long as these differences are defined by an interval-level variable.

- There are two basic *t*-tests: one for related samples and the other for independent samples.
- The independent samples *t*-test comes in two versions, depending on the equality of the group variances.
- A preliminary test, a version of the *F*-ratio test, is done to determine which of the two independent samples *t*-tests to use.
- The *t*-test makes some critical assumptions about the data and can easily be used incorrectly.

---

[8]There is a version of the *t*-test for a "one-sample" test. As with the Chi-square statistic, the single variable (sample) is compared to a hypothetical second group. For instance, it would be possible to measure age in a sample and then compare the sample age to census age figures.

CHAPTER 13

Testing for Significance in Multiple Groups: The Analysis of Variance Statistic

Key Concepts

- analysis of variance

- between groups

- within groups

- sums of squares

- mean squares

- multiple comparison tests

Now that you are familiar with testing groups for differences in their means, we'll take a look in this chapter at one of the most popular, and useful, of the significance tests: the Analysis of Variance (abbreviated as ANOVA or ANOVAR). Not only is this test frequently used on its own, but it works in conjunction with other statistics in a family of techniques called the *General Linear Model*. You may have not have noticed in the last chapter, but there was a comment that the *t*-test is related to ANOVA. Because a *t*-test can only be used on two groups, another test is needed for instances in which there are more than two groups, referred to in statistics as *k-samples*. That test is the ANOVA.

WHY COMPARE MULTIPLE GROUPS ALL AT ONCE?

It may have occurred to you that the *t*-test could still be used with multiple groups, just in a two-at a time fashion. If that doesn't make sense, try this. A comparison of three groups (we'll call them A, B, and C) would result in three *t*-tests for differences between A and B, A and C, and B and C. So, surely that could be done? That would save you from having to learn this statistic. As I'm sure you have anticipated, the answer is that you can't do that. The reason has to do with error. Before providing a technical explanation, see if this makes sense. Each individual test has a certain amount of error allowed (usually .05). What if you make a succession of three tests on essentially the same thing? Would the error amount change? If you said "yes," you would be correct. Now for the technical reason.

The usual alpha-level probability of .05 means that one in 20 results will be in error—that is, your chance of being wrong when you think something is real is pretty small. If you have to make several tests on the same variables, each result appears to be the same interpretation of probability, but it is *not* because of the multiple tests you are making. The individual probabilities actually *under-represent* the chance of your making an error. This is called an *experiment-wise error rate* problem. The true amount of error is related to the fact that you thought you only had a 1-in-20 chance of being wrong, but your collective error is 3-in-20 (three tests, remember?).

Thus, we want to continue using a single test to keep our error rate (probability) at the normal level. The answer to this problem is to use the ANOVA statistic, which examines all group combinations at once and gives us a single, collective probability. When used with one independent variable (the grouping variable), the test is referred to as the *One-Way ANOVA*. We won't discuss this here, but it is possible to have more than one independent grouping variable and the name of the statistic becomes the *Two-Way ANOVA*.[1]

THE ANALYSIS OF VARIANCE

Though the ANOVA can be used for a two-group comparison, it makes more sense to use the *t*-test for that. As a result, the statistic is normally used for a comparison of means among three or more groups. A typical use would be testing whether different size cities (for example, in four groups represented by "rural," "small," "medium," and "large") have different crime rates. The dependent variable has to be measured at the interval level because group means will be compared.

This sounds good so far. Unfortunately, as you might have guessed, nothing is without its problems. There are two drawbacks to doing all group comparisons in *one* test:

An Important Point

A two-tailed hypothesis must be used. The potential complexity of a one-tailed hypothesis would cause problems. Imagine trying to test a hypothesis like "Rural areas will have lower crime rates than large cities but higher crime rates than medium-sized cities and equal crime rates compared to small cities." There are simply too many opportunities to be incorrect. And, if you are incorrect at any point, the hypothesis is unsupported—there is no such statistical creature as a partially correct hypothesis.

(continued)

---

[1] Sometimes you will see the multiple variable test referred to as *n-way analysis of variance*. After all, the two-way term does seem incorrect for more than two independent variables.

(continued)

A significant result does not tell you which groups are different. The single test merely indicates that, somewhere among the various group combinations, there is at least one significant difference.[2] If you see a significant probability for ANOVA, the issue is to determine which group comparisons are significantly different. Only one might be. So, once the ANOVA test shows significance, a follow-up test is necessary to locate any significant differences between the groups.

What Is Being Compared?

ANOVA extends the logic of the *t*-test to multiple groups. Therefore, it is concerned with the same two sources of variation: within and between groups. This time, though, there is only one version of the test regardless of the inequality of the within variances.

Thinking back to our earlier discussion of the variance statistic (measure of dispersion), the idea was to sum the individual squared distances of each score from their mean (we'll now call this "sums of squares") to establish a collective measure of variation. Using the same concept, ANOVA establishes the total variation for all groups as the "total sums of squares." Then using each individual group's mean, it determines the average distance from the grand mean (the mean for the entire sample) for each group and totals this. This becomes the *between sums of squares* (BSS). After this, the internal group variation is calculated as sums of squares and this becomes the *within sums of squares* (WSS). The BSS is the comparison of group means and the one we are interested in when we test a statement like "city size affects crime rates." The other, WSS, becomes "error" and is used to make a judgment of a real effect versus error.

These sums of squares, representing the effect of an independent variable (the BSS) and the overall variability within the groups (the WSS), are compared to each other. Because of differences in the number of items making up each sums of squares, this comparison cannot be made directly. In our city size example above,

---

The Analysis of Variance Dilemma

If the ANOVA test probability is significant, *which group comparisons are significant?*

With the four city size groups in the text, for instance, we would be comparing groups 1 with 2, 1 with 3, 1 with 4, 2 with 3, 2 with 4, and 3 with 4—a total of six comparisons. Are all significant? Only one? Or some combination of them?

---

[2]It is very rare, but possible, to have an overall significant effect across all groups with no two groups appearing to be significantly different. That circumstance can occur when all groups are "almost" significant and group sample sizes are relatively small.

Sums of Squares in the Analysis of Variance

There are two main "sums of squares":

✓ *Within sums of squares:* Used to measure the dispersion within each group to be compared—treated as error.

✓ *Between sums of squares:* Used to measure differences between groups—the test of the hypothesis.

there are only four groups to make up the sources of between variation. On the other hand, the within variation is a product of all the cases in the data (or, the sample size) and therefore has *many more sources* contributing to the total variation. The BSS value will almost always be smaller than the WSS value, so the number of sources (number of groups, number of cases) is divided into their respective sums of squares leading to the "mean squares"—between mean squares (BMS) and within mean squares (WMS).[3] This final result provides us with a standardized comparison of the two. If BMS (our measure of an effect) is reasonably larger than WMS, we can say that the independent variable affects the dependent variable.

ANOVA Results

This comparison is made, statistically, using the *F*-test to judge the size of the difference when BMS is divided by WMS. In keeping with virtually all inferential test interpretations, we do the following:

1. Propose a two-tailed hypothesis. (Don't forget—two-tailed *only!!*)
2. Examine the probability value:
   a. If the probability level is *equal to or smaller than your alpha level*, accept your hypothesis (the means of the groups are significantly different).
   b. If *p* is *larger than your alpha level*, reject your hypothesis and accept the null hypothesis (there is no difference in the means of the groups).

Using the Sums of Squares

The BMS is our measure of an effect; WMS is our measure of error. So, we check to see if our effect is larger than our error. Or,

$$\frac{\text{BMS}}{\text{WMS}} = \text{relative size of effect}$$

The *F*-ratio

---

[3]This process is similar to what we did in creating the variance statistic. The number of "items" is divided into the total difference to standardize the result.

TABLE 13.1 Example of ANOVA Results

How Much Problem is Crime in Your Community?

	Sum of Squares	*df*	*Mean Square*	*F*	*Sig.*
Between Groups	241.950	2	120.975	20.868	.000
Within Groups	4910.155	847	5.797		
Total	5152.105	849			

An example of ANOVA results from a comparison of respondents in three different city sizes, and their estimates of their community crime problem is in Table 13.1. The mean squares (*between* is the top one) suggest that the "effect" is much larger than the error (within). The *F*-ratio reflects this, with a value for the BMS more than 20 times the size of the WMS. The associated probability level for an *F* of 20.868 is less than .001, which is significant.

Assumptions of ANOVA

Just as with the *t*-test, the ANOVA has several critical assumptions. First, it assumes interval-level data. Second, the dependent variable must be normally-distributed. If the variable is not normally-distributed, ANOVA can produce an estimate of probability that is actually lower than the real probability. In other words, it will *underestimate* the amount of error. Because the statistic is relatively robust, it can handle mild departures from normality without much error. Be careful of data that are clearly not normal, though. A third assumption is something called *homogeneity of variances*—the variances within the groups are presumed to be drawn from populations with equal variances. Nonhomogeneous (heterogeneous) variances are referred to as being *heteroscedastic*, a term we will encounter later in a brief discussion of regression. These assumptions may be violated, within reason, with little error in ANOVA results as long as the "independent variable" groups are equal in size. For unequally-sized groups, the violation effect is another matter altogether.

If there are problems with violations of assumptions, the data should be tested with an ordinal-level statistic (the Kruskal Wallis H-test, see Appendix C). In addition, the use of ANOVA *should* be limited to independent samples. It can be used in experimental design if one compares randomly-assigned treatment and control groups to each other, but not if the comparison is made to multiple measures within a single group (that would constitute related measures, i.e., a pre- and post-test comparison for the same group).

An Example of an ANOVA Test

Using output from SPSS, let's look at an ANOVA using education and income. Our two-tailed alternative hypothesis will be:

Educational levels affect income.

TABLE 13.2 ANOVA Results for the Effect of Education on Income

Approx Family Income for Last Year

	Sum of Squares	df	Mean Square	F	Sig.
Between Groups	3098.456	4	23274.614	37.760	.000
Within Groups	755694.5	1226	616.390		
Total	848793.0	1230			

Table 13.2 presents the same format of ANOVA results as you have already seen. Let's go through it piece by piece.

Note the second column from the left, the between groups and within groups sums of squares. These are the original, unstandardized measures of variation, BSS and WSS. Remember we said that BSS would likely be small and WSS large because of the number of sources? That's precisely what happened. There were only five education groups compared to over 1,200 respondents in the sample. So, let's standardize the results for each sums of squares on their number of sources. The column entitled "Mean Square" is the result of dividing the sources of varia-tion $(df)^4$ in the third column from the left into the sums of squares, thereby stan-dardizing the sums of squares.

$$\text{BMS} = 93098.456 \div 4 = 23274.614$$
$$\text{WMS} = 755694.5 \div 1226 = 616.390$$

Now let's get to the really important stuff—the F-ratio value (or the F-value) and the probability. The F-value of 37.760 is produced by dividing the BMS (23274.614) by the WMS (616.390). "Sig." represents the probability level associ-ated with that F-value.

If your professor doesn't ask you to do the calculations that produced the table, all you need is the probability level. A probability less than .001 is obvi-ously smaller than the .05 we usually use for significance; therefore, we can say education affects income.

And, now for the final issue: We don't know *which* education groups are different from each other. All we know is that one comparison is significant. It's a good bet that the comparison of the two groups with the biggest difference—in this case the educational groups with the highest and lowest income levels—will be significant, but we don't know about the others. Let's now discuss how this problem is handled.

---

[4]Don't worry about the fact that the number of sources for the BSS is 5 and the df is 4 (or that WSS sources are a few cases larger than their df. The actual df formulas are $(K-1)$ and $(N-K)$, where K is the number of groups and N is the number of cases.

HOW DO YOU DETERMINE WHICH GROUPS ARE SIGNIFICANTLY DIFFERENT?

Once we have used the ANOVA to determine whether a significant difference exists among the groups, another test is necessary to establish where those differences are. These tests are called *multiple comparison tests* and are specially adapted to handle the experiment-wise error rate problem. Another name is "post hoc" tests (for "after the fact"). There are actually a lot of them. So many, in fact, that we will focus on just one. Some of the others are mentioned in Appendix D, along with a way to make choices among them.[5]

Multiple Comparison Tests

As with all statistics, multiple comparison tests have assumptions, too. Some are designed to be used with equal or unequal variances, small samples, for groups with unequal sample sizes, and so forth. We will use the Bonferroni test as an example. This multiple comparison test uses *t*-tests adjusted for an experiment-wise probability and allows you to compare all possible groups without having a greater chance of error just because of the multiple comparisons (as the *t*-test would). Let's look at the Bonferroni results (on the next page) for the ANOVA test above, based on output from the SPSS program (these tests are on the "Post Hoc" button in SPSS).

An Example of a Multiple Comparison Test

First, the results in Table 13.3 represent all possible comparisons. Each education group is represented in the first column, with all other groups next to this comparison group. Probability is located in the fourth column under "Sig." Now let's look at the first set of group comparisons.

The first set of comparisons falls under the "Less than High School" box (the heading group). All of the other education groups are listed to the right of the heading group. In each case, the heading group is the value (mean income level here) that all other groups will be compared to. Our results indicate that mean income levels for "Less than High School" respondents are not significantly different ($p = 1.000$, fourth column) from those with "High School Diplomas." Income is expressed in thousands in the data, so the difference between the two means was only $1.51K (second column), with the "LT HS" group barely lower than the HS Diploma respondents. Because the comparison wasn't significant, we would say that there is no income difference between those with less than high school educations and those with a high school diploma.

On the other hand, the LT HS group had incomes significantly lower than the other three education groups (Some College, College Degree, and

---

[5]A common multiple comparison test is the Scheffé test. In the field of psychology, it is exceedingly popular. The problem is that it has some serious assumptions and is frequently unable to provide an accurate result. The one chosen for an example here is a multipurpose test.

TABLE 13.3 Example of a Multiple Comparison Test

Multiple Comparisons

Dependent Variable: Approx Family Income for Last Year Bonferroni

(I) SCHOOL	(J) SCHOOL	Mean Difference (I−J)	Std. Error	Sig.	95% Confidence Interval	
					Lower Bound	Upper Bound
LT HS	HS Diploma	−1.51	2.264	1.000	−7.87	4.86
"group 1"	Some College	−8.71*	2.157	.001	−14.77	−2.64
	College Degree	−21.62*	2.493	.000	−28.63	−14.61
	Graduate Degree	−26.15*	3.145	.000	−34.99	−17.30
HS Diploma	LT HS	1.51	2.264	1.000	−4.86	7.87
"group 2"	Some College	−7.20*	1.841	.001	−12.38	−2.03
	College Degree	−20.11*	2.226	.000	−26.37	−13.85
	Graduate Degree	−24.64*	2.938	.000	−32.90	−16.38
Some College	LT HS	8.71*	2.157	.001	2.64	14.77
"group 3"	HS Diploma	7.20*	1.841	.001	2.03	12.38
	College Degree	−12.91*	2.116	.000	−18.86	−6.96
	Graduate Degree	−17.44*	2.856	.000	−25.47	−9.40
College Degree	LT HS	21.62*	2.493	.000	14.61	28.63
"group 4"	HS Diploma	20.11*	2.226	.000	13.85	26.37
	Some College	12.91*	2.116	.000	6.96	18.86
	Graduate Degree	−4.53	3.118	1.000	−13.30	4.24
Graduate Degree	LT HS	26.15*	3.145	.000	17.30	34.99
"group 5"	HS Diploma	24.64*	2.938	.000	16.38	32.90
	Some College	17.44*	2.856	.000	9.40	25.47
	College Degree	4.53	3.118	1.000	−4.24	13.30

* The mean difference is significant at the .05 level.

Graduate Degree). (The output from SPSS conveniently notes all significant mean differences in the "Mean Difference" column with an asterisk [*], so they are easy to find.) Don't forget that it is not only important to say that the differences are significant, but also to say whether a group has a lower or higher income level in making these comparisons.

Multiple comparison tests make all possible comparisons. As a result, these tables have many duplications. For instance, the "LT HS and HS Diploma" comparison is found again under "HS Diploma and LT HS," the reverse of the first one. You need to work your way through them to determine *all* significant differences so a final, summary conclusion may be made. For the sake of simplicity, let's refer to educational groups by numbers (1 = LT HS, 2 = HS Diploma, 3 = Some College, 4 = College Degree, and 5 = Graduate Degree). A final statement would look like this:

- H_a: Education affects income levels. The hypothesis is supported by the ANOVA test and there is a significant relationship between education and income.
- There are only two educational group comparisons that are not significant, those being group 1 and group 2, and group 4 and group 5.
- Groups 1 and 2 are significantly lower than groups 3, 4, and 5. Group 3 is significantly lower than groups 4 and 5.
- On the whole, then, income tends to increase as level of education increases (note: this "directional" statement is *not* one you can usually make about the results of these tests).

SUMMARY

ANOVA is a very useful and popular three-plus group significance test. The test resolves the problem of combining multiple error rates when multiple groups are compared by making a single test across all of the groups. The assumptions are similar to the *t*-test, with the exception of adding an equality of variance assumption. It is fairly robust when these assumptions are violated, but multiple violations at once cause accuracy problems. While the ANOVA is easy to interpret, it can only provide evidence that there is a difference somewhere among the groups in the comparisons. As a result, only two-tailed hypotheses can be made and tested with ANOVA.

Multiple comparison (post hoc) tests are required to tease out information about which group comparisons are significantly different. Those tests supplement the ANOVA by providing the group comparison details and provide interpretations of the effect of the grouping variable (the independent variable) on the dependent variable.

ANOVA can accommodate multiple independent variables. For example, suppose in our attempt to use education to explain what affects income levels we added other variables that might be important, such as gender, race, or even attitudes. Not only would a two-way ANOVA provide us with information on the additional effect of those variables, but we could also determine their effect relative to each other. In other words, we could locate the variables that contributed the most to explaining income levels. Imagine if you had to do a study on possible gender discrimination in the workplace where some people claimed that they were paid lower salaries merely because of their gender—here is your statistical tool to examine that claim!

Another important fact to remember about ANOVA is that it is part of what is called the *General Linear Model*. An entire family of our most important and best known statistics are derived from this model. If you know ANOVA, you have a partial understanding of most of the rest of these techniques.

This chapter concludes the discussion of inferential statistics. In an earlier chapter, we said that inferential statistics are used to determine whether an observed effect is "real," or statistically significant. They cannot, however, tell us how strong that effect is. That is the job of statistics called *measures of association*. The next chapter begins the discussion of association (relationship).

KEY POINTS OF THE CHAPTER

The ANOVA statistic is the most popular of "multiple group" significance tests. It requires interval-level data and has other assumptions that suggest caution in using it.

- ANOVA tests two-tailed hypotheses because it examines several group comparisons at once to avoid an experiment-wise error rate problem.
- ANOVA requires dependent variables with normal distributions and equal variances across the groups.
- Once a significant result is found with ANOVA, a multiple comparison test must be used to locate the groups with significantly different comparisons.

CHAPTER 14

The Concept of Association

Key Concepts

■ association

■ correlation coefficient

■ proportionate reduction of error

■ indirect PRE

■ symmetric relationship

■ asymmetric relationship

Earlier in Chapter 8 we discussed tables and relationships. Another term for a relationship is to say that two variables are "associated" with each other. That is, an *association* exists. The inferential statistics in previous chapters actually determine whether that is true (within error bounds, of course).[1] Just knowing that there is an association is important (there is a "significant difference" or effect), but it is insufficient information. After we have established that two variables are related, the next task is to determine how *strong* the relationship is. That's what a measure of association does.

MEASURING STRENGTH OF RELATIONSHIP

You probably are wondering why establishing that a relationship exists is not enough. The answer is not immediately obvious, but can be illustrated by discussing two different research problems.

Example I

Let's say that staff in a large juvenile detention facility have been complaining about the toilet paper. As an administrator, you can purchase one of two alternate brands available in the approved supply catalog. Instead of making a unilateral decision about which one to purchase, you decide to test which brand is preferred by the staff. The existing toilet paper is replaced for 1 week by one of

---

[1]If you have read through a discussion on causality in a research methods textbook, the term used is *covariation*. That simply means the variables vary with each other. If one variable "varies" and the other doesn't, then they aren't related (associated) and do not "covary."

the alternate brands and for another week by the other. After this you ask the staff which one they prefer. When you get the results, you run a Chi-square test, find that there is a significant difference in preferences, and order the one with the greatest preference. Do you bother with strength of the relationship? Probably not. It's just not important enough (in fact, you might even be questioning whether the use of a Chi-square test was even necessary). Put another way, the costs of being wrong are negligible.

Example 2

One of your state legislators has a "major contributor" who does self-esteem training for prisoners and the legislator has introduced a bill to fund a mandatory self-esteem program in all of the state prisons and local jails. If research shows it to be effective, the funding will be in the amount of $500,000,000—much of which will come from existing prison programs. The legislative budget board has hired you to evaluate a pilot self-esteem program for 10,000 prison inmates and determine if it will reduce recidivism. You construct an appropriate research design, collect the data, and run inferential tests. You find a statistically significant decrease in recidivism among those inmates who went through the pilot program. The legislator and contributor say that's enough evidence and begin lobbying for the expensive bill. Now do you conduct a test of strength of relationship? Absolutely!

You already know from earlier chapters that a large sample size can have low probability estimates (therefore, tests are frequently statistically significant). But, we also said that the size of any probability is a function of both a true relationship and sample size. In short, a very small difference can produce a significant probability level. You want to know how strong the self-esteem/recidivism relationship is because a substantial amount of money is going to be spent in a public policy change. So, you use a measure of association and discover that the strength of the relationship is on the order of a 0.003 decrease in recidivism for every $100,000,000 spent. The effect is so small that no reasonable person would recommend the program (and you don't even know if something else might have accounted for that small effect). The "cost" of being wrong in this example is very high.

Comparison of Different Effects

It may also have occurred to you that strength of association could be used to assess which of several alternative "causes" you might prefer. From the second example above, there are obviously many other possible prison programs that might affect recidivism rates. Wouldn't it help in deciding which ones to fund and use if you knew how strongly each program affected recidivism? You would want to keep and increase funding for those programs most strongly associated with decreased recidivism. To know they all have a "statistically significant effect" is not much help in making such decisions.

Criminologists have studied the causes of crime and delinquency for a long time. It is a fact that each modern theory explaining these causes has found statistically significant support. Yet, many of these theories are in opposition to each other. Once again, it would be helpful to have a measure of the strength of support for each theory and then you could compare them to help you decide what should guide crime policy in the United States. How do you do this?

How Do You Estimate Strength of Association?

Measures of association estimate strength of association by providing a number between zero and one.[2] These numbers are called *correlation coefficients*. Zero means that there is no relationship (in other words, "not significant"). One (1.0) means that there is a perfect relationship. Because of sampling and measurement error, it is almost impossible to get a zero estimate, even when there really is no relationship. That is why we use a test of significance first—to see if the "difference" that seems to be present is "real" or just random error around the zero position.[3] A perfect 1.0 is also unlikely—because it would mean that one variable is *perfectly* related to another. Or, put another way, one variable would perfectly "predict" the other.[4] Most relationships, then, are somewhere between zero and 1.0, with most of them closer to zero than 1.0. In fact, in the social sciences in general, many relationships are in the (0.1, 0.2) range.

Before we leave this section, here's something to remember: a measure of association requires a measure of significance first to determine if the observed relationship is a "real" one. We are always concerned with measurement error, so if the reported correlation coefficient values are not significant, then there is insufficient evidence that the values are not due to error.

In such a case, the reported values are considered to be merely chance fluctuations around zero. Don't comment on such values as if they were real. In fact, if probability is not significant, don't comment on them at all!

Nonsignificant Correlation Coefficients Are Interpreted as Zero Values

If the measure of significance tells us that the difference between the two variables is not significant, then the relationship between the two variables is zero (no relationship).

---

[2]There are some older measures of association that require certain conditions to achieve this 0–1.0 range. If these conditions don't exist, they cannot reach 1.0 as a measure of a perfect relationship. Worse, some will report different numbers for the same proportionate relationship simply because the sample size is different in two tests you want to compare (or the number of cells and rows are different). These are generally undesirable for use and should be avoided.

[3]It is possible to use a measure of association without a test of significance when correlating variables drawn from nonrandom samples. If that is done, however, there is no way to know if the correlation is real or a product of error.

[4]The issue of association is more complicated than the discussion in this chapter suggests and this is particularly true of the concept of a *perfect* relationship. Different statistics may be designed to detect certain types of associations—leading to different results when you compare them.

INTERPRETING MEASURES OF ASSOCIATION

Because we either want to (1) make an understandable statement about the strength of a relationship or (2) compare results of various relationship tests, reliable interpretation of these measures is important. Years ago, researchers were trying to put words to correlation coefficients in an effort to interpret their meaning. Some said that a relationship in the range of .10 to .20 was a "weak" relationship; others called it a *moderately weak* relationship and yet others referred to it as a *moderate* relationship. The term *strong* was used to discuss relationships anywhere from .4 to .9—a wide discrepancy. Attempting to standardize the interpretation of correlation coefficients, in 1956, J. P. Guilford added a table in his statistics textbook (see Box 14.1). It became popular and some people still use it today.

Proportionate Reduction of Error

At about the same time as Guilford produced his table, two statisticians, Leo Goodman and William Kruskal, were working on an interpretation of a measure of association they had developed (Lambda). Their remarks and references to a "proportionate reduction of error" interpretation were used by Herbert Costner in 1965 to create our preferred modern-day approach to correlation coefficients.

Proportionate reduction of error is now commonly abbreviated as PRE, and there is general agreement that PRE measures of association are the "best" statistics. That is because they are the easiest to interpret. Instead of trying to figure out whether a correlation of .17 is a "weak" or "moderately weak" relationship, it is easier to use the number directly. And that's what PRE statistics do. A correlation of .17 between income and criminality can be roughly interpreted as 17% of the variance being accounted for. You could compare this, for example, to a correlation of .20 between education and criminality and you know that the second correlation accounts for 3% more variation than the first one. Because the coefficients translate into percentages, it is much easier to figure out their relative positions.

BOX 14.1

EARLY VERSION OF INTERPRETING CORRELATION COEFFICIENTS

Guilford's Table

Less than 0.20	Slight, almost negligible relationship
0.20–0.40	Low correlation; definite but small relationship
0.40–0.70	Moderate correlation; substantial relationship
0.70–0.90	High correlation; marked relationship
0.90–1.00	Very high correlation; very dependable relationship

Now for a bit more technical, and accurate, explanation of PRE. When we say that there is a percentage of variance explained, the reference is really to two or more variables.[5] For the sake of simplicity, we'll use two variables. Because correlation/association is a relationship between two variables, the actual statement using our income/criminality .17 correlation above should be:

> *Income explains (or predicts, or accounts for) 17% of the variance in criminality.*

In the case of the other correlation above, between education and criminality, we would say that education explains 20% of the variance in criminality. If we could explain 100% of the variance in criminality, then we would be able to perfectly predict your crime propensity by knowing how much education you have.

The reason that PRE is so readily interpretable is that it gives us a *linear* correlation with every one unit increase equal to every other one unit. In other words, you can compare the magnitude of correlations. The correlation coefficients of some statistics simply do not convey magnitude, even though they appear to. Others, like Pearson's *r*, cannot be interpreted directly but when squared become linear (i.e., PRE interpretable).

Wouldn't It Be Nice If Everything Were Interpreted the Same Way?

At this point, we have been discussing PRE interpretations as if all measures of association were translated the same way. That would be nice but, unfortunately, that isn't the case. However, the good news is that, aside from the measures that shouldn't even be used today, almost all of the statistics you will see have a PRE interpretation. In order to distinguish between those that are directly PRE, we'll use the very creative term *direct-PRE* statistics. A few don't translate directly and those, being very creative again, we'll call *indirect-PRE* statistics. Because this sounds like a big problem, be assured that it isn't. All you have to do to the *indirect-PRE* statistics is to *square their coefficients*.

> **The Format of a PRE Interpretation (for Hypothesis Testing)**
>
> You can simplify the way a correlation coefficient is interpreted and reported by using the following "fill in the blank" statement.
>
> [*Independent variable*] explains_____ % of the variance in [*Dependent variable*]. (E.g., "*Learning from peers* explains *26%* of the variance in *delinquent behavior.*")

---

[5]The term *explained* doesn't mean actual explanation (or cause)—it means to account for the covariance between variables.

Now here is another "unfortunately." Both of the two measures of association we will discuss are indirect PRE. They are *Phi* (a nominal-level statistic) and *Pearson's r* (an interval-level statistic).[6] Just remember to square their values and you'll do fine. In other words, a Phi value of .5 would be a PRE value of .25 when squared, and the interpretation would then be that one variable explains 25% of the other variable. It is easier to refer to these as *Phi-squared* and *r-squared* so we remember what we have to do to interpret them.

The Issue of Symmetry

Interpreting relationships so far has been about the coefficient itself. There is, however, another important thing: *symmetry*. Relationships can be symmetric or asymmetric. A symmetric relationship is one that has no assumed cause and effect. It's *just* a relationship. In other words, there are no independent and dependent variables, just variables being correlated with each other. An example might be the moon and night—they are highly correlated because most people only notice the moon at night. The moon doesn't cause night and night doesn't cause the appearance of the moon. An asymmetric relationship, on the other hand, is a directional one—as in the causal direction implied in a hypothesis from independent variable to dependent variable. This relationship is a one-way statement of effect. Now let's translate this into statistics.

Symmetric Correlations

A statistic that is *symmetric* effectively has no idea which variable is the independent and which one is the dependent variable. That is important because we normally try to use one variable to "explain" or "predict" the other. There are two possible relationships in any two-variable statement: A → B and B → A. As a result, a symmetric statistic has to calculate the relationship between the variables *both* ways and produce an average relationship. Using our example above, we would have a relationship between income and criminality, and then between criminality and income (rest assured that both relationships are probably *not* the same value, although they might be close). Phi and Pearson's *r* are both symmetric statistics, so their correlations give us average relationships. It

The Format for Reporting a PRE Symmetric Analysis

The formula for making a statement about the results of a symmetric analysis when you really have no hypothesis is:

The covariation between (variable 1) *and* (variable2) *accounts for* (number) *percent of the total variation of the two variables.*

---

[6]Actually, if we calculate Pearson's *r* on a 2 × 2 table, the result is the same as calculating Phi—so, in reality, there is only one indirect-PRE statistic (Pearson's *r*)!

might occur to you that if you can make a hypothesis, then you really aren't working with a symmetric statement. That statement would be something like this: "A and B vary together."

Asymmetric Correlations

A statistic that is *asymmetric* is able to calculate each relationship direction separately and provide a separate correlation coefficient for each direction. This means any hypothesis test is a perfect candidate for an asymmetric statistic. Because a correlation is being provided for A $\rightarrow$ B *and* B $\rightarrow$ A, the more specific estimate of the relationship is more accurate (less error). All you have to do is make sure you are using the correct one.

So what's the bottom line on this symmetry/asymmetry thing? Simple, if you can make *any* hypothesis with the two variables, you have discovered which is independent and which is dependent. If so, use an *asymmetric* version of a statistic if one is available. Because you can tell which one is the dependent variable, you can reduce your error in determining the "real" relationship and get a closer estimate. Usually, computer-based statistical output will tell you when an asymmetric version of a statistic is available.

Let's look at the edited statistical output below in Table 14.1. The measure of association isn't important, so we won't discuss it except to say it is direct PRE. We're interested in the symmetric/asymmetric interpretations. The two variables are the race of the survey respondents and their estimate of a crime problem in their community.

There are three different correlation coefficients present in the table under the "Value" column. Notice that the column to the left begins with "Symmetric." This is the line with a calculation of a symmetric relationship (or the average of both one-way relationships). If you had no hypothesis and were merely using race and crime problem estimates as a "what's there?" kind of analysis, the value of .024 tells us that the two variables share about 2.4% of the total variance between them. (Not too good for prediction, is it?) However, I'm sure you can figure out a hypothesis for race and crime problem estimates—perhaps something like this two-tailed version: "Race affects crime problem estimates." Testing that merely requires looking at the "Approx. Sig." (probability) column and finding the .000 estimate. That's significant, so we go to the strength of the relationship

TABLE 14.1 Example of Symmetric and Asymmetric Correlations

		Value	*Approx. Sig.*
Uncertainty coefficient	Symmetric	.024	.000
One of these is → *your dependent* *variable* →	Race Dependent	.045	.000
	How much of a problem is crime in your community? Dependent	.016	.000

under "Value." We look for the one matching our hypothesis and find it under "How much of a problem is crime in your community? Dependent." That's the one that matches our dependent variable. The associated correlation coefficient is .016—significant, but very poor as an effect of race on crime problem estimates.[7] We conclude that race explains 1.6% of the variance in community crime problem estimates.

Stating a hypothesis in which crime problem estimates affect someone's race could be pretty weird—that's equivalent to saying that as people's estimates of crime problem change, their race will change (a biological impossibility). But let's do it anyway. The correlation coefficient for that one is significant and .045—the highest of the three coefficients. But that isn't a reasonable hypothesis and certainly not one we are interested in. So, one lesson here is not to go searching for the highest of the coefficient values—the independent/dependent variable combination might not make sense.

The other thing to notice in this table is the relationship of the three correlations. If the symmetric value is an average, it must fall between the other two values. Correspondingly, one of the asymmetric values has to be the highest of the three and the other the lowest. You'll see that is the case in our example.

DIRECTION OF THE RELATIONSHIP

The final piece to interpreting correlation coefficients is to check the direction of the relationship. The direction is indicated by a "+" or "−" sign in front of the coefficient value (actually, there is no "+" sign, so the absence of a sign usually means "+"). Even though nominal-level statistics don't have a "direction," Phi is sometimes reported with a directional sign because of its relationship to Pearson's r. That will be the case in examples used in this book, but you should be careful when looking at Phi from other sources—don't automatically assume a "no-sign" value means a positive direction.

To rehash from Chapter 9, a positive value means that the relationship between the two variables is in the same direction, that is, both increasing or both decreasing. A negative value means the relationship between the two variables is in opposite directions, as one increases the other decreases or as one decreases the other increases. Having a directional sign attached to the coefficient is a valuable piece of information. If you are trying to interpret the results of a crosstabulation analysis, you don't have to look at the table and try to figure out direction—it's already there.

Just in case, don't make the mistake of using the positive and negative signs as they are normally used in math problems. For instance, a correlation of +.45 is exactly the same strength as a correlation of −.45, the signs only denote the *direction* of the relationship.

---

[7]This is a good example of our earlier discussion of statistical significance, strength of relationship, and sample size. Even a sample size of 1,000 will produce significant and virtually meaningless relationships.

Routine Steps for Interpreting Measures of Association

1. Examine the variables and determine their level of measurement. Use the statistic appropriate to the *lowest* level of measurement. This means if *one* variable is at the nominal level and one is at the interval level, you have to use a nominal-level statistic.

2. Check probability to make sure the observed relationship is significant.

3. If you have proposed a hypothesis, use the correct version of an *asymmetric* statistic. If you have no hypothesis, use a *symmetric* version of the statistic.

4. Examine your hypothesis to make sure that the relationship is in the *correct direction*. If it is not, stop and reject the hypothesis.

5. Determine whether the measure of association is *indirect or direct* PRE. If indirect, square the value.

6. If you have a hypothesis, interpret the value as a percentage of the vari- ation of one variable "explained" by the other variable.

   a. Don't forget to add an explanation of the direction of the relationship. For example, suppose that you found that the relationship between age and crime had a Pearson's *r*-square of −.25. This is commonly interpreted as "age explains 25% of the variation in crime, such that as age increases, crime decreases."

   b. The "formula" for interpretation is:
   (independent variable) explains (number) percent of the variation in (dependent variable), *such that as* (independent variable) (*increases/decreases*), (dependent variable) (*increases/decreases*).

7. If you do *not* have a hypothesis, interpret the value as the percent of the total variation "explained" by the covariation between the two variables.

SUMMARY

Association is a very useful concept for statistical research in criminal justice and criminology. In statistics, association is expressed as a correlation coefficient, and the statistical techniques that do that are called *measures of association*. These correlation coefficients produce estimates that range from 0 to 1.0—or from a nonrelationship to a perfect relationship.

Unfortunately, not all measures of association are easily interpretable. We prefer the ones that have a proportionate-reduction-in-error interpretation because they can be translated into a percentage effect of one variable on another and then compared to other percentage effects. Although most of the PRE-interpretable statistics have a direct percentage interpretation, a few must be squared to gain such an interpretation—these are called *indirect-PRE measures*.

When data are at the ordinal level of measurement or higher, measures of association also provide the direction of a relationship. Positive correlations mean there is a positive (same direction) relationship between the variables and negative correlations mean there is an opposite relationship between the variables.

With this information, you no longer have to examine crosstabulations to decipher the direction of a relationship (sometimes almost an impossibility).

Now that you have a good idea of what association is and how correlations work, it is time to explore a measure of association. We'll begin with the Phi statistic in the next chapter. That is a good beginning choice because it works with a 2×2 table, making it easy to relate the results to what can be seen in the table itself. It also is directly related to Chi-square.

KEY POINTS OF THE CHAPTER

Measures of association are designed to determine the strength of relationships. They are normally used after an inferential statistic produces a statistically significant result.

- The best measures of association have a PRE interpretation.
- A PRE interpretation provides us with a percentage estimate of the effect of one variable on another.
- The correlation coefficients used with ordinal and interval data have positive and negative signs that can be used to determine the direction of relationships.
- Measures of association may produce symmetric or asymmetric correlations. Asymmetric measures are preferred when independent and dependent variable can be identified.

CHAPTER 15

Testing for Association: Phi

Key Concepts

■ Phi

■ natural dichotomy

■ indirect PRE

Association at its most basic level is a simple determination of which category a case occupies across the joint values of two variables. This means that if we use two variables in a crosstabulation, one variable is being used to predict which cases fall into the categories of the second variable. For instance, if gender is used to predict whether someone has ever committed a criminal act (the dependent variable), we might hypothesize that males are more likely to have done so. Thus, we predict that the cases in the "criminal act" category are males and that the cases in the "no criminal act" category are females. If we are perfectly correct, gender will predict all cases in both the criminal act and no criminal act categories. Our results are unlikely to be this perfect, so we expect the results to fall somewhere in between no relationship and a perfect relationship. The question, of course, is how well we did with our prediction.

The concept of association at the nominal level of measurement, as you would expect, focuses on categories and uses crosstabulations just as our discussion above suggests. In Chapter 8, we noted that a relationship, as depicted in a crosstabulation, tends to use the table diagonals. Thus, the concept of association at the nominal level is that as the number of cases in the table cells of one of the values increases, the corresponding number should decrease in cells of the other values. In a 2×2 table, a relationship is easy to see. Once the table gets larger, it becomes more difficult. As a result, we begin our discussion of the first measure of association with a special purpose, 2×2 table statistic.

A NOMINAL-LEVEL CORRELATION: PHI

Phi (Φ) is a rather old statistic, and there is some debate whether it was created by statisticians Pearson or Cramér. You have already seen Pearson's name associated with the Chi-square statistic and it is perhaps no accident that Phi is associated with him as well. That's because Phi is based on Chi-square. Because Chi-square cannot be used directly to estimate the strength of relationships, Phi is an adaptation that allows an easy calculation of strength. Remember, in the days before computers, easy calculation was an important ingredient in statistical analysis. Phi is also a *nonparametric* statistic because it doesn't assume linearity in the relationship between variables.

Phi is a rather special purpose statistic and has only one use: to measure the association between *natural dichotomies*. In other words, it can be used only for a 2×2 table. The variables in the table should be ones that haven't been artificially collapsed into a dichotomy. For example, gender is a natural dichotomy. "Young" and "old" as a measure of age is an artificial dichotomy (at exactly what age do you declare someone to be young and someone to be old?). The reason a natural dichotomy is required is that by splitting any ordinal, or higher level, variable in two groups and correlating them with another variable, you could "create" the results. Using the age example, the sample of respondents might have a relationship with a second variable if you split them at age 35, but not if you split them at 45. Exactly where you create the split could easily be a product of your own bias (you could have a vested interest in the results). So, to keep Phi (and yourself) "honest," natural dichotomies are used.

When you think about it, a statistic restricted to a 2×2 table with natural dichotomies as variables is *really* restrictive. But, when you have data like that, Phi is the correlation of choice. It also may help to know that there are a lot of natural dichotomies in the social sciences and, certainly, in criminal justice and criminology. For instance, victimized or not, reported a crime or not, committed a crime or not, arrested or not, convicted or not, recidivated or not, and so forth are all reasonable variables for use with Phi.

The Formula for Phi

Let's look at the formula for Phi, not just because we want to do the calculation, but to see how the statistic uses the data. There are two, one based on Chi-square and the other a calculation without knowing Chi-square in advance (the "actual" formula).

The easy calculation formula for Phi is: x^2/n (Chi-square divided by sample size)

The actual formula is: $\phi = \dfrac{(ad - bc)}{\sqrt{(a + b)(c + d)(a + c)(b + d)}}$

A close look at the second formula tell us that Phi is comparing the cells in a 2×2 table along the two diagonals (a and d, b and c). Just in case you need a reminder, the cells and diagonals in a 2×2 table are arranged as in Box 15.1.

Phi and the Diagonal Relationship

If the relationship is perfectly on the "a" and "d" diagonal, then there will be no cases in the "b" and "c" cells (the other diagonal). If this is the case, the numerator contains the equivalent of all cases minus zero. The denominator in the formula contains all possible sources of variance both across and down the four cells. The end

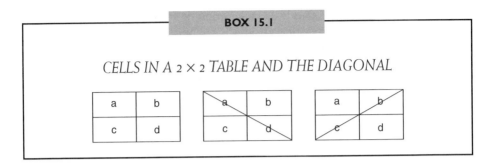

BOX 15.1

CELLS IN A 2 × 2 TABLE AND THE DIAGONAL

result is dividing the variance we are interested in (the cases on the diagonal) by the total variance. If the relationship is perfect, then we get $1.0 \div 1.0 = 1.0$ for the correlation. If there is absolutely no relationship, then the result is $0.0 \div 1.0 = 0.0$ for the (lack of) correlation. Obviously, most real relationships are somewhere in between 0.0 and 1.0. Box 15.2 contains a visual depiction of this diagonal relationship issue.

In one sense, the most desirable definition of a perfect relationship is that all cases occur exactly where we expect them (along the diagonal). If any case is not on the diagonal, that case represents an error (it is not where it is supposed to be) and the relationship is a partial one. Phi achieves a perfect relationship value of 1.0 only when all cases are on the diagonal, so it does exactly what we want a statistic to do when measuring relationships.

Proportionate-Reduction-in-Error Interpretation

Another characteristic of Phi is the ability to achieve a proportionate-reduction-in-error (PRE) interpretation of its calculated value. However, the actual value of Phi cannot be used in this fashion because the relationship "strength" implied

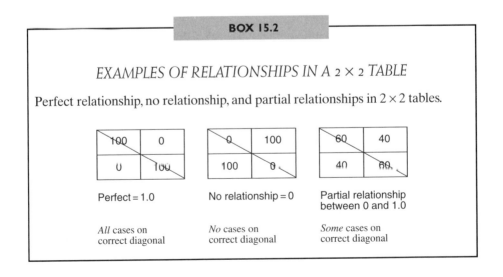

BOX 15.2

EXAMPLES OF RELATIONSHIPS IN A 2 × 2 TABLE

Perfect relationship, no relationship, and partial relationships in 2×2 tables.

Perfect = 1.0   No relationship = 0   Partial relationship
                                                    between 0 and 1.0

All cases on   *No* cases on   *Some* cases on
correct diagonal   correct diagonal   correct diagonal

FIGURE 15.1 Image of Phi Coefficients Before Squaring

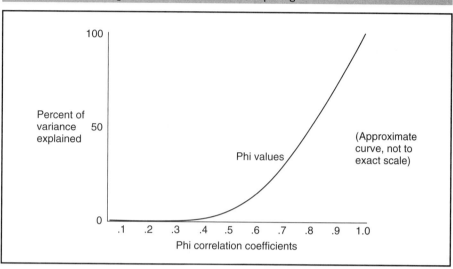

by its values looks like an exponential distribution (see Figure 15.1, above). These values are closer together toward the zero point and get progressively further apart toward the perfect relationship point (1.0). Fortunately, there is an easy solution to distributions like this—squaring the values results in a straight line. This is what must be done with Phi coefficients. Thus, Phi is referred to as an *indirect-PRE* statistic.[1]

Symmetry

Phi is a symmetrical statistic, estimating the overall relationship present in the table. There is no formula, or adaptation, to estimate the one-way relationship between an independent and dependent variable. That is, you are stuck with an estimate of the average relationship between the two variables, without taking into account which is independent and which is dependent. This doesn't mean you can't use hypotheses with Phi—you just have to remember that it loses some accuracy because of its symmetric nature.

Use with Larger Tables

Because of the 2×2 table restriction, statisticians in the 1920s attempted to generalize the concepts behind Phi to larger tables. The problem in using Phi with larger tables is that it can attain a value larger than 1.0 for a perfect relationship. Cramér, one of the original statisticians behind Phi itself, developed a version for tables larger than 2×2. That version is referred to as the Cramér's V statistic. Regardless of the number of rows and columns, V can attain unity (1.0).

---

[1]In fact, this status is actually not because of the properties of Phi itself, but because another statistic (Pearson's r) calculated on the same data for a 2×2 table results in exactly the same value. Pearson's r has an interval-level, indirect-PRE interpretation and we borrow that fact to interpret Phi.

Unfortunately, it doesn't have a clear PRE interpretation because Pearson's r produces no equivalent result, thus making V very difficult to interpret.

PROBLEMS WITH PHI

"Natural Dichotomies" Revisited

Because the concept of "natural dichotomies" is so important when using Phi, it is worth visiting the subject again in a bit more detail. Remember, the concept means that a variable's two groups (values) are not arbitrary ones. For instance, Phi is properly used with the variable gender; using it with the variable age collapsed into two values (say ages 15–31 and 32–85) wouldn't be acceptable. The reason for this is that creating an arbitrary dichotomy out of a continuous variable may result in an association that is merely a product of the choice used to create the two values. In the age example above, there is no good reason for separating age into two values representing "young" (ages 15–31) and "older" (ages 32–85). Other ages could just as easily have been used to create the two groups, so any relationship Phi might find is as likely to be a product of *which* ages were chosen as it is anything real. To illustrate this point, Table 15.1 contains the results of two Phi calculations of the relationship between fear of crime and age, with age split at 32 in one and at 55 in the second. As you can see, the coefficients are different. One is a negative .146 and the other is a positive .263. While the correlations are not large, swinging from a negative correlation to a positive correlation just because of the choice of where to make age into a dichotomy is a notable effect.

TABLE 15.1 Example of the Effect of an Artificial Dichotomy on Phi

Variable Split	*Fear of Crime—Phi Value*
Age split at under 32 and 32+	−.146
Age split at under 55 and 55+	+.263

The two examples below demonstrate both good and bad dichotomy variables for use with Phi.

Example of a "Good" Dichotomy for Phi		*Example of a "Bad" Dichotomy for Phi*	
Variable: Were you a victim?	Yes	Variable: What is the	1 − 500,000
	No	size of your city?	500,001+

It makes sense that asking someone if they have been a victim would naturally elicit "yes" and "no" answers—that's a good dichotomy. On the other hand, asking someone the size of their city or town by using only two categories of "less than 500,000" and "more than 500,000" is bad. There is no reason why 500,000 should be chosen to create the two groups except for convenience—and that's rarely a good reason for a methodological decision. There may be, for instance, differences in people's opinions in rural and small towns compared to cities of

100,000 or more. If so, you would have lost the relationship by breaking city size into two groups at 500,000.

While it is possible to use Phi with a continuous variable that has been collapsed into two groups, the split has to be at some rational point that "makes sense."[2] Again, the issue is that you want to measure a real relationship, not one that is merely a product of the choices you made.

Chi-Square Problems

The other major issue with Phi is the fact that it is Chi-square based. Therefore, all the problems of Chi-square come into play with Phi. The two primary ones are sample size and marginals. Small sample sizes lead to error in estimating relationship strength. In fact, the smaller the sample size the more Phi is likely to overestimate strength of association. If at all possible Phi should be used with larger sample sizes. The marginal problem is common among older statistics developed for tabular analysis. As with Chi-square, unequal marginals cause an overestimation of strength of association. The greater the inequality, the worse the problem is. It is not a good idea to use the statistic when the marginal split is more extreme than 80/20 percent. Actually, if you have a crosstabulation that is a poor choice for calculating Chi-square, that logic should be extended to Phi.

EXAMPLE OF THE USE OF PHI

Let's use two dichotomous variables appropriate for Phi: gender and voting. Table 15.2 contains the results from a survey question asking people if they had voted in the last election.[3] Our hypothesis will be a one-tailed one:

> H_a: *Females are more likely to vote than males.*

The data in the crosstabulation, then, not only need to show a difference but a difference in the direction of females being more frequent voters.

First we look at the crosstabulation below and conclude that, as we hypothesized, females are more likely to vote than males:

Females voting = 84.1%
Males voting = 75.8%

The direction of our hypothesis is correct. Next we examine the probability ("Approx. Sig.") value of .000 (the statistical program truncates the results at

---

[2]While this has been mentioned previously, a variable with multiple values meets the requirements of a natural dichotomy if it can be collapsed into two theoretically meaningful categories. In other words, the choice of where to split the values is specified beforehand and not a biased or artificial choice on the researcher's part.

[3]As a methodological comment, notice that the percentage who say they voted is very high. This would have been record voting behavior and was not likely to be real. So, what caused the exaggerated reports of voting? Most likely it was an effect of what survey researchers call a "socially-desirable" question. In the United States, voting is a good, responsible duty of citizens. Most people, then, will tend to paint a favorable image of themselves and will say they voted even when they didn't.

TABLE 15.2 Example of Phi Results

Sex of Respondent* Vote Crosstabulation

| | | | Did You Vote in Last Election? | | Total |
			No	Yes	
Gender	Female	Count	101	534	635
		%	15.9%	84.1%	100.0%
	Male	Count	123	385	508
		%	24.2%	75.8%	100.0%
Total		Count	224	919	1143
		%	19.6%	80.4%	100.0%

Symmetric Measures

		Value	Approx. Sig.
Nominal by Nominal	Phi	.104	.000
N of Valid Cases		1143	

three digits after the decimal) and conclude that it meets or exceeds an alpha level of .05, so gender has a significant effect on voting . Finally, we examine the Phi value of .104 and interpret it. Remembering that Phi must be squared to get a PRE interpretation, we do so and get a rounded value of .011.

$$(.104) \times (.104) = .011 \quad [= 1.1\%]$$

That means that gender explains 1.1% of the variance in voting and females vote more than males. If you think this is a very small relationship, you are correct (notice the large sample size).

A Guideline for Determining Significance

For this statistic, and other correlations, you will see a column labeled "Approx. Sig." in the statistical output from SPSS. Most of the time, the figure in that column will be calculated by dividing the statistic's value by an estimate of its standard error and then using a common statistical distribution to find the probability level. In the case of Phi, it is obviously the Chi-square distribution that is being used. For other correlations, it will most likely be the *t*-distribution. When interpreting the analytical results, you can simply use this associated probability level to make a statistical significance decision. In the unlikely event you are actually using a statistical analysis program yourself, you can request an appropriate inferential test and continue to use probability as we have discussed in previous chapters. The choice is yours.

The Critical Facts about Phi

Assumptions:

✓ Data represent a natural dichotomy.
✓ The table is 2×2.
✓ Those of Chi-square.

Advantages:

✓ Easy to compute (directly from Chi-square).
✓ Indirect-PRE interpretation (square the value).
✓ 2×2 table counterpart of Pearson's *r*.
✓ Will reach unity (1.0) only if entire diagonal is zero.

Disadvantages:

✓ Limited to 2×2 tables (in other tables Phi can reach values larger than unity).
✓ Those of Chi-square.

This is also a good time to revisit our earlier discussion of the way in which sample size affects probability. If you remember, the size of the calculated probability is a function of both sample size and the existence of a relationship. In the case above, there were over 1100 cases, so the sample size is fairly large. Thus, the random error on which probability is based is fairly small. This allows a detection of smaller real relationships in the data and the probability of something less than .001 is a product of these two factors. If someone mistakenly used probability for the strength of the relationship, she might conclude that the relationship was quite strong (what people seem to be saying when they erroneously use the term *highly significant*). Just remember that the larger the sample size, the more likely it is that a tiny relationship will be found to be real (significant).

A Final Note about Nominal-Level Correlations

Phi works well for the special case of a 2×2 table, as long as the marginals are approximately equal. What do you do, however, when you have variables with more than two categories? That situation is actually more common than the 2×2 case. There are two basic choices for nominal-level data: Goodman and Kruskal's Lambda (λ) and the Uncertainty Coefficient (U). Either one will handle variables with multiple values and both are direct-PRE statistics, so you don't have to square the results. Lambda, for all of its good attributes, has problems with unequal marginals, much like Phi. The Uncertainty Coefficient doesn't depend on the marginals for its calculations and seems to be the equivalent of an all-purpose nominal-level correlation. For a brief overview of these statistics, see Appendix E.

One of the greatest difficulties with any correlational measure for nominal data is dealing with the concept of direction. Technically, there is no such thing as direction yet we frequently propose hypotheses that provide direction by suggesting movement "toward" a category. As a result, we can discuss movement from female to male (independent variable) affecting attitudes (dependent variable). The problem is that we have to look in the crosstabulation and decipher directional movement ourselves. For a 2×2 table (and Phi), this is easy; for larger tables, it becomes very difficult. Obviously, it would be better if the statistic itself could tell us something about the direction of the relationship. Because the concept of direction belongs to ordinal or higher measurement, statistics designed for those levels can solve the problem for us. Two ordinal-level statistics are briefly discussed in Appendix F. An interval-level statistic, Pearson's r is discussed in the next chapter.

SUMMARY

Phi is very handy and intuitively understandable measure of association for nominal-level data—but only for 2×2 crosstabulations. The variables must be naturally dichotomous or the results depend on the choice of where to split the data values. It reports correlation coefficients ranging from zero to 1.0 and, when squared, has a PRE interpretation. There is no asymmetrical version, so the coefficients are symmetrical ones, reporting average relationships across the two variables involved.

Because Phi is only used for 2×2 tables, it has limited utility. Attempts to generalize Phi to larger tables have not proven very successful. The generalized statistics based on Phi (V) are sensitive to the number of cases and the number of rows and columns in a table, and therefore their results are limited to identical conditions for comparison purpose.

The analysis of data in larger tables and nontabular data is the subject of the next chapter. Pearson's r requires interval-level measurement (magnitude and distance), but it is the most frequently used measure of association.

KEY POINTS OF THE CHAPTER

Phi is a useful measure of association as long as you understand its limitations. It is:

- Used with 2×2 crosstabulations only
- Requires natural dichotomies for variables
- Is symmetric only
- Can be indirectly interpreted as a PRE measure by squaring the calculated value
- Has assumptions tied to Chi-square, so be especially careful about marginals and sample size

CHAPTER 16

Testing for Association:
Pearson's r and Regression

Key Concepts

■ pearson's *r*

■ regression

■ *parametric statistic*

■ correlation coefficient

■ linearity

■ homoscedasticity

■ slope

■ regression coefficient

It is safe to say that Pearson's *r* has been the most popular research statistic in criminal justice and criminology for a long time. Moreover, it is the basis for many other, more complex statistics at the multivariate level. Pearson's *r* is also a *parametric* statistic, so called because it assumes linearity in the relationship between the variables. You might have already heard about this statistic, perhaps under the term *regression*. It is also possible that *r* is on your handheld calculator.

PEARSON'S *r*

Pearson's *r* (also referred to as the *Pearson Product-Moment Correlation Coefficient* or *regression*) is a correlation for two interval-level variables. It reports the *linear* relationship, not just any relationship. The statistic is used with raw data rather than tables (just imagine the size of the tables if you crosstabulated variables like age with income!), and examines pairs of observations based on the magnitude of their scores.

For example, we might test the notion that age group proportions in cities affect their crime rates. Our expectations, based on previous information, are that crime rates increase as the proportion of the population in the 15–25 age group increases. For this, we need measurements on every city's census proportions in the 15–25 age group and crime rates for the city. Thus every city has a pair of observations: one is the population proportion of those in the 15–25 age group and the other is the crime rate. Cities with lower population proportions of this age group should have lower crime rates. That would look something like this:

City	City Proportion of People in the Age Group 15–25	City Crime Rates
Sasquatch	.25	227.8
NFL City	.16	175.2
Bigville	.34	259.1
Rainfall West	.22	207.8

In the example, Bigville has a proportion of young people at .34, paired with a crime rate of 259.1. That pairing can be compared to Sasquatch with young people/crime rate figures of .25 and 227.8. We are interested in seeing if a rise in the proportion of young people is related to an increase in crime rates. If you examine the data above, you will see that it is—as a city's proportion of young people increases, the crime rate also increases (just in case, these are "made-up" data, although Sasquatch really does have that much crime and the Pearson's r correlation for this is .990).

As an overview of what is coming up, Pearson's r provides a correlation that ranges from 0 to ± 1.0 but needs to be squared (known as r-square) for interpretation purposes. The closer to ± 1.0, the stronger is the correlation; conversely, the closer to 0.0, the weaker is the correlation. Zero represents "no relationship" and ± 1.0 represents "perfect relationship." When r-square is used, the number tells us the proportion of variance explained in the dependent variable (by the independent variable). However, it is a symmetric measure of association only. Now's let's look at the formula to see what it does.

The Pearson's r Formula

There are multiple ways the formula for Pearson's r can be expressed. Here are just a few:

1. As the ratio of the covariation between the two variables (X and Y) to the square root of the product of the variation in X and Y:

$$r = \frac{\Sigma XY}{\sqrt{(\Sigma X^2)(\Sigma Y^2)}}$$

Where: X is an individual's score on variable 1
Y is an individual's score on variable 2

2. As the ratio of the explained sums of squares to the total sums of squares (TSS):

$$r = \frac{\Sigma(Y_P - \overline{Y})^2}{\Sigma(Y - \overline{Y})^2}$$

Where: Y is an observed score of variable Y
   Y_p is a predicted score of variable Y
   $\overline{Y}$ is the mean of variable Y

3. And, as the linear regression of Y on X:

$$Y = \alpha + bx$$

Where: x is a score of variable X
   b is the slope of X on Y
   α is the intercept of X on Y

The first of these formulas is perhaps the easiest one to make sense of, the second one is better explained using a graph, and the third is commonly known as the "linear function" and you may have seen it in your math course. This linear function is used to estimate the actual amount of effect variable X will have on variable Y, *for each unit increase in X* (we'll discuss this later).

The first formula version, expressed in words, is an attempt to take the variation present *between* variables X and Y (covariation) and compare it to the total amount of variation in the X and Y variables in the sample. The logic is that if the amount of covariation between X and Y equals the total variation, then X and Y are perfectly related. If there is *no* variation between X and Y, then there is no relationship. Otherwise, *some* X and Y covariation will mean a partial relationship when divided by the total variation. The resulting product of the division gives us the value of r.

The second formula is just another way of saying something you have already seen before: the sums of squares in the Analysis of Variance (ANOVA). Remember, we took the squared differences between the group means (the independent variable) and compared that to the total squared individual differences from each group mean. These were then called the *between sums of squares* (BSS) and the *within sums of squares*. Adding both together yields the total sums of squares (TSS). If you are having trouble seeing this, look again at Table 13.2. The essence of this is that the r correlation is a calculation of the ability of X and Y to vary together (the BSS) compared to the total amount of variance in X and Y. The more X and Y vary together, the stronger the correlation is. So, here's the conclusion to this: the formula can be rewritten as

$$r = \sqrt{\frac{\text{BSS}}{\text{TSS}}}$$

Where: BSS is the between sum of squares
   TSS is the total sums of squares

And here's another good part to this version. You know that we have to square r to interpret it. All that is necessary is to remove the square root sign in the box above and you have *r-squared*. Now you know a bit about the so-called General Linear Model—the ANOVA and Pearson's *r* use primarily the same calculations.

What are the Advantages of Pearson's *r*?

The most important advantage of using Pearson's *r* is that, because it uses interval-level data, it is sensitive to the magnitude of change between pairs of scores. This means that the *amount of change* in one variable can be used to predict the amount of change in another. Actually, then, *r* not only can provide a correlation coefficient as a measure of the average *linear relationship* between the variables but also an estimate of the *amount of effect* one variable has on the other. We'll discuss more of this aspect later.

A second important advantage of *r* is that it can easily be extended to a multivariate statistical technique, incorporating multiple independent and control variables. This means that the effect of the original independent variable on the dependent variable can be examined while simultaneously "controlling" for the effect of other variables. Because bivariate relationships just don't have enough information when you are looking for what causes something, this is a great advantage.

We've already noted that the statistic can be interpreted in a proportionate-reduction-in-error (PRE) fashion, though it is indirect through the necessity of squaring the correlation. And you already know that the statistic is part of the General Linear Model, so there are many extensions and techniques related to it. Finally, Pearson's *r* has been so popular that almost everyone who does, or reads, research is very familiar with it. In other words, *r* is a "must-know" statistic, particularly in criminal justice and criminology.

What are the Assumptions of Pearson's *r*?

For all its popularity and frequent use, Pearson's *r* has a relatively stringent set of assumptions. In one sense, these assumptions are common among virtually all parametric statistics and include linearity, normality, and equal variances. If they are not met, it is best to use an ordinal-level correlation, such as Somers' *d*, which is briefly described in Appendix F. These assumptions are found in the box below.

Assumptions of Pearson's *r*

✓ *Linearity*—the data are best represented with a straight line relationship

✓ *Homoscedasticity*—the variances of the dependent variable are equal for each value (or "group") of the independent variable

✓ *Normally distributed data*—both variables must be normally distributed

✓ *No serious outliers* in either variable

✓ *The residual variance* (what is left over after the independent variable is introduced) *is uncorrelated with the independent variable*

One last note about these assumptions. If you'll remember, we mentioned in Chapter 4 a potential problem with using the interval-level mean. If there are extremes present in the data (outliers), then the mean moves away from representative scores and toward the extreme scores. All interval-level inferential and association statistics use the mean in their formulas; thus they are "harmed" by outliers.

Fortunately, the statistic is fairly robust to violation of assumptions. Moreover, there is a substantial amount of research on the effect of violations and how to interpret the statistic. Multiple violations of assumptions will cause serious problems, though. Violations of each of the above causes underestimation of association, and the problem gets worse as violations mount.

What are the Disadvantages of Pearson's *r*?

On the whole, the greatest problems in using *r* are related to the stringent assumptions made by the statistic. The fact is that there are really very few instances in social science research in which one could expect all of these assumptions to be met. While its tolerance of violations is high, the statistic normally encounters data in which several assumptions are violated. Violation of one assumption might not result in too much error; violation of multiple assumptions results in exploding error. In addition, a lot of criminal justice data have been measured at the nominal and ordinal level, not the interval level required for the statistic. Some procedures to handle data at lower levels of measurement have been established, but many data are still suspect.

AN EXAMPLE OF A PEARSON'S *r* CORRELATION ANALYSIS

Let's take a look at a typical research problem for which Pearson's *r* can be used. We will examine the relationship between people's educational level and how they rate their chances of becoming a crime victim in the coming year. This is our alternative hypothesis:

> *People with more years of education will rate their chances of becoming a crime victim higher than those who have fewer years of education.*

The direction is positive, requiring both variables to increase together. Table 16.1 contains the information from an SPSS output of a Pearson's *r* analysis.

Note that there are two rows and two columns of numbers, each one representing either the crime victim variable or the education variable. In fact, the diagonals duplicate the information in the table. This is true of all "correlation matrices"—there is a grouping of correlation results in the top half *above* the left/right diagonal and a duplicate version in the bottom half *under* the diagonal. If we look at the entries in the table representing the first cell in the column

TABLE 16.1 Pearson r Correlation Between Education and Crime Victimization

Pearson r Correlations

		Crime Victim?	Years of Education
Crime Victim?	Pearson Correlation	1	.086*
	Sig. (Two-Tailed)		.003
	N	1160	1147
Years of Education	Pearson Correlation	.086*	1
	Sig. (Two-Tailed)	.003	
	N	1147	1168

** *Correlation is significant at the 0.01 level (Two-Tailed)*

These two are identical

where "years of education" and "crime victim" cross, there are three numbers: the Pearson's *r* correlation, probability (sig.), and the number of cases (*N*) as follows.

1. The *r* for this relationship is .086,
2. the probability is .003,
3. and the sample size is 1,147 cases.

The positive *r* of .086 tells us that the *direction* of the hypothesis is correct (as education increases, victim chances increase). Our hypothesis also turns out to be significant as the probability is .003, which is well below our required alpha of .05. Thus, we accept our hypothesis. Now we need to interpret *r* as the strength of the relationship.

In order to get a PRE version for interpretation, the *r* of .086 needs to be squared.[1]

$$.086 \times .086 = .0074$$

We do that and obtain a value of approximately .0074—which means that, by knowing years of education, we can account for 0.74% (remember to move the decimal point over two places to change a proportion to a percent) of the variation in ratings of victim chances over the next year.

Obviously, education accounts for a *very* small amount of variation in victim chances but, nonetheless, that small amount is real and not merely a product of random error because it is statistically significant ($p = .003$). Thus, our attempt to *explain* victim chances by using education is statistically significant but not worth much. There is a tremendous amount of *unexplained* variance ($100\% - 0.74\% = 99.26\%$), or what is otherwise known as *error*.

---

[1] Just a math reminder: If you square a proportion (numbers below 1.0), the result will be *smaller* than the original number. Here's an intuitive version of that. A proportion of .50 squared will be .25—it is the equivalent of taking half of a half (.50) and getting a quarter (.25). In percentage terms, half of 50% is 25%. As another example, squaring .10 is equivalent of taking 10% of 10%, which is 1%.

TABLE 16.2 Choosing the Best Predictor

Correlations

		Age	Years of Education	Intolerance Scale	Punitiveness Scale
How willing are you to serve on a criminal jury?	r	−.202	.186	.094	.045
	Sig. (Two-Tailed)	.000	.000	.002	.147
	N	1078	1085	1061	1062

Now let's try another example, this time with several relationships at once. We're going to look at the results of calculating a Pearson's *r* on four bivariate relationships, but each one using the same dependent variable—willingness to serve on a criminal jury. The independent variables are age, education, intolerance, and punitiveness. Our goal is to find the independent variable that best "predicts" (has the best relationship with . . .) willingness to serve. Table 16.2 has the results of these analyses.

Because we are trying to find the best predictor, the process is equivalent to testing a group of two-tailed hypotheses and then comparing the results. The significance tests are two-tailed because we don't care what direction a predictor takes, just that it predicts. The first step is to look at the probability levels in Table 16.2 (the row labeled "Sig. (two-tailed)"). Variables meeting our .05 significance criteria are age, education, and intolerance. Punitiveness, as it turns out, does not have a significant relationship with willingness to serve on a criminal jury (because this is real data, that's actually a good sign).

Now let's compare the *r* values. Age has a correlation of −.202 with willingness to serve, education a correlation of .186, and intolerance an *r* of .094. The answer to our question, what is the best predictor, is easy—the variable with the highest correlation. That variable is obviously age. Before we finish here, though, it would be wise to change the results to *r-square* so they can be interpreted. Squaring −.202 yields .0408, so age explains about 4% of the variance in willingness to serve on a criminal jury. Looking at the negative sign,[2] we also have to conclude that as age increases, people are less willing to serve on a jury. On the whole, though, 4% is not a very good predictor, so if you really wanted to predict jury service, you would need to keep searching for variables.

GRAPHING RELATIONSHIPS AND ESTIMATING EFFECTS

One of the advantages of using Pearson's *r* is that the results can be graphed in a scatterplot so a visual representation is available. If you remember, we said that *r* is a correlation of the *linear* relationship between two variables. That means the

---

[2]Because *r-square* will always be positive, you need to get direction of the relationship from the original *r* value.

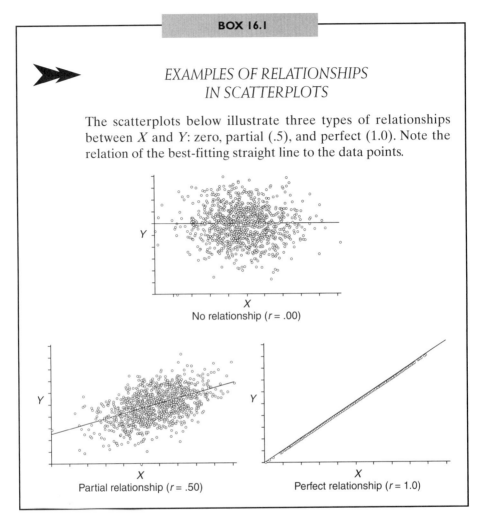

BOX 16.1

*EXAMPLES OF RELATIONSHIPS
IN SCATTERPLOTS*

The scatterplots below illustrate three types of relationships between *X* and *Y*: zero, partial (.5), and perfect (1.0). Note the relation of the best-fitting straight line to the data points.

No relationship ($r = .00$)

Partial relationship ($r = .50$)

Perfect relationship ($r = 1.0$)

relationship is measured as if it were a straight-line function. One of the terms used in some discussions of *r*, and regression, is "the best-fitting straight line." The idea is to take all data points (on a graph, the *X* and *Y* points) and fit a straight line through them. The one line that comes closest to all of the data points is the one that is used. Look at the graphs in Box 16.1 for an illustration of this concept.

As you can see in the three graphs, the closer the line comes to touching all of the data points, the higher the *X/Y* correlation is. Conversely, the further it is from all data points, the lower the *X/Y* correlation is. A true zero correlation will have a group of points with no discernable linear pattern whatsoever.

REGRESSION

Regression is actually a product of Pearson's *r* in that it provides an estimate of the magnitude effect of one variable on another. The term *regression* comes from the concept of "regressing" a variable on another. The idea is that, for a linear relationship, there ought to be a constant relationship between the two variables. That enables you to answer the question "If X increases by 1, what will Y be?" As an example, suppose you are a parole administrator trying to maximize your manpower because the parole agents have high workloads. Through research, you know that there is a strong negative correlation between age and recidivism. This opens up the possibility that older parolees who recidivate less might not have to be supervised so closely, thereby decreasing parole agent workload. The problem is you don't know what age is "safe" to use. A regression of recidivism on age would tell you what you need to know. It would produce a measure of decrease in recidivism for every year of parolee age.

We had said earlier in this chapter that we would revisit the second formula. The general concept of that formula version is to say that, if variables X and Y are related, knowing a score of X would help you to better predict the variable Y. Examine the graph in Box 16.2 for an illustration of this along with an explanation.

Regression Line with Actual and Predicted Data Points

The relationship between the regression line (best-fitting straight line) and *r-square* is illustrated below. The best prediction of any Y score, with no other information, is to guess it is at the mean of Y. If X is related to Y, then it will help improve prediction. The graph below shows only one data point (Y) with the regression line used to predict where that point should be (Yp). It "varies" from Y because the two points aren't identical. An improvement over guessing the mean of Y is "explained" variance. The distance left over from the predicted point, Yp, and Y is "unexplained" variance. The PRE-measure *r-square* is the same as explained variance, but is the average explained variance for all data points in the sample.

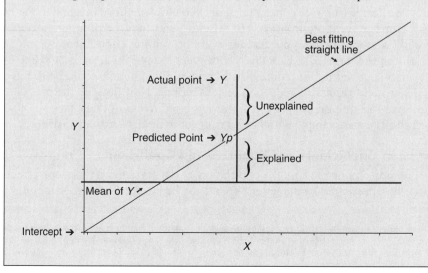

Slopes and Regression Coefficients

This approach is frequently referred to as *linear regression* (also *ordinary least squares regression*) because it uses a straight line to represent the regression of Y on X. The angle of the straight line, or the *slope* (known as b), shows the relative effect of X on the movement of Y. Put another way, one variable may have relatively strong impact and another may have little impact—even though the correlations of both are perfect. The third formula, the linear function, is an important part of this discussion. If you don't remember it, here it is again:[3]

$$Y = \alpha + bx$$

Some general statements about the slope (b) of the regression line are as follows:

- If b (the slope) is 1.0, and X and Y are measured the same way (equal units), then the angle of the slope is at 45 degrees.
- If b is >1.0, and X and Y have equal units, then the angle of the slope is >45 degrees.
- If b is <1.0, and X and Y have equal units, then the angle of the slope is <45 degrees.

"Units" are units of measurement. For example, if both X and Y are measured in years, then the measurement units are equal. If X is measured in proportions (0–1.0) and Y is measured in miles, the measurement units are not equal. This latter example is the most common situation (such as trying to use the proportion of males in various cities to predict crime rates, measured in number of crimes per 100,000 population). Remember that the scale of measurement for both variables must be the same before the angle of the slope in relation to the value of b holds true.

In general, the further the b is away from 1.0, the stronger the X effect on Y. In terms of angles and degrees, any angle larger than 45 degrees (b of 1.0) means that a smaller than 1 unit change in X has a greater than 1 unit effect on Y. That would be a desirable effect if you were concerned about economy of effort. Imagine trying to create a crime prevention program. You would prefer that the program not only work well (i.e., reduce crime) but that for every prevention effort, there is a major effect on crime. In terms of dollars, this is equivalent to saying that you would like to have every expended dollar reduce, say, 10 crimes. Even better would be to have every dollar spent result in a reduction of 1,000 crimes. Now imagine the opposite, that for every $1 million dollars spent, there is a reduction of one crime—not so good, right? The last example is a slope, or b, of substantially *less* than 45 degrees.

Regression Coefficients and Standardized Coefficients

The regression coefficient (not the correlation, r) is a measure of this slope effect. It is usually represented by the letter "b" and can be interpreted as the amount of

---

[3] The linear equation can be a little misleading because it is an ideal function. We already know that measurement is never perfect; further there are likely influences on any relationship in addition to the simple bivariate effect of X on Y. Thus, it makes sense to add an error term (e) to the regression formula so the "real" formula is $Y = \alpha + bx + e$.

change in Y as a product of X. Thus, the formula $Y = \alpha + bx$ is a direct expression of the effect on Y of a change in X. If, for instance, X changes 4 units and the effect on Y is a change of 1 unit (and we assume that α, the intercept, is zero), then an X of 16 would represent a Y of 4. A b is referred to as an *unstandardized* regression coefficient because X and Y are in their original units (however they were originally measured). If you have several independent, or predictor, variables, the unstandardized bs from each relationship cannot be compared directly to each other, unless all of the independent variables have the same units of measure. That means the b from a variable measured on a scale of 1–10 cannot be compared with the b from a variable with a scale of 1–100. For that reason, there are "standardized Bs," usually referred to as *Betas*, that can be calculated to allow the comparison of relationships created by any independent variable no matter what their units of measurement are.

In interpreting either unstandardized or standardized coefficients, it is necessary to remain aware of the r values as a measure of the degree to which the coefficients are reliable. An impressive b can have a low r value, indicating that while X has a large effect on Y, the reliability (or strength) of that effect is very low—or, it has a large amount of error. Large bs are often a simple product of a large difference between the units of measurement for X and Y, even if the relationship is a very weak one.

AN EXAMPLE OF A REGRESSION OUTPUT

Before looking at a regression, the first step is to examine what is called the *scatterplot* of the graphed relationship between the two variables. A scatterplot is an X and Y axis graph with dots representing the location of each case on both the X and Y variables. Figure 16.1 below is a typical example of a scatterplot. This one is created by the X-Y plot of a person's worry about crime (the Y axis) and a measure of learning to be concerned about crime from a spouse.

The results demonstrate a visible relationship between the two variables—one apparently learns from one's spouse to be worried about crime, but the relationship is not a strong one. There is a tendency for an individual's worry about crime to increase as learning about worry from the spouse increases. This particular result is statistically significant ($p \leq .001$), with a Pearson's r of .334 (r-square of .112). The slope, or b, is represented by the line through the data and has a value of 0.125. In other words, for every 1 unit increase in learning about worry from a spouse, there is a 0.125 increase in personal worry about crime. Using the intercept (α) and the linear formula, $Y = a + bx$, we can estimate a person's level of fear if on a 0–30 scale their spouse is at 5. The answer would be a predicted fear level of 1.60—a fairly low level. The calculations for this result are below.

$Y = a + bx$
$Y = .975 + .125(5)$
$Y = .975 + .625$
$Y = 1.60$

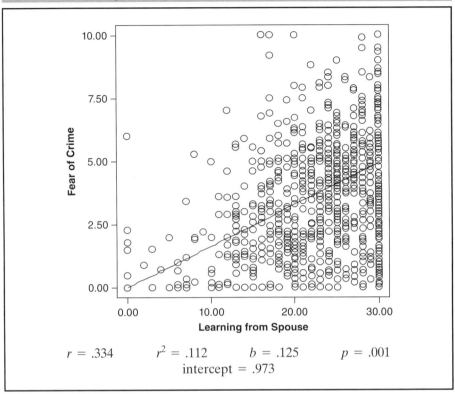

FIGURE 16.1 Regression Results

$r = .334 \qquad r^2 = .112 \qquad b = .125 \qquad p = .001$

$\text{intercept} = .973$

From this, you can see that a much stronger relationship is needed before predictions are very useful. If this were a policy issue, it wouldn't be worth the effort. Sometimes a very high level of accuracy is required—as for instance, attempting to predict prison admissions in a coming year. Being off in the prediction by even a small bit when you are dealing with thousands of people could have serious effects. Imagine what even a 10% error would mean with 3,000 inmate admissions. An entire wing of a prison might contain 300 inmates and cost over 10 million dollars. The point is that you need to know both the correlation coefficient and the regression coefficient in order to assess prediction results.

SUMMARY

Pearson's *r* and regression are very useful measures, assuming you have approximately interval-level data that can be reasonably interpreted as a linear effect. The statistic provides us with both an estimate of the strength of a relationship and the strength of the effect of *X* on *Y*. The usefulness of Pearson's *r* is a bit restricted by its assumptions, particularly the need for interval data and normally distributed variables. Fortunately, it is reasonably able to withstand the effect of violating one of those assumptions. More than a single violation, however, results in an unknown amount of error and, likely, an exponential increase in error.

As part of the General Linear Model, Pearson's *r* can also be easily calculated from ANOVA results and the *F*-ratio is frequently the measure of statistical significance used with *r*. This connection with the larger model allows for an expansion into multivariate analysis—a more realistic view of modern research than a series of bivariate analyses.

The final chapter explores a bit of the world of multivariate analysis, using elementary layered crosstabulations and a quick look at multiple regression.

KEY POINTS OF THE CHAPTER

Pearson's *r* is a popular and useful measure of linear association. It is used with two interval-level variables and provides a magnitudinal measure of relationship.

- The correlation coefficient *r* is an indirect-PRE statistic—*r*-square is necessary to interpret the results.
- Assumptions include normality in the data and a linear relationship between the variables.
- Regression is an adaptation of Pearson's *r* that allows an estimation of the degree of effect per unit of the independent variable, rather than just an overall average relationship provided by the correlation.
- *r* and *b* together allow estimates by which to evaluate attempts to predict scores of a dependent variable.

CHAPTER 17

Doing Real Research: Elementary Multivariate Relationships

Key Concepts

■ layered table

■ partial relationship

■ multiple regression

■ partial regression

Because this has been a textbook focusing on elementary statistical concepts, all of the statistics and examples have been either univariate or bivariate ones. While these are necessary for beginning any analysis of research data, you should consider such statistics a *beginning* in answering research questions. This final chapter is a short introduction to two common techniques used in multivariate analysis. There are many more types of multivariate statistics, many of which are designed for very special situations. These two techniques were selected because you are already familiar with tabular analysis and regression. Let's see how they work.

WHY DO MULTIVARIATE ANALYSES?

Though they might sound difficult or complex, multivariate analyses are not necessarily any more difficult to do, or interpret, than most bivariate analyses. The basic difference is that there are at least two variables in addition to the dependent variable. Once you look at a bivariate relationship, a natural question emerges: Is this relationship a real one or is it the product of another variable that affects both the independent and dependent variables? One way to look at this is that variables *A* and *B* vary together because they are both caused by *C*. There is also another possibility, that multiple variables affect the dependent variable—something common in real-life situations. Multivariate statistics can assist in answering these questions for us. Sometimes, though, a multivariate analysis is just an elaboration created by adding another variable to a table.

160

LAYERED TABULAR ANALYSIS

As suggested above, there is nothing to keep a researcher from adding additional variables to any bivariate crosstabulation. Analysts refer to such tables as *layered* tables. In a sense, the addition of a variable makes these tables a type of "multi-variate" analysis. In their simplest form, we use layered tables to determine the effect of a third variable on the original relationship. The method constitutes a form of *partial relationship* analysis. Let's look at the real research example below to see how this is done.

Parole agents have long said that gang affiliation is related to parole outcome (higher failure rates to be specific). Let's take a quick look at some data to see if this holds up. Our hypothesis is that parolees who have gang affiliations are more likely to fail parole. The simple crosstabulation for our test is below in Table 17.1 (sample and cell sizes have been omitted to save space).

As you can see, gang-affiliated parolees have a failure rate (70.8%) that is higher than that of parolees without gang affiliations (57.0%). The direction of our hypothesis is correct. In addition, the calculated Fisher's Exact Test probability (good for a 2×2 table) is less than .001, so it is significant and we accept the hypothesis.

Now it occurs to us that gang-affiliated parolees are generally younger and, also, that younger parolees are more likely to fail parole. Could it be that it is age and *not* gang affiliation that affects parole failure? Probably not, but this calls for a multi-variate analysis in the form of a layered table to check our suspicions. Table 17.2 below is the layered crosstabulation (once again, we'll omit the number of cases for economy of space).

Because there are four age categories, the layered table actually produces four versions of the previous bivariate table. For convenience, each of the internal tables is separated with a double line and the appropriate cells, the ones containing gang-affiliated parolees, are the ones with a gray background. If you look at the first table in the age layer, the one with parolees aged 21 and under, 70% of the gang-affiliated parolees fail compared to 58% of the non–gang affiliated parolees. So, within this age group, the youngest parolees' gang affiliation has an affect separate from age and significant at .025. Looking at each age group layer in the large table, the same finding occurs—gang-affiliated parolees have higher failure rates than those who are not affiliated with gangs. However, the last comparison with parolees aged 40 or more is not significant (primarily because

TABLE 17.1 Gang Affiliation with Parole Outcome

	Parole Outcome		
Gang Affiliation	*Failure*	*Success*	*Total*
Not gang affiliated	57.0%	43.0%	100.0%
Gang affiliated	70.8%	29.2%	100.0%
Total	59.1%	40.9%	100.0%
Fisher's Exact Test p < .001			

TABLE 17.2 Gang Affiliation with Parole Outcome by Age at Release

Age at Release	Gang Affiliation	Parole Outcome		Total (%)	*Prob.
		Failure (%)	Success (%)		
21 and under	Not gang affiliated	58.2	41.8	100.0	
	Gang affiliated	70.1	29.9	100.0	
	Subtotal	64.0	36.0	100.0	.025
22–29	Not gang affiliated	61.9	38.1	100.0	
	Gang affiliated	72.6	27.4	100.0	
	Subtotal	64.4	35.6	100.0	.000
30–39	Not gang affiliated	56.1	43.9	100.0	
	Gang affiliated	78.4	21.6	100.0	
	Subtotal	58.3	41.7	100.0	.000
40+	Not gang affiliated	51.8	48.2	100.0	
	Gang affiliated	59.1	40.9	100.0	
	Subtotal	52.1	47.9	100.0	.326

*Fisher's Exact Test (1-tailed)

there are not many gang-affiliated parolees in this age group), so for that group we'll have to say that there is, officially, no difference. Still, it looks good for our original hypothesis that gang affiliation results in higher parole failure rates, even when controlled by age.

While there are some problems in controlling relationships for a third (or more) variable in a crosstabulation analysis, it does provide evidence necessary to discard threats to a hypothesis. It can also be used to "explain" or "interpret" a bivariate relationship, by figuring out such things as which layered group has the strongest relationship.

PARTIAL AND MULTIPLE REGRESSIONS

Though layering tables as a method of controlling for the effect of variables on a relationship is a good idea, it is limited by the sample size and the large number of cells created by ever-increasing new tables every time we add a variable. Actually, even with large sample sizes, getting beyond four variables is almost unheard of. Things just get too unwieldy and the very small cell sizes cause error rate problems. Further, imagine trying to create tables with interval-level variables. But, interval-level variables can be analyzed with Pearson's r, right? How could that be handled?

Let's try this example for a possible solution. We know that if a city is broken up into various neighborhoods, those neighborhoods with higher income levels are likely to have lower crime rates—a negative relationship. We also know that the same thing can be said about neighborhoods with higher educational levels, higher home values, and two-parent households. Each one of these variables could constitute an independent variable used to explain crime rates. And, of course, each of those relationships with crime rates would be a bivariate one. If we wanted to explain crime rates even better, couldn't we just add the correlations of those four variables to get a total effect on crime rates? While adding their individual effects is a good idea, simple addition won't work.

Here's why. Does it occur to you that each of these variables might be measuring at least part of the same concept—perhaps some kind of "people with greater opportunities" phenomenon? If so, then each variable "shares" property space with the others. Figure 17.1 illustrates this problem, using neighborhood income and education levels.

FIGURE 17.1 Independent and Shared Conceptual Property Space

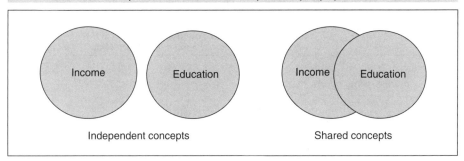

Independent concepts   Shared concepts

If each variable measured a truly independent concept, then each would stand by itself. If, however, the two variables share measurement, then the properties of the two concepts may be shared. Actually, doesn't it make sense that income and education may be partially measuring the same thing? It's not just that they are correlated, as much as it is that the variables themselves are partly duplicating each other.

This sharing of measurement and concept space is the reason why adding correlations to get a total effect can't be done. You would be adding some parts of each correlation multiple times. In order to "add" the effect of multiple variables on a single dependent variable, the measurement they share must somehow be taken into account. That's what multiple and partial regressions do. Let's begin with one independent variable and one "control" variable to determine the "non-shared" measurement in the independent variable.

Partial Regression

The technique of *partial regression* is conceptually simple. The name comes from the idea of "partitioning" variance in the dependent variable by the effects of independent and control variables. For instance, assuming you are interested in the income levels and crime rates relationship, we have already noted that there are other factors that might influence the basic relationship (educational level, two-parent households, and home values). All three are potentially related to income. If you are using income levels to explain crime rates, you don't want to be using the "co-effect" of other variables as part of the relationship with crime. Partial regression offers the opportunity to control for (partial out) the effect of these variables, thus leaving your basic income/crime relationship independent of shared measurement. The general effect is analogous to having the $A \rightarrow B$ relationship minus the effect of C, D, and E variables. Statistical output generates a bivariate r (the original relationship) and a partial r (original relationship minus the effect of the control variables). Here's how this works.

Let's start with a bivariate Pearson's r for the income and crime rate relationship—we'll say that was .0544 with a significant probability of .045. Now we need to "control" for the effect of potential shared measurement variables on the bivariate relationship. We enter the independent variable, three control variables, and the dependent variables into a partial regression. The outcome is in Table 17.3, below.

TABLE 17.3 Example of a Relationship with Three Control Variables

Variable	Bivariate r with Crime Rate	Bivariate Prob.	Third Order Partial r with Crime Rate	Partial Prob.
Independent: Neighborhood income level	.0544	.045	.0424	.098
Controls:				
Home values	−.0130	.550		
% two-parent Household	−.0418	.103		
Educational level	−.0848	.017		

The interpretation of the table above is that, controlling for three variables (third order partial r), the relationship between unemployment rate and crime rate changes from .0544, which is statistically significant ($p \leq .05$), to .0424. That is not much of a reduction in effect but, most important, the partial r is no longer significant ($p > .05$). Now we can say there is no relationship between income levels and crime rates once the effect of home values, two-parent households, and educational levels is removed from the original relationship. As you might have already noticed, even the bivariate "significant" correlation is nothing to get excited about—after squaring Pearson's r to get the proportion of variance "explained" in the dependent variable, this one is only .0029 or less than 3/10s of 1% of the variance.

Now that you have seen how it is possible to control for the effect of other variables on a relationship, let's examine the possibility of adding all of variables together to see how strong the effect of a *combination* of them on a dependent variable might be.

Multiple Regression

If your task is to determine the effect on the dependent variable of a group of independent variables, then *multiple regression* (R)[1] is the most commonly used technique. This approach is very similar to partial regression, and can provide those results also, but focuses on the combined effect of variables. The statistical

---

[1]Multiple regression is always identified by a capital R. Another thing to remember about R is that it cannot show direction ($+$ and $-$) because it may have to add both positive and negative relationships.

approach can also be used to test multiple independent (or predictor) variables to see which one is the *best* predictor.

Say, for instance, you are interested in trying to explain crime victimization. You find several variables in an existing data set. The first thing to do is to look at the bivariate relationships and determine which variables appear to have the "strongest" relationships with victimization. Then you would use multiple regression to add all of these variables into one relationship with the dependent variable. This will give you two products of interest: the multiple *R* value and information on the effect of the individual variables (especially partial *r*). The *R* provides the total effect of all variables and, if squared, the proportion of variance explained by all the variables. The individual variable information will tell you what each variable contributes to the entire relationship and whether it is a significant contribution.

There is one caveat here, though: The variable with the strongest bivariate correlation is automatically entered first, then the one with the remaining largest correlation after removing the effect of the first, and so on. This is *not* the same as a partial correlation—if you want to know the independent effect of each variable you have to request partial correlations and then report those. Multiple *R* can also be used to enter groups of variables together as a block, or as if they were a single variable. Let's look at an example.

We'll try to explain victimization by using these variables:

- whether an individual's significant other was victimized during the past year
- how many "worry definitions" are provided by the media
- how important an individual perceives media to be
- how important the opinion of others is to an individual
- the number of general safety precautions taken

Table 17.4 below presents the results of the *total* correlation (all five variables at once) with victimization.

The first result to examine is the last column ("Sig. F Change") because that is the probability level of the multiple regression. It is significant. Next you want to look at the *R* value. In our table it is .459 and, squaring it (the next column, *R*-squared), we find that all variables together explain 21% of the variance in victimization. There are other pieces of information below but, for this example, these are the important ones.

TABLE 17.4 Multiple Regression Summary

Model Summary

Model	R	R Square	Adjusted R Square	Std. Error of the Estimate	Change Statistics				
					R Square Change	F Change	df1	df2	Sig. F Change
1	.459[a]	.210	.206	1.82895	.210	52.169	5	979	.000

[a]*Predictors: (Constant), general safety precautions, media impact function, significant other victim during past year, bonding—importance of social factors, media worry definitions scale*

TABLE 17.5 Example of Individual Variable Results from a Multiple Regression

Coefficients[a]

Model		Unstandardized Coefficients		Standardized Coefficients			Correlations		
		B	Std. Error	Beta	t	Sig.	Zero-order	Partial	Part
1	(Constant)	1.652	.455		3.628	.000			
	Significant other victim during past year	.334	.021	.454	15.727	.000	.453	.449	.447
	media worry definitions scale	−.004	.004	−.049	−.823	.411	−.041	−.026	−.023
	media impact function	−.009	.042	−.012	−.212	.832	−.049	−.007	−.006
	bonding importance of social factors	−.005	.005	−.026	−.892	.373	−.067	−.028	−.025
	general safety precautions	.000	.017	.000	−.005	.996	.049	.000	.000

[a]Dependent Variable: victim during lifetime

Now let's look at a second table of results from the same multiple regression (Table 17.5).

There are multiple columns of information with each of the variables on the side of the table. The probability level for each of the variables can be found in the fourth column ("Sig.") from the right. Ignoring the "Constant" row because it actually is the regression line intercept, our focus is on significant variables. Of the five variables, only one has a significant effect on victimization—whether an individual's significant other was a victim in the past year. None of the other four variables are significant. Now let's look at a few of the other columns starting from the left. The "B" is the same as a regression coefficient or slope and you can use it to find the magnitude of effect on victimization just as with the bivariate level. The "*Beta*" column is the standardized slope. These coefficients can all be directly compared to each other to determine their magnitude effect. Under the "Correlations" heading, the first column is labeled "Zero-order." That is the bivariate correlation ("zero"-order because there are no control variables used) or Pearson's *r*. At .453, you can see that significant other victimization has what is clearly the strongest bivariate relationship with an individual's own victimization. Because none of the other variables are significant, we'll ignore the other bivariate correlations. The middle column is "Partial" and this is the partial *r*, or the relationship between each variable and victimization controlling for all other variables. The significant other victimization variable, controlling for the other four variables, has a slightly lower relationship with the individual's victimization (.449) than its original bivariate one (.453). Our conclusion is that it doesn't have much shared measurement with the other variables or the control effect might have been much lower. In all, it appears that the one variable helps us predict about 20% of the variance in an individual's victimization.

Though not every research report using regression will present identical information, all of this is available from most statistical programs (this is one you *definitely* don't want to calculate!). Moreover, the authors of most reports will at least provide information on *R* and *Beta*, even if they don't give you the partial *r* details. The assumptions of regression remain as stated in the previous chapter, and multiple/partial regression adds even more restrictions because of joint normality requirements between all variables. Even though there are serious data limitations on regression analyses, you will see partial and multiple regression in the research literature with great frequency.

SUMMARY

The examples in this chapter of using both tabular and statistical control are based on the ways a researcher might actually analyze data. Bivariate analyses are important and necessary. But, although they help you to understand the data and elementary relationships, they are only the beginning to a real analysis. Too many variables affect each other, too many variables share measurement properties, and there are too many types of causality for us to do simple bivariate analyses and make conclusions about relationships.

Layered tabular analyses represent a good way to explore the effect of interrelated variables on a dependent variable, but only if they are all nominal- or ordinal-level variables. They really aren't much different than creating subsamples of data based on the categories of a third variable, so they aren't really "controlling" for the effect of a third variable. But, at least such analyses provide a sense of what happens to the original two-variable relationship *within* the categories or layers of the third variable.

A better form of multivariate analysis for interrelated variables is regression, both multiple and partial. Because these work primarily with interval- and ratio-level data, their use is limited—but when they can be used, they work very well and provide substantial amounts of information about relationships. Both are merely an extension of bivariate Pearson's *r* into the realm of multivariate analysis. As a result, they have similar assumptions and are members of the General Linear Model statistical family. Multivariate techniques don't stop here, however—there are many more multivariate approaches depending on what the data will support.

The overall intention behind this book has been to get you to the point where you can appreciate the use of, and the analytical purpose behind, statistics. We want to know *objectively* when differences between phenomena exist, when relationships exist, and whether other factors affect those differences and relationships. Rather than knowing all about the hundreds of statistics and how to calculate them, the focus here has been on understanding the concepts behind them. If you know the basics and something about interpreting results, you will be able to read research reports and grasp statistical results. That's important in criminal justice and criminology. Criminal justice system policies and political pronouncements about crime and criminals are big issues and, more importantly, emotional ones. We need as much objective analysis as possible. As someone who will likely have a college degree in these fields, it is up to you to make better objective decisions so that our criminal (and juvenile) justice system becomes fairer, more efficient, and better at reducing crime. Knowing statistical analysis will help you do that.

KEY POINTS OF THE CHAPTER

Multivariate analyses are more like the "real world" than bivariate analyses.

- There are always outside relationships with other variables that affect the relationship we are interested in.
- Multivariate analyses help us to control for the effects of these outside variables.
    - Layered crosstabulations can be used to interpret categorical relationships.
    - Partial regression is used to control for the effects of interval- or ratio-level variables.
- Multivariate analyses, such as multiple regression, help us to see the joint relationship among several variables at once and a single dependent variable.

APPENDIX A

Box Plots

A complex, but very useful, statistical graphic is the *box plot*. This technique is a relatively new one, created by statistician John Tukey as part of what he called *exploratory data analysis*, an approach designed to suggest relationships present in data and subsequent hypotheses to be tested. Box plots are also referred to as *5-number plots* because they provide five pieces of numerical information:

- the highest score,
- the 75th percentile (upper hinge),
- the median,
- the 25th percentile (lower hinge), and
- the lowest score.

They are very useful because of the amount of information conveyed in the graph.

TWO-VARIABLE BOX PLOT

Figure A.1 illustrates a typical box plot graphic. For this, and the examples that follow, we will use "successful days in the first year of parole" as the measurement variable (the one being measured in the box). The idea is to explore parole success to see what parolee characteristics are associated with success. We begin with a simple two-group plot, using the experience of violating parole in a previous parole term as a criterion for creating the two groups. One group is "new parolees" only and the other is all previous "violators." Using the adage that past behavior predicts future behavior, we'll expect the violators to be less successful this term as well.

The "box" itself is the middle 50% of the data. The top of the box (upper hinge) is the 75th percentile and the bottom of the box (lower hinge) is the 25th percentile. The dark line is the median or midpoint of the data. The lines at the top (none here in this plot) and bottom of the box are called the *whiskers* and represents the distance to the highest and lowest scores (of successful days in this example). If the lowest (or highest) score is further away than 1.5 times the distance from the median to its hinge (the bottom of the box in this case), then the whisker stops at that point. This gives us these parts to compare across the two groups:

- the medians
- the "size of the box" representing spread of "central cases"
- the upper and lower hinges (where the ends of "central cases" are)
- the whiskers (the more extreme scores)

FIGURE A.1 A Simple Two-Group Box Plot

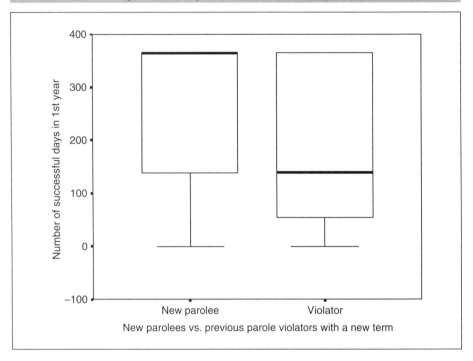

The first piece of information we use in Figure A.1 is the median experience of the two groups. This is represented by the dark horizontal line within each "box." As you can see, the "new parolee" box has a dark line at the *top* of the box. Because the upper part of the box from the median to the highest score would be the upper 50% of the scores, this means that 50% of those parolees were fully successful during the entire first year (365 days). On the other hand, it is easy to see that the median line for previous parole violators is much lower, and looks to be around 130 successful days or so. In fact, in comparison to the new parolees, the *bottom* of their box (lower hinge) is at virtually the same number of successful days as the *median* of the previous violators. Or, only 25% of the new parolees (lower hinge to the end of the whisker) do as poorly as 50% of the parole violators.

Another piece of information is contained in the actual length of the box. Longer box lengths mean that the data in that category are spread more; shorter boxes mean that the data are more alike. You can also see where the spread is occurring by comparing the length of the upper and lower portions of the box. If the median to upper hinge is longer, then the data are "skewed" (topic taken up in Appendix B) on the high end. If the median to lower hinge is longer, then the skew is toward the lower scores. Finally, the length of the entire box also conveys the middle 50% of the data—a way to see what is occurring with what we might consider the "core" of the variable or relationship. This is because the distance between the top hinge (75th percentile) and the bottom hinge (25th percentile) is 50%.

In our example, it is obvious that the boxes themselves are different and the new parolee box is smaller (less spread out) than the violator box. There are also differences in the size of the "below" and "above" the line segments of the box (the 25–50 percentile and 50–75 percentile areas). We have already noted that the upper 50 percentile of new parolees are all compacted into 365 days of success. This also means that the spread among new parolees is in the area below the median. Meanwhile, the violators are more spread out above the median than below.

Looking at the whiskers (extremes) of both boxes, it is evident that there are no extremes to the high end (more successful days), primarily because one year was used as the term of parole. Unless there are extreme circumstances, we would expect a number of parolees to be successful. The differences in whiskers come at the lower end. New parolees have a lower hinge (25th percentile) at about 130 days versus violators at about 50 days. Therefore, it stands to reason that the lower extremes of violators would be more compact—because there are lots of them failing between 50 and 130 days, they have fewer days for a whisker to represent. Now let's add a third variable to see what a slightly more complex box plot looks like.

TWO VARIABLES WITH THREE-GROUP BOX PLOT

In Figure A.2, the idea is to see if the number of successful days on parole are different, based on a parolee's prior arrests. If so, a researcher might be interested in trying to explain this variation or a parole administrator might want to see if this could be used to help classify parolee risk. Note that box plots cannot *test* hypotheses, but they can provide the initial evidence by which you would create a later hypothesis.

The box plots in the figure clearly show that the median (average) number of successful days decreases as the number of prior arrests increases (at least among the three categories we are using). The median line is at the top of the first box (0–3 arrests) because of the great number of parolees in that category who are successful for the entire first year. The top of the box for all three groups is at 365 days (the number of days in a year) because the 75th percentile (box top or upper hinge) is at that point. The 25 percentile (box bottom or lower hinge) varies more across the three groups, with the second and third boxes showing 25% of the parolees succeeding for fewer than 100 days. As a result, the 0–3 arrests box also has information below the lower whisker—these are cases that are extremely low compared to the others in that category.

Considering the overall shape of the boxes, it is obvious that greater differences in successful days occur when there are four or more prior arrests. Overall, all of the indicators point to three or fewer arrests being a potentially important indicator of success on parole. Those with four or more prior arrests are more spread over the continuum of possible successful days but also, on average, more likely to fail earlier. Now let's take what we know about these data and add a gender variable.

FIGURE A.2 Three-Group Box Plot

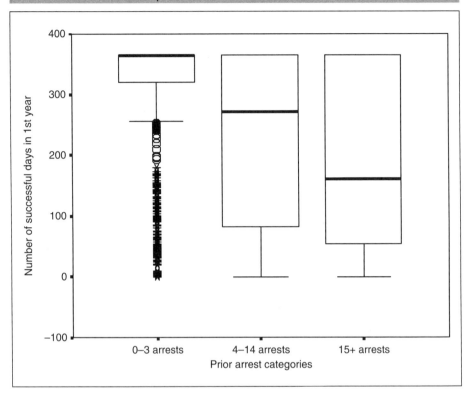

THREE-VARIABLE BOX PLOT

We now turn to an example of a three-variable analysis, using a box plot to illustrate possible relationships between successful days, prior arrests, and gender. For this example, we are especially interested in whether the apparent relationship found above is true for both males and females. Figure A.3 adds the third variable, gender, to the box plot by giving us two boxes for each category of prior arrests.

The first thing you might notice is that there is no *box* for females in the 0–3 prior arrests category. That is because almost all females in that arrest category are fully successful (all 365 days); the number of less than fully successful females here is so few that they can all be represented by asterisks. Thus, there is a "box" but the upper and lower hinges are the same as the median (and the highest score as well). Looking at the entire table, you also might notice that the average (median) female is more successful than the average male across all categories. Females are also centrally spread across fewer days than males.

FIGURE A.3 Box Plot with Three-Groups and One Layer Variable

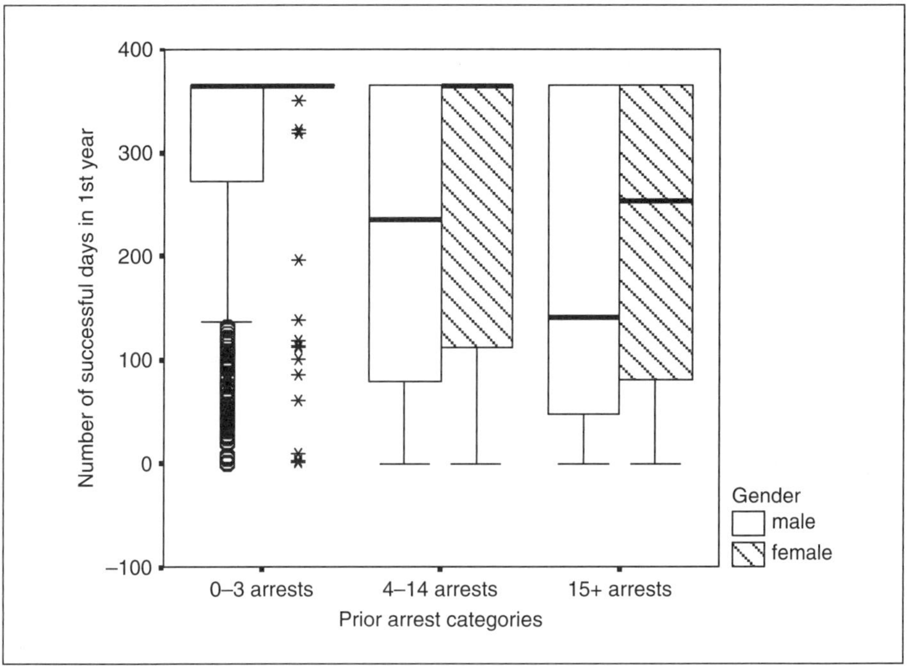

USING BOX PLOTS

With these examples, you can see how much information can be conveyed graphically if the charts are well-thought-out. Dr. Tukey obviously had in mind a combination of graphical techniques that would work well with ordinal-level data because he used a median as the measure of central tendency. However, box plots also work well with interval- and ratio-level data. They are best used to "explore" data prior to more sophisticated analyses. In fact, box plots are very useful prior to conducting an analysis of variance (see Chapter 13).

APPENDIX B

Statistics for the Normal Curve

A normal curve is a theoretical distribution with counterparts in the real world. The theoretical curve has special features; key among them are the symmetry of the curve and the height of the curve in relationship to the shape of the tails. Rather than having to look at the shape of a sample distribution and guess whether it is normal, there are two old, but simple, statistics designed to measure a curve to see if it has normal properties or not. These are called *skewness* and *kurtosis*. There are other statistics to see if a sample curve deviates from normal, but those are too complex to be treated at this stage.

SKEWNESS

One of the key properties of a normal curve is a symmetrical distribution. That is, both ends of the curve look alike. If a normal curve were split at its mean (also the high point of the distribution), the resulting halves could be folded over each other and would be identical. The result would be as if you were looking at only one half of a curve. To the extent that a curve, split at its mean, does not produce identical halves, there is a degree of skewness present. So, we can easily define skewness as *the lack of symmetry in a curve*.

There are two kinds of skewness: positive and negative. They receive their names from the direction of the tails (the ends of the curve). A normal curve has ends defined by their relation to the mean. The end of the curve above the mean is considered *positive* (thus, the "positive tail"), and the end below the mean is *negative* (thus, the "negative tail"). As a result, a skewed curve has a tail that extends in a positive or negative direction, as in the illustrations below.

The Two Forms of Skewness

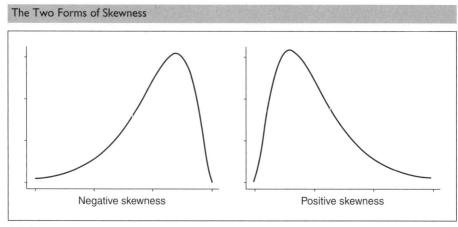

Negative skewness   Positive skewness

KURTOSIS

Kurtosis refers to the height, or peakedness, of the middle of the curve relative to its tails. The issue for kurtosis becomes whether the height (or amount of data in the middle of the curve) is substantially more or less than would be the case if the curve were a normal one. Thus, a normal curve is used as the comparison for all other curves. There are three kinds of kurtosis: mesokurtic curves, leptokurtic curves, and platykurtic curves. A *mesokurtic* curve is the "middle" curve, or the normal curve. A *leptokurtic* curve is one with a greater amount of data in its middle and less in its tails than is expected in the normal curve, thus a higher peak. The *platykurtic* curve has less data in its middle and more in its tails than is expected in a normal curve, thus it is flatter or lower. The illustrations below represent the three forms.

The Three Forms of Kurtosis

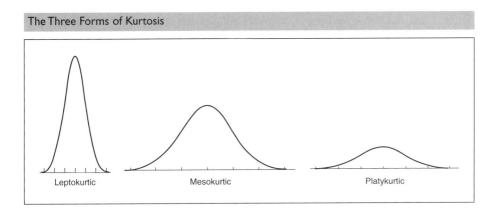

Leptokurtic   Mesokurtic   Platykurtic

Even though these illustrations provide examples of leptokurtic and platykurtic curves, there is another way to visualize them. An ideal type, or perfect example, of each would actually be a straight line. The perfectly leptokurtic curve would be represented by a vertical line—all scores would be the same. On the other hand, the perfectly platykurtic curve is a completely flat horizontal line—all values would have the same number of cases (or, there is no peak at all).

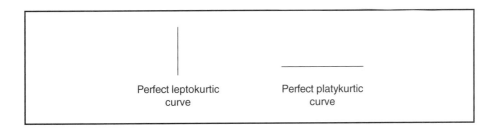

Perfect leptokurtic   Perfect platykurtic
curve   curve

THE QUANTITATIVE APPROACH TO SKEWNESS AND KURTOSIS

Certain statistics you will learn about later, such as the *t*-test, the analysis of variance, and Pearson's *r*; assume that data are normally distributed. If this assumption is incorrect, the results from these statistics will have error. The amount of error depends on how far away the distribution is from a normal one. An easy method of checking a data distribution is to calculate the skewness and kurtosis statistics. We will not deal with their calculation here, just how to interpret them (computer programs do the calculations for us).

Both statistics have a similar interpretation. They range around zero, which is the arbitrary score for a normal curve. Because curves cannot be expected to be perfectly normal, the statistics almost never provide a zero score. The question, then, becomes "how different from zero does the score have to be before it can no longer be treated as a normal curve?" Some arbitrary point is necessary in order to answer that question. If the score gets too large on either side of zero, for example ±2.6, then the curve might be considered non-normal. The commonly accepted cut-off point for a normal curve is considered to be ±1.0. *Anything larger than ±1.0 is no longer a normal curve.* The closer to zero the score is, the closer to perfectly normal the curve is.[1]

A curve that is positively skewed (or leptokurtic) would have a score beyond +1.0. A negatively skewed curve (or platykurtic) would have a score beyond −1.0. Because curves are rarely *perfectly* normal (or zero), some leeway must be given in using statistics that assume normality, else we would almost never be able to use them. Therefore, the ±1.0 range is a useful criterion for determining when normal-curve statistics can be used.

---

[1]It should be noted that the kurtosis statistic actually ranges around 3.0 and is usually corrected to range around zero. Some statistical programs use the uncorrected version; therefore, you should determine which version is being reported before you draw conclusions about the shape of your data (large positive kurtosis figures are usually a tip-off).

APPENDIX C

Ordinal-Level Tests of Significance

O rdinal-level data do not have the full information required for the direct use of scores. Because all this level of data can provide is information about rank or order, all *ordinal* tests examine differences in *ranking* (order of the scores) rather than the actual scores. Even if the data are interval-level, the "scores" will still be converted to ranked data and compared. This is because the actual scores themselves have no meaning other than being more than or less than the previous score.

Ordinal statistics are usually referred to as *nonparametric* statistics. This term means that such statistics *do not assume data approximate linear parameters* (that is, do not assume any relationship is linear and, therefore, normally-distributed).

Often they are called *distribution-free*, but these statistics *do* make assumptions about the shape of population distributions because that is what their probability sampling distributions are based upon.

WHICH TEST DO YOU USE?

Deciding which test to use is always a problem, but there are so many nonparametric tests that it can indeed be a *big* problem. Normally, you can use the answers to these two questions to help narrow your choices (actually, this works with any type of statistic).

- How many *groups* (in statistical terms, *samples*) are you comparing? One, two, or more (*k*-samples)?
- Are the groups/samples *related* (such as pre- and post-tests) or *independent* (the usual type of random samples from a population)?

In addition, as with other statistics, some of these tests have some specific features that others do not (that is, they have more or less power, are capable of specifying a particular distribution for comparison, or can analyze particular forms of variance). Some of these statistics actually assume that the data are more than basic ordinal and "almost" convey actual magnitude (metric ordinal). If one of these issues is present in the data, you must choose the appropriate test.

For our purposes in this Appendix, we will only be concerned with two of these tests—the *Mann–Whitney U* and the *Kruskal–Wallis H* tests.

MANN–WHITNEY *U*-TEST

This test is one of the most common of nonparametric, ordinal-level statistics. It is also a very powerful test, particularly when the data are metric ordinal (almost interval). Because the Mann–Whitney *U*-test is a good alternative to the parametric *t*-test, it should be used when the dependent variable is ordinal-level or the data are interval-level but not normally distributed. This means that you should not just automatically use the *t*-test because violations of its assumptions cause error in the results. Consider the *U*-test whenever there is some suspicion that data are not "quite right" for a parametric test.

Like the *t*-test, it requires two categories (e.g., males and females) on which to compare the dependent variable scores. Thus, this is a test of whether two independent samples (groups) are from the same distribution. Or, are these two groups equal?

The formula for the Mann–Whitney *U*-test is a bit complicated (common among nonparametric statistics). It is:[1]

$$\text{Smallest } U \text{ of:} \quad U_a = N_a N_b + \frac{N_a(N_a + 1)}{2} - \Sigma R_a$$

$$U_b = N_a N_b + \frac{N_b(N_b + 1)}{2} - \Sigma R_b$$

Assumptions

Now let's discuss the assumptions of the *U*-test. There are really only two. The first is common to every test discussed in this book—the two groups' data must be *independent* (no related data). The second is that the data in the dependent variable (or the measured variable) should have an underlying *continuity*. This means that data that are simply discrete (categories and nothing else) cannot be used. In fact, the best case scenario is that the data are interval-level (automatically continuous). This is why the test does better with metric ordinal information (or higher), rather than basic ordinal data. If you use it with a basic ordinal variable, continuity must theoretically be present in the variable (like education when grouped into several categories). The fact is that the greater the number of categories (values) in the dependent variable, the better the test works.

Advantages

Now, let's get to the important part—why would you want to use the Mann–Whitney *U*-test? Here are several reasons:

- The statistic works well with *both* small and large samples.
- It is more powerful than the *t*-test when normality assumptions are violated.

---

[1] If you make these calculations by hand and have to use a sampling distribution table, the largest group size is called "*m*," the smaller one "*n*," and the *U* in the table represent the largest possible *U* value for a significant result (usually at .05). This means your smallest calculated *U* has to be smaller than or equal to the value in the table—the *opposite* of what you would normally expect.

- The *U*-test is the most powerful nonparametric inferential (two-sample) statistic. In fact, when the *t*-test is at its best (the sample size is large and *all* assumptions of the *t*-test are met), the Mann–Whitney *U*-test is approximately 95.5% of the power of the *t*-test. Because perfectly meeting all *t*-test assumptions is rarely the case, the *U*-test is usually more powerful.
- It has a correction for ties (when scores in both groups are the same). However, this correction should be used only when the number of ties is quite large because the uncorrected test is more conservative in its estimate of probability.

Given all this, you almost have to ask the question "Why isn't the *U*-test used most of the time, rather than trying to use a *t*-test with its stringent assumptions?" And, there is no good answer to this, except perhaps that social and behavioral scientists are not too familiar with nonparametric statistics.

Disadvantages

So when is it a bad idea to use the *U*-test? That is pretty simple. Don't use the test when

- there are discrete data—noncontinuous, just categories (this is because of the over-conservative estimates of probability the test will provide).
- there are a large number of tied scores (even though there is a tie-correction formula, there is still a loss of power).

There are other nonparametric test alternatives for these circumstances, and one of those should be used.

An Example of the Mann–Whitney *U*-Test

Now let's look at an example of the *U*-test results for a typical criminal justice research problem. We know that most of the evidence points to females committing fewer crimes than males. But does this also mean that females will be less likely to have violations while on parole? We'll examine this possibility by using a measure of the number of successful days on parole (Hypothesis: Females will have a higher number of successful days on parole than males).

Table C.1 contains the results for this analysis. The "Mean Rank" column in the first part of the table is the one we examine first. The hypothesis proposed that females would have a *higher* number of successful days and that is the case (males have a lower rank, therefore fewer successful days). The "Mean Rank" is the result of changing the actual number of days for each case (interval level) into a rank score across both groups and then calculating the mean of those ranks for males and females. For instance, if the lowest score is assigned the rank of 1 and the second a rank of 2 (and so on . . .), all female ranks can then be added and divided by the number of cases to produce a mean rank (the average rank of successful days for the group). If females are distributed mostly among the higher ranks (more successful days), then their mean rank will be higher.

TABLE C.1 Results from the Mann-Whitney U-test

Ranks

	Gender	N	Mean Rank	Sum of Ranks
Number of successful days in 1st year	Male	3326	1897.15	6309922.00
	Female	539	2154.22	1161123.00
	Total	3865		

Test Statistics[a]

	Number of Successful Days in 1st Year
Mann–Whitney U	777121.000
Asymp. Sig. (Two-Tailed)	.000

[a]*Grouping Variable: Gender*

This is just like using a mean to compare the two groups for the *t*-test, only with ranked scores.

Now that we know the direction is correct, the second part of the table has the probability associated with the calculated *U*-test value. Note that the reported probability is two-tailed, but at a probability value smaller than .001, there is no need to divide the result for our one-tailed hypothesis. This is obviously significant. So, we can say that our hypothesis—females will have a higher number of successful days on parole than males—is supported.

Now let's turn to a nonparametric statistic for comparing more than two groups.

KRUSKAL–WALLIS ONE-WAY ANALYSIS OF VARIANCE (H-TEST)

As with the Mann–Whitney *U*-test, this test is an ordinal level alternative to a popular parametric test, in this case the analysis of variance (ANOVA). The Kruskal–Wallis statistic is also a powerful test and is best used in two instances:

- when the dependent variable is measured at least at the metric ordinal level, or
- when the dependent variable does not meet the normal distribution assumption of the ANOVA.

Where the Mann–Whitney *U*-test assumes there are only two groups on which we compare the rankings of the dependent variable, the Kruskal–Wallis *H*-test assumes there are more than two groups (as with White, Black, and Hispanic respondents). This test is formally used to determine equality of sample distributions in cases where the number of samples (groups) exceeds two.

The formula for the statistic is:

$$H = \frac{12}{N(N + 1)}\left(\frac{\Sigma R_1^2}{N_1} + \frac{\Sigma R_2^2}{N_2} + \frac{\Sigma R_3^2}{N_3} + \ldots \frac{\Sigma R_k^2}{N_k}\right) - 3(N + 1)$$

If you notice the equation term, ΣR_n^2, then you can see that the mean squared ranks of each group are being compared to each other. Actually, the H-test is an extension of the U-test to multiple groups.

Assumptions

As with other nonparametric or "distribution-free" tests, the Kruskal–Wallis H-test has a few critical assumptions. The groups (k-samples) must be independent of each other, with no related measurements. And, of course, the data (dependent variable) must be measured at the ordinal level or higher. Merely ordinal discrete data, though, exacerbate the problem of ties and the test assumes an underlying continuity in the data. As a result, the data really should be *metric* ordinal or higher.

Advantages

The H-test shares with the U-test a high degree of power. It almost equals the ANOVA statistic when all of that statistic's assumptions are met (particularly normality and equal group variances), with approximately 95% relative power. When ANOVA assumptions are not met, the H-test is more powerful. That being the case, the statistic would appear to be the best choice for situations in which the groups to be compared have unequal variances and sample sizes.

Disadvantages

The H-test shares a problem with all analysis of variance tests: a significant result is merely the result of an overall test and cannot indicate *where* a difference lies. However, there are possibilities for subsequent multiple comparison tests. These range from applying the Bonferroni test when group variances are equal or a Dunnett's test if group variances are unequal to using individual U-tests (not a good idea) or specialized tests recently designed for the H-test.[2] There is also the traditional ordinal-level problem with ties, which reduce the power of the test. The result of a large number of ties will be to produce a conservative estimate of p. A tie-correction procedure exists, but it should probably be used with caution because it does not improve the situation much. Finally, the test has not been generalized to multiple variables as the ANOVA has.

An Example of the Kruskal–Wallis H-Test

For an example of the statistic's use in criminal justice research, we need a dependent variable at the metric ordinal level or higher and at least three groups in the independent variable. Let's use the same dependent variable, number of successful days on parole, as in the U-test example. For an independent variable, we'll need to switch the gender variable for one with more

---

[2]If you ever need one of these tests, simply consult the statistical literature.

categories. Prior arrests are also one of the "good" predictors of committing future crimes, so we'll see how well the variable does in predicting success on parole. To make the example easy, prior arrests have been collapsed into three categories: 0–3 arrests, 4–14 arrests, and 15 or more arrests.[3] We'll propose a traditional analysis of variance two-tailed hypothesis: "Prior arrests affect the number of successful days on parole."

The SPSS output for our Kruskal–Wallis H-test is shown in Table C.2. The first part of the table shows the mean ranks of each of the three prior arrests groups. While we weren't predicting a direction (we had a two-tailed hypothesis), it is evident that those parolees in categories with greater numbers of prior arrests have progressively lower success on parole. The mean ranks drop from 2,436 for the 0–3 arrests group to a low of 1,621 for the group with the greatest number of arrests. Now we need to determine if this is a significant difference (if not, there are *no* differences among the groups). The second table shows a Chi-square value with an associated probability level.[4] This is a two-tailed probability, as is our hypothesis, so we interpret it directly. With a probability lower than .001, the result is significant and we can say that prior arrests affect the number of successful days on parole. Of course, we don't know *which* groups are different without using a multiple comparisons test.

TABLE C.2 Sample Results from a Kruskal–Wallis H-test

Ranks

	Prior Arrests	*N*	*Mean Rank*
Number of successful days in 1st year	0 to 3 arrests	775	2436.91
	4 to 14 arrests	2300	1874.97
	15+ arrests	795	1621.83
	Total	3870	

Test Statistics[a,b]

	Number of Successful Days in 1st Year
Chi-Square	254.835
df	2
Asymp. Sig.	.000

[a]*Kruskal Wallis test*
[b]*Grouping variable: prior arrest categories*

---

[3]These categories aren't as arbitrary as they might seem. A prior research study found that these cut-off points were the best age groupings for maximizing the effect of prior arrests on parole success (although not with this "number of days" variable).
[4]Because the H-test sampling distribution closely approximates the Chi-square distribution, the latter is commonly used to determine probability levels. The H-test value is substituted for the Chi-square value.

WHEN WOULD YOU USE ONE OF THESE STATISTICS?

Both tests are alternatives to their parametric cousins, the t-test and the ANOVA. You should have a dependent variable measured at the metric ordinal level or higher.

Use the *Mann–Whitney U-test* for two groups when:

- The dependent variable is not normally distributed in each of the two groups.

Use the *Kruskal–Wallis H-test* for multiple groups in any of these conditions:

- The dependent variable is not normally distributed in each of the groups, or
- The dependent variable doesn't have equal variances within the groups, or
- The sample sizes of the groups vary widely.

APPENDIX D

Multiple Comparison Tests

The main issue for multiple comparison tests is how to choose one. For the most part, the critical ingredient is whether the variances among the three-plus groups you are comparing are equal (homoscedastic) or not (heteroscedastic). Some statistics programs make this relatively easy for you and you don't have to remember which test assumes what. In the SPSS statistical program, equal or unequal variances is actually the primary heading for the different sets of multiple comparison tools it offers for analysis. In order to make a choice, you obviously need to know whether the groups have equal variances, so that test will have to be done. SPSS offers the Levene's Test (just as it does with the t-test) to make such a determination. Let's look at that output below.

Test of Homogeneity of Variances

Approximate Family Income for Last Year

Levene statistic	$df1$	$df2$	Sig.
7.394	4	1018	.000

You have already seen the Levene's Test for the equality of variances used with the t-test. This version is almost identical, except there are more than two groups. So, it compares all group variances (at one time) and provides us with a probability that they are equal. In the output example above, family income is used across five educational groups. Looking at the probability above ("Sig." is .000, which is smaller than .05), we conclude that the incomes vary substantially across the five educational groups. Thus, the best thing to do is treat the variances as if they are unequal. You would then use one of the multiple comparison tests with no assumption of equal variances and interpret as above. While the choices vary with the statistical program and version, here are the choices in one version of the SPSS program. As you can see in the screen capture, if you can't assume equal variances, the proper tests are Tamhane's T^2, Dunnett's T^3, Games-Howell, and Dunnett's C. As with all of these tests, it is a wise idea to find out what other assumptions they make and match your choice to your data. However, they all can be interpreted in pretty much the same way.

For the sake of an example, let's continue with the education and income analysis. We already know that the analysis of variance (ANOVA) test was significant and that the variances are not equal, meaning that we will have to use one of the four tests at the bottom of the menu below. The first test, Tamhane's T^2, generally gives a pretty conservative estimate, so let's use that one. The multiple comparisons table

Choices of Multiple Comparisons Tests in a Version of SPSS

One-Way ANOVA: Post Hoc Multiple Comparisons   ☒

Equal Variances Assumed

☐ LSD	☐ S-N-K	☐ Waller-Duncan
☐ Bonferroni	☐ Tukey	Type I/Type II Error Ratio: 100
☐ Sidak	☐ Tukey's-b	☐ Dunnett
☐ Scheffe	☐ Duncan	Control Category: Last
☐ R-E-G-W F	☐ Hochberg's GT2	Test
☐ R-E-G-W Q	☐ Gabriel	◉ 2-sided ○ < Control ○ > Control

Equal Variances Not Assumed

☐ Tamhane's T2   ☐ Dunnett's T3   ☐ Games-Howell   ☐ Dunnett's C

Significance level: .05

Continue   Cancel   Help

below shows the output for a multiple comparison of income across our education groups with the Tamhane statistic. Note that the output is almost identical in appearance to the equal variance Bonferroni test we used in the ANOVA chapter.

Looking at the results, we would conclude that every level of education has a significantly different mean income from every other level, except the college

Multiple Comparisons

Dependent variable: Household Income in Thousands Tamhane

(I) Education Collapsed	(J) Education Collapsed	Mean Difference $(I-J)$	Std. Error	Sig.	95% Confidence Interval	
					Lower Bound	Upper Bound
IT HS	HS grad	-9.34^*	2.107	.000	-15.29	-3.40
	Some college	-18.20^*	2.160	.000	-24.29	-12.11
	College deg	-31.83^*	3.603	.000	-42.00	-21.66
	Adv. deg.	-28.73^*	2.788	.000	-36.63	-20.83
HS grad	IT HS	9.34^*	2.107	.000	3.40	15.29
	Some college	-8.86^*	2.080	.000	-14.70	-3.01
	College deg	-22.49^*	3.555	.000	-32.52	-12.45
	Adv.deg.	-19.39^*	2.726	.000	-27.11	-11.66

(continued)

(*continued*)

Some college	IT HS	18.20*	2.160	.000	12.11	24.29
	HS grad	8.86*	2.080	.000	3.01	14.70
	College deg	−13.63*	3.587	.002	−23.75	−3.51
	Adv.deg.	−10.53*	2.767	.002	−18.36	−2.69
College deg	IT HS	31.83*	3.603	.000	21.66	42.00
	HS grad	22.49*	3.555	.000	12.45	32.52
	Some college	13.63*	3.587	.002	3.51	23.75
	Adv.deg.	3.10	3.996	.997	−8.17	14.37
Adv.deg.	IT HS	28.73*	2.788	.000	20.83	36.63
	HS grad	19.39*	2.726	.000	11.66	27.11
	Some college	10.53*	2.767	.002	2.69	18.36
	College deg	−3.10	3.996	.997	−14.37	8.17

**The mean difference is significant at the .05 level.*

degree and advanced college degree comparison. Further, it appears that the lower the level of education, the lower is the income. If you reflect back to Chapter 13, these are the same variables used in the example of the ANOVA and Bonferroni tests. Comparing the Bonferroni and Tamhane test results (and we now know the latter should have been used because of unequal group variances), the Bonferroni failed to find the significant difference between the less than high school and high school graduate groups. So, you see, using the correct statistic *can* make a difference, though not always.

APPENDIX E

Nominal-Level Measures of Association

In Chapter 15, we examined only one statistic, Phi. Because determining association between variables that don't fit into a 2×2 table is very common, here are a couple of tests that can be used for that purpose. Actually, this appendix will end up recommending only one of them, but the other has been traditionally useful as a way to see what occurs when trying to measure association between nominal-level variables with multiple categories.

GOODMAN AND KRUSKAL'S LAMBDA (λ)

Lambda is a measure of association used to predict one variable from another. In one sense, it is historically significant because it was the statistic used to establish the concept of a proportionate-reduction-in-error (PRE) interpretation for correlations in both Goodman and Kruskal's original research and Herbert Costner's classic 1965 article. Lambda can be used with any size table (any number of rows and columns), and it has asymmetric versions.

There are two formulas for Lambda because of its asymmetric capability:

$$\text{Symmetric Lambda: } \lambda = \frac{\Sigma fr + \Sigma fc - (Fr + Fc)}{2n - (Fr + Fc)}$$

$$\text{Asymmetric Lambda: } \lambda = \frac{\Sigma fi - Fd}{n - Fd}$$

Where: fr = largest row frequency
fc = largest column frequency
Fr = largest row marginal frequency
Fc = largest column marginal frequency
n = number of observations
fi = largest frequency within each subclass of the independent variable
Fd = largest frequency within the dependent variables totals

As you can see from the explanation of the symbols in the two formulas, Lambda is using the marginals to compare total variance to the "real" variance we are interested in. The asymmetric version is a shorter equation because it only looks at one diagonal for its estimate of relationship—of course, you have to know which variable is your dependent variable.

Lambda is a marginal-based statistic and achieves its maximum power when marginals are equal and sample sizes are fairly large. It remains reasonably accurate with small sample sizes as long as marginals are relatively equal. Lambda also has the desirable property of being an asymmetric statistic—the relationship being proposed can be separated into two, depending on which variable is the dependent variable. Other than the dependence on marginals, the statistic has no other assumptions that are critical for its use.

The statistic is, as has already been noted, a PRE measure of association. It ranges from 0 to 1.0, with partial relationships in between those proportions. By multiplying the Lambda value (the proportion of predictive error being reduced) by 100 to change it into a percent, it is interpreted as the percentage of variance in the dependent variable accounted for by the independent variable. Or, in other words, a straightforward PRE interpretation. Any Lambda may be compared to any other Lambda in order to estimate which independent variables best "predict" the dependent variable. For instance, if we are trying to predict the crime rates in various cities, a Lambda value of .37 for the relationship with "poverty" would be a better predictor than a .25 value for a "percent minority" relationship.

Problems with Lambda

The major issue with Lambda is that it loses sensitivity (power) when the marginal totals are not approximately the same. When marginal totals are substantially different, Lambda will underestimate the association present in the table. In the worst cases, those in which almost all cases are within a single row or column, Lambda will not only underestimate the association but will likely provide a zero result (meaning no relationship).[1] This can happen even when there is an obviously strong relationship present. As a result, Lambda should be used with care and never without examining a table to see how the marginals are distributed.

An Example of Using Lambda

A survey provided a scenario for a felony crime. Respondents were asked questions about their attitude toward criminals (which created a scale for punishment orientation toward criminals) and a question about their willingness to serve on a jury. Here is the hypothesis we will use:

> H_a: *Punishment orientation toward criminals affects willingness to serve on a jury.*

In this example, the hypothesis is a two-tailed one. Therefore, there is no need to check the direction of the relationship in the table (at least not yet). We do, however, need to determine which variable is the dependent one—and according to our hypothesis, that is "willingness to serve on a jury." The next step is to find the line in the "Directional Measures" table with "Willingness to serve on a jury" used as the

---

[1]The reason Lambda underestimates association under this condition is that it was designed to use the modal category (of the independent variable) as a baseline for prediction. In other words, if you knew nothing else about the dependent variable, the modal category would be your best guess to predict any individual case. Lambda's PRE capability is oriented around improving predictability of the dependent variable with the modal "guess" as the zero point. When almost all cases are in the modal category, there is little by which to improve the prediction.

Crosstabulation of Punishment Orientation Toward Criminals with Willingness to Serve on a Jury

			Willingness to serve on jury			
			Low	Medium	High	Total
Punishment Orientation Toward Criminals	Low	Count	68	153	119	340
		%	20.0%	45.0%	35.0%	100.0%
	Medium	Count	79	118	157	354
		%	22.3%	33.3%	44.4%	100.0%
	High	Count	86	115	167	368
		%	23.4%	31.3%	45.4%	100.0%
Total		Count	233	386	443	1062
		%	21.9%	36.3%	41.7%	100.0%

Directional Measures

			Value	Asymp. Std. Error	Approx.I	Approx.Sig.
Nominal by Nominal	Lambda	Symmetric	.055	.022	2.483	.013
		Punishment orientation Dependent	.055	.023	2.327	.020
		Willingness to serve on jury Dependent	.055	.026	2.066	.039

dependent variable. That line is on the bottom of the table. Looking at the calculated probability ("Approx. Sig.")[2] for the possible relationship, we conclude that a *p* of .039 is lower than the standard alpha level of .05; thus, the hypothesis is accepted.

To determine the size of the relationship, we look for the asymmetric Lambda value for "willingness" as the dependent variable. That value is .055—multiplying it by 100, we get 5.5%. Finally, we interpret the relationship by saying that punishment orientation accounts for 5.5% of the variance in willingness to serve on a jury.

Note that this example used two variables with a reasonably uniform distribution across the rows and columns. That made a calculation of Lambda possible. Because variables are frequently not distributed this way, it is not uncommon to see at least one of the Lambda values at .000. Let's now examine a nominal-level measure of association that does not have this problem.

UNCERTAINTY COEFFICIENT (*U*)

The uncertainty coefficient (also known as Theil's *U*) is specifically designed to measure association between variables in a contingency table. Like Lambda it will predict one variable from the other and has a PRE interpretation in its asymmetric versions.

---

[2]The probability associated with Lambda is derived from dividing the Lambda value by its standard error and using the result as if it were a *t*-test value.

Summary of Lambda Features

Assumption of Lambda:

✓ Equality of marginals (particularly in the independent variable).

Advantages of Lambda:

✓ PRE measure (direct)
✓ Useful with any size tables
✓ Has both symmetrical and asymmetrical formulas

Disadvantages of Lambda:

✓ Loses sensitivity when marginals are not equal
✓ Will give incorrect results when almost all cases are in the same row or column (underestimates association and can even give an erroneous value of zero)

The formulas for U are much more complicated than those of the other statistics we have examined, and it is very laborious to calculate by hand. Therefore, they are shown here merely to illustrate the statistic.

The symmetric formula for U is:

$$U = \frac{2[H(X) + H(Y) - H(XY)]}{H(X) + H(Y)}$$

The two asymmetric formulas are:
Row to column U

$$U = \frac{H(X) + H(Y) - H(XY)}{H(Y)}$$

Column to row U

$$U = \frac{H(Y) + H(X) - H(XY)}{H(X)}$$

Where: X = the column variable
Y = the row variable
$H(X) = -SUM_j[(r_j/n)*ln(r_j/n)]$
$H(Y) = -SUM_k[(c_k/n)*ln(c_k/n)]$
$H(XY) = -SUM_jSUM_k[(n_{jk}/n)*ln(n_{jk}/n)]$
n = sample size
r_j = the row totals (marginals) for rows $1 \ldots j$
c_k = the column totals (marginals) for rows $1 \ldots k$
n_{jk} = the cell count for row j, column k
ln = the symbol for the natural log function

This statistic is a nonmarginal based, maximum-likelihood test—meaning that it focuses on the odds of a case being in one of the cells relative to the other cells.

Compared to other nominal-level measures of association, U is a more recent statistic and its inclusion in major statistical programs, like SPSS, has made it more popular.

As is evident in the formulas above, it has asymmetric versions allowing us to more accurately test any hypothesis. Moreover, it has a direct PRE interpretation with the usual range of 0–1.0 and proportions in between signifying a partial relationship. As a result, the relationships of a dependent variable with multiple independent variables (calculated one-by-one in bivariate tables) can be compared to see which is strongest. Finally, U does not lose much power when small samples are used and can be efficiently used with virtually any sample. As always, though, very small samples have large amounts of error and one should be careful with estimating relationships when using them. The Uncertainty Coefficient is, overall, a good choice for measuring the relationship between two nominal-level variables.

Problems with the Uncertainty Coefficient

Because U does not rely directly on marginals, a common feature of tabular statistics, there are no express issues associated with its use in testing relationships between variables with nonuniform category distributions. As opposed to other statistics, however, U is based on the concept of entropy (another name for it is the *entropy coefficient*). In most instances, it will yield a larger value than Lambda.

Example of the Uncertainty Coefficient

A survey asked if respondents would be willing to serve on a jury and, given a scenario of a felony crime, whether they would vote to convict if they were serving on the jury for that case. We'll create the following one-tailed hypothesis:

> H_a: *Those with greater willingness to serve on a jury are more likely to vote for conviction.*

Looking at the crosstabulation below, we are faced with trying to ascertain direction because of the nominal nature of the data and our test. If the direction of the hypothesis is correct, then respondents with high levels of willingness to serve should have the highest percentage in the "Yes" vote-to-convict column. Indeed, that appears to be the case, though not by much. The opposite, low willingness to serve, results in more voting *not* to convict, is barely correct, and you have to consider the "not sure" category as well. However, we'll say the direction is okay.

Having determined that the direction matches our hypothesis, we now need to examine the probabilities associated with the U values. Before doing that, though, we need to decide which U value will be used (the "Directional Measures" table below). Because the test is an asymmetric one, there are three values. We look for the row matching our hypothesis, with voting to convict as the dependent variable. That row is the one at the bottom of the table. The probability associated with the U value is .001, which is significant. The hypothesis is accepted, but we need to check the strength of the relationship. For that, we go to the U value itself, which is .031, and interpret it as a direct PRE measure.

Crosstabulation of Willingness to Serve on a Jury with Decision to Convict Based on Felony Scenario

| | | | Felony Scenario—Would you Vote to Convict? | | | |
			No	Not Sure	Yes	Total
Willingness to Serve on Jury	Low	Count	3	27	160	190
		%	1.6%	14.2%	84.2%	100.0%
	Medium	Count	2	27	291	320
		%	.6%	8.4%	90.9%	100.0%
	High	Count	5	15	343	363
		%	1.4%	4.1%	94.5%	100.0%
Total		Count	10	69	794	873
		%	1.1%	7.9%	91.0%	100.0%

The .031 means that willingness to serve on a jury accounts for 3.1% of the variance in voting to convict, and as willingness to serve increases, voting to convict increases. As we have found several times already, the percentage of explained variation is not very high and this is not a very strong relationship.

Directional Measures

			Value	Asymp. Std. Error	Approx. I	Approx. Sig.
Nominal by Nominal	Uncertainty coefficient	Symmetric	.015	.007	2.171	.001
		Willingness to serve on jury dependent	.010	.005	2.171	.001
		Vote to convict? Dependent	.031	.014	2.171	.001

Summary of the Uncertainity Coefficient Features

Assumptions of U:

✓ None known but *may* be slightly sensitive to marginal problems with small samples.

Advantages of U:

✓ Direct-PRE interpretation for the asymmetric versions.
✓ Both symmetric and asymmetric versions.
✓ Does not appear to be sensitive to unequal marginals.
✓ Does not use the modal category as a prediction baseline.

Disadvantages of U:

✓ Difficulty of computation.
✓ Relatively new and not yet popular.

APPENDIX F

Ordinal-Level Measures of Association

In Chapter 15, you saw how nominal-level measures of association work. Most are designed for use in crosstabulations. That is also true of ordinal-level measures, primarily because, even though using ordinal-level data, they still handle discrete rather than continuous information (although metric ordinal data may be an exception). All ordinal statistics, as was noted in our discussion of ordinal inferential tests in Appendix C, have a special problem to overcome in measuring relationships—they measure the association between *ranked scores* rather than the relationship between actual scores (interval-/ratio-level data). Therefore, there is some difficulty in interpreting their results because, theoretically, we are referring to the prediction of ordered pairs of scores, not the individual scores. Most of the time, though, you can ignore this problem and just deal with explained variance in the normal way.

WHAT IS BEING MEASURED?—THE CONCEPT OF ORDINAL ASSOCIATION

Due to this ranked pairs issue, most ordinal correlations are based on the idea of *concordant* and *discordant* pairs. A concordant pair is a set of ranked scores from A and B that match in their ranking on both A and B. The ranked scores may also have to increment correctly (increase or decrease in the same way) in order to be called concordant. A discordant pair is a set of ranked scores that don't match or pairs that do not increment correctly. With this in mind, an intuitive way to calculate correlations (predicting one set of ranked scores from another) is to know how the ranked pairs match up. Here's an example of this concept using five individuals who are measured on two different variables:

Variable 1		Varibale 2		
Score	*Rank*	*Score*	*Rank*	
9	1	23	2	⇐discordant
12	2	10	1	⇐discordant*
13	3	25	3	
15	4	30	4	
25	5	47	5	

*May not be discordant under the concept of correct increments, i.e., the next score is higher.

Looking at the example above, the first task is to order all of the scores in variable 1 in order of low to high. Having done that, we can see that the first individual had a score of 9 on variable 1 and 23 on the variable 2. The second individual scored 12 and 10, respectively. Now we need to rank all of the scores in variable 1. Our first individual with a score of 9 had the lowest ranked score on variable 1, so that score is assigned a rank of 1. The same individual's score on variable 2 is 23, which is the second lowest score giving it a rank of 2. Once the ranks are assigned for both variables, we can compare the ranks.

It is obvious that three of our individuals have the same ranking across both variables. Out of five individuals, if we guessed that the rank of variable 1 would predict the rank of variable 2, we would be 60% correct ($3 \div 5 = .6$). Assuming our requirement for prediction is that all of the ranks match perfectly, 60% is our prediction accuracy. Put another way, 60% of the cases are concordant.

However, you might have noticed that in terms of incrementing correctly once we go beyond the first individual all scores are lower than the next score (not counting the highest score, of course). Put another way, even though the second pair of scores misses the correct rank, the lower-to-higher criterion still applies. Rank 1 is indeed lower than rank 3, and so on. If we use strictly a *correct increment criterion,* then four of the five individuals' paired ranks are matched in their rank increments. That would give us 80% predictability or 80% concordance. Depending on the criterion we use for association, then, a correlation should be somewhere in the range of .8–.6.

Now that we have the concept of what is being measured (ordered pairs), let's discuss two other ordinal association characteristics. In comparison to nominal-level statistics, where there is no reporting of the direction of a relationship unless you decipher the crosstabulation percentages, ordinal statistics provide *direction* of relationship. For instance, in our example above, 60–80% of the paired ranks match in their direction. Therefore, this is a *positive* relationship. Now consider that the paired ranks had moved in opposite directions, but with the same results, like this:

Variable 1	Variable 2
Rank	*Rank*
1	5
2	4
3	3
4	1
5	2

We would get the same level of predictability, but with a negative correlation instead. This is a good development because it means we no longer have to look at the data, or at percentages in a table, to decipher direction. An ordinal correlation will be either positive or negative and we can interpret that directly.

The second characteristic is essentially a problem. The statistics, even though used with discrete ordered data, actually assume underlying continuity in the data. That is, no two scores are alike. For most ordinal data, we know that isn't true (think of a traditional Likert scale, with its strongly agree to strongly disagree categories). In fact, it is common for *most* of the data to have similar scores. Those shared scores create *tied ranks*, and when ranking scores you now have to figure out how to assign a rank to several individual scores that are the same. There is no "best way" to do this and, as a result, values that are *tied* present a difficult problem for ordinal statistics. Given that most of these statistics assume that *ties are absent*, correlations can be inflated (overestimated) when a substantial proportion of the cases have tied scores on a variable.

Now let's use what we know to understand two ordinal measures of association: Gamma and Somer's *d*.

GOODMAN AND KRUSKAL'S GAMMA (γ)

Gamma is a bivariate test of association between two ranked variables. While it is traditionally calculated with discrete data, like those in crosstabulations, the tied ranks problem can affect results. For this reason, a better test is Somers' *d*, which will be discussed later. Gamma, however, can be sometimes found in the criminal justice and criminology research literature, and it is easy to see how it measures association in a table.

Here are the formulas for Gamma:

Formula for 2×2 table:

$$\gamma = \frac{ad - bc}{ad + bc}$$

where the table cells are designated as below:

a	b
c	d

Gamma formula for larger table:

$$\gamma = \frac{\sum fa - \sum fi}{\sum fa + \sum fi}$$

where: fa = total sum (sum of all cell frequencies below and to the right of each cell times the frequency of the cell)

fi = total sum (sum of all cell frequencies below and to the left of each cell times the frequency of the cell)

The 2×2 table formula is the easiest to see. Gamma uses each diagonal, *a–d* and *b–c*, to create a comparison between them and the total variance on the diagonals. If all scores are on one diagonal, for instance *a–d*, then subtracting or adding the other diagonal would be subtracting or adding zero. In other words, everything

(1.0) would be on the one diagonal and dividing by everything (1.0) would produce a correlation of 1.0. If any scores are not on the diagonal, the correlation shrinks. When the table is not a 2×2 version, then the "agreements" and "inversions" are the equivalent of the concordant and discordant scores we looked at previously.

Assumptions

Gamma has three major assumptions about data. We already know that it assumes a contradiction, that is, discrete data with no ties. The product of this is that a *few* ties are okay—but as the number of ties increases, problems increase. The statistic is also best used with larger tables (crosstabulations with a "larger" number of cells) or with variables that have a large number of "groups." In short, Gamma is a large sample, discrete data, and no-ties statistic.

Advantages

Even though Gamma is a large sample statistic, it can be used without much error in smaller tables. In addition, the tables can be square ($2 \times 2, 3 \times 3, 6 \times 6$) or nonsquare ($2 \times 3, 4 \times 8$), and the calculations still work to produce a reasonable correlation. This is not true of some ordinal-level measures of association. Cell frequencies can also be small and that has little effect on accuracy. Further, in the unlikely event a researcher might have to calculate a Gamma by hand, computation is simple. Now, for the best news, Gamma is a direct proportionate-reduction-in-error (PRE) statistic and, as you already know, has an attached directional sign—all of which makes it easy to interpret. There have also been attempts to extend Gamma to "partial" correlation (more than bivariate relationships), but these haven't been too successful.

Disadvantages

Gamma has two distinct disadvantages and a minor one. First, it has a problem similar to many statistics used in crosstabulations—unequal marginals result in error. In this case, the error is in the form of liberal estimates of association. That is, Gamma will overestimate association (produce a higher correlation) when marginals are unequal. The second serious problem is that of ties and Gamma itself has no tie correction available. Again, the error that results will create an overestimation of the association. These two problems in combination can produce a correlation much larger than should be the case. A final issue is that the statistic is a symmetric one, with no asymmetric version. This is not a major issue, as there are many similar statistics (even Pearson's *r*) with the same feature. You simply have to keep in mind that any Gamma value will be an average of the two possible dependent relationships.

Example of Using Gamma

For an example of how Gamma is used, we'll look at the relationship between the educational level variable previously used and a measure of punitive attitudes toward criminals. Using a rationale that those who are better educated

TABLE F.1 Crosstabulation of Two Ordinal Variables

Crosstabulation of Educational Level with Punitiveness Attitude

			Punishment Attitude			
			Low	*Medium*	*High*	*Total*
Education	LT HS	Count	6	20	127	153
		% within education collapsed	3.9%	13.1%	83.0%	100.0%
	HS grad	Count	5	32	280	317
		% within education collapsed	1.6%	10.1%	88.3%	100.0%
	Some college	Count	8	44	313	365
		% within education collapsed	2.2%	12.1%	85.8%	100.0%
	College deg	Count	7	35	178	220
		% within education collapsed	3.2%	15.9%	80.9%	100.0%
	Adv. deg.	Count	8	23	75	106
		% with education collapsed	7.5%	21.7%	70.8%	100.0%
Total		Count	34	154	973	1161
		% within education collapsed	2.9%	13.3%	83.8%	100.0%

might be more tolerant and/or more likely to see the value in treatment, we'll hypothesize that "Higher education will result in lower punitiveness attitudes." For this test, we'll need to check direction first and because this is an ordinal statistic that can be done by looking at the sign associated with the Gamma value in Table F.2. The value is negative, which is the direction of our hypothesis. In addition, we could also examine the crosstabulation in Table F.1. Looking at that table, we find a higher percentage of those with higher education levels have lower punitive attitudes than those with low educational levels. Further, there is a trend in the high punitive attitude level toward increasing percentages of lower educational levels. As you can see, the relationship in the table is nowhere near a perfect one. Thus, we would also expect the Gamma value to be fairly low.

The next step is to determine if the relationship is a real one, that is, statistically significant. Table F.2 contains the probability associated with our presumed relationship. With a probability value of .005, the relationship is a real one and the hypothesis is accepted. Now all that remains is to determine the strength of the relationship. The Gamma coefficient is −.170, which translates to 17% of the variance. Thus, we can say that educational level explains 17% of the variance in punitive attitudes and, as educational level increases, punitive attitudes decrease.

TABLE F.2 Gamma Results

	Value	Asymp Std. Error	Approx. T	Approx. Sig.
Ordinal by Ordinal Gamma	−.170	.059	−2.827	.005
N of valid cases	1161			

SOMERS' d

This ordinal statistic is an extension of Gamma. It was developed by Robert Somers as a resolution to Gamma's problem with ties. The resulting statistic corrects for ties. The tie correction can be used for both variables or either variable, creating three formulas. Perhaps the best part of Somers' approach is that it results in asymmetric versions of the new statistic. If you look at the formulas below, you can see the Gamma large-table formula buried within them—so, we might say that Somers' d statistic is essentially Gamma corrected for ties.

The formulas are:

$$\text{Symmetrical: } d = \frac{\sum fa - \sum fi}{\sum fa + \sum fi + \frac{1}{2}(tx + ty)}$$

$$\text{Asymmetrical: } dyx = \frac{\sum fa - \sum fi}{\sum fa + \sum fi + ty}$$

$$dxy = \frac{\sum fa - \sum fi}{\sum fa + \sum fi + tx}$$

Assumptions

Somers' d has the same assumptions as Gamma, so it requires equality of marginals, and prefers large samples. When used with tables, it obviously works best with a large number of cells—continuous data are even better than ordinal data. With the tie correction factor, there is no assumption of tied ranks, but an absence of ties in the data is always best.

Advantages

As is true of Gamma, Somers' d has one of the most desirable traits for a correlation measure—a direct-PRE interpretation. Because of the tie correction factor, the statistic has both symmetric and asymmetric versions. In short, if Somers' d can be used, it is a good choice for ordinal to metric ordinal data. Similarly, if interval/ratio data are clearly not normally distributed and the use of Pearson's r is questionable, Somers' d will also be the measure of choice.

Disadvantages

The primary disadvantage of Somers' d is related to its assumption of equal marginals. Therefore, it is sensitive to marginal inequality and will produce liberal estimates of the true correlation between variables. Because larger samples and continuous data are also preferred, the combination of small samples, few variable categories, and marginal inequality will seriously inflate correlations.

An Example of Somers' d

To illustrate Somers' d, let's use the same crosstabulation of data in the Gamma example (Table F.1) to avoid creating another crosstabulation. The two variables are educational level and punitive attitude toward criminals. We had previously found that the relationship was going in the correct direction for our hypothesis (those with higher educational levels will be less punitive toward criminals) and was statistically significant. Looking at Table F.3, we find the same results. The Somers' d value has a negative sign and the probability of .005 is significant. Note that the crosstabulation itself is not actually required for us to make decisions about the hypothesis.

What remains is make a decision about which Somers' d value will be used and then interpret it. Because we are predicting punitive attitudes, that is obviously the dependent variable, so we use the row of values across from "Punishment Dependent." The Somers' d value is −.048, which interprets as educational levels explain 4.8% of the variance in punitive attitudes. Of course, we already know that the negative sign means that the two variables move in opposite directions.

Before we leave the discussion of Somers' d, let's compare the Gamma correlation of −.170 to the Somers' d correlations. You already know that the categories in the table were not continuous; in fact there were only three in the dependent variable and five in the independent variable. With 1,161 cases (see Table F.1), there were a *lot* of ties. Therefore, we can conclude that Gamma gave us an inflated correlation—but inflated by how much? The equivalent

TABLE F.3 Somers' d Correlations

			Value	Asymp. Std. Error	Approx. T	Approx. Sig.
Ordinal by Ordinal	Somers'd	Symmetric	−.071	.025	−2.827	.005
		Education dependent	−.133	.046	−2.827	.005
		Punishment dependent	−.048	.017	−2.827	.005

correlation for Somers' *d*, the symmetric value (−.071), helps us answer that question. If we subtract the Somers' *d* correlation, corrected for ties, from the Gamma correlation, we have an estimate of inflation error. This would yield:

> *.170 − .071 = .099 (error estimate) (Note: the signs are not used)*

It seems that the inflation error is actually *larger* than the actual correlation.

But, if you remember the hypothesis and the dependent variable, the appropriate asymmetric value for Somers' *d* is even lower, on the order of −.048. So, if we use that to estimate the total error in choosing Gamma as the correct statistic, the result would be:

> *.170 − .048 = .122 (error estimate)*

As you can see, Gamma can be the wrong choice to measure the strength of relationships when you have a hypothesis and ties exist in the data. Use Somers' *d* instead of Gamma and you'll have a much better estimate of the true relationship.

Index